A Question of Community

A Question of Community

Religious Groups and Colonial Law

Edited by
Amrita Shodhan

Samya

A QUESTION OF COMMUNITY:
Religious Groups and Colonial Law,
by Amrita Shodhan was first published in
January 2001 by SAMYA,
16 Southern Avenue, Calcutta 700 026

ISBN 81-85604-43-6

Distributed by Popular Prakashan Pvt Ltd
Mumbai, Calcutta, Delhi

Designed and typeset by Compuset International
85 Park St, Calcutta 700 016 and printed by
Webimpressions (India) Pvt Ltd,
34/2 Beadon St, Calcutta 700 006

Published by Mandira Sen for SAMYA,
an imprint of Bhatkal and Sen,
16 Southern Avenue, Calcutta 700 026

Acknowledgements

THIS BOOK WOULD not have been possible without the generous help of those who taught me at the University of Chicago and all my friends on whose time and energy I have drawn so heavily. I am happy to acknowledge my intellectual debt to Professor Cohn whose insightful comments and questions have taught me to think in new and critical ways. Professor Inden's criticisms and careful readings pushed me to think through many arguments and achieve some clarity regarding what I wanted to say. I know I have not done full justice to my debt to Professor Naim. He has been a guide in the often cold and confusing world of the university, from reading chapters with careful attention, to celebrating festive occasions.

I am indebted to all my colleagues from whom I have learnt as much as I have from my teachers. I would especially like to thank Arshia Sattar and Sanjay Iyer for having consistently read my work from proposal to write-up and giving it meaning and form, Achyut Yajnik for sharing his knowledge of and interest in the history of Gujarat; Rudolf C. Heredia S.J. for demanding outlines that helped me to organize my work to organizing activities that demanded my time. I am grateful also for the help I received from Jim Nye and William Alspaugh of the University of Chicago library who have made numerous resources available. I thank the staffs of the BJ and Vidyapeeth libraries in Ahmedabad, the Bombay University library and the

Pharbus Gujarati Sabha libraries in Bombay and of the Bombay Archives and the Bombay High court Archives.

While writing the book, my life in general was made meaningful and worthwhile in numerous ways. I would especially like to acknowledge the work of Shakti and India Alert (Chicago), Setu (Ahmedabad), Social Science Center, FAOW and Vacha (Mumbai). I am indebted to both my families for believing in my work and patiently requesting me to 'finish', my parents for their faith in me and their vital and generous perspective on life. Life in Chicago and Mumbai would have been cheerless indeed without sustaining telephone conversations with Sheela Shodhan-Shah, the dynamic and 'quickening' presence of Shobha Shrinivasan, Bindu T. Desai, Meenal and Bashir Mamdani and without Sanjay Gupta it would have been often impossible to go on at all.

Contents

Introduction

THIS BOOK INTERROGATES the category 'community', and analyses its use as a model to understand religious groups. In order to do so, it takes up two religious groups and examines disputes within them, the public articulation of the disputes and their legal 'settlement' in a colonial court of law. Tracing how the model of 'community' evolved in colonial knowledge and administration, it demonstrates how its use structured the complex interaction between the colonial court, indigenous elite and lay members of their social organizations. It studies the Khojas and the Vallabhacharya Vaishnavas (also known as Pushtimargis) in the mid-nineteenth century. Both groups were divided over questions regarding their religious beliefs and over the behaviour of their religious authorities. These differences were extremely severe, could not be resolved internally, and resulted in court cases. Among the Khojas there were several cases, the most important and definitive was the Aga Khan Case in 1866. Among the Pushtimargis it was the Maharaj Libel Case (MLC), preceded by the Bhatia Conspiracy Case. The libel case has been celebrated as a milestone in the reduction of the power of maharajas or gurus over their devotees.[1] It was (and is) also seen as the victory of modernity over Hindu superstition.[2] The Aga Khan Case was seen as important only to the Khojas.[3] Since the Aga Khan won the case, it could not be claimed in the general story of Reform and Improvement, even though subsequent to the case, the Aga Khan himself encouraged modern education in English and other aspects of Reform.

Examining how the judicial courts dealt with the 'polities' of the Khojas and the Pushtimargis as 'communities' within Islam and Hinduism respectively, the book notes that firstly, the Khojas and the Pushtimargis were treated as 'communities'; and secondly, they were examined in a context of a court-determined true Islam and Hinduism. The treatment of the 'polities' as communities and the definition of 'true' Islam or Hinduism were neither natural nor obvious in the early nineteenth century in the Bombay Presidency. This micro-juridical point is traced through examining the silences in judicial proceedings and marking the establishment of dominant categories on members of the Khoja and Pushtimarga polities. Thus the primary focus is to understand the particularities of the Khojas and the Pushtimargis in law. The Conclusion draws out some of the implications of these details for understanding the law and posits that the analysis of micro-juridical processes actually suggests new ways of looking at the category of 'community'.

To keep the focus firmly on the idea of community the book examines the meaning of the term, which is used advisedly, as it captures the idea of the collective as encapsulated in the judicial proceedings and also because it is employed in a similar way today to refer to religious collectives in South Asia. The book also examines the concepts of *jamat*, *jnati* (caste), sect and *sampradaya* as used in the nineteenth century and characterizes their governed as well as ungoverned natures as polities. The second chapter analyses how the Bombay Presidency Regulations in 1827 came to represent castes as the only relevant category in which to recognize collective governance in indigenous society. Within this category were included tribes and sects, as well as castes in the narrower sense. 'Caste groups' were represented to be partly self-governing and therefore exercising a limited jurisdiction over internal affairs. This acceptance of caste was itself a denial of other kinds of authorities that were involved in making decisions or settling disputes. Villages, religious figures like maharajas, or trading groups were either not accepted at all or were very marginally accepted within colonial legal administration as possessing the necessary authority to settle disputes.

Chapters 3, 4 and 5 discuss how the Khojas and the Pushtimargis were treated during the examinations of the Aga Khan Case (1866) and the Maharaj Libel Case (1862) respectively. By 1862 common law and equity were accepted as the rules of decision in most civil disputes. The principle of interrogating caste in court to determine its law was discarded. The reformers and participants in the debate considered caste itself a regressive category. While religious groups were assumed to be free of the government's interference, the courts did settle civil disputes within religious groups. In order for the courts to hear disputes within religious groups, litigants had to reformulate them so that they were seen as concerning primarily 'public' issues. The plaintiffs of the Aga Khan Case and the Maharaj Libel Case and their British lawyers had to do so. Then the disputes were reformulated again within the judicial process itself. During the legal proceedings the Khojas and the Pushtimargis were represented as sects of larger religious communities of Hindus and Muslims, employing colonial knowledge of Islam and Hinduism.

Chapter 3 discusses the employment of sectarian categories to resolve disputes within the Khojas in 1866. The employment of the sect-in-Islam classification required individual Khojas to define their beliefs in terms of Islam. The court drew upon various Orientalist histories of Islam to determine whether the Khojas were followers of the Shia Ismaili or Sunni versions of Islam. Thus, the Khojas, instead of describing themselves through their historically grounded practices had to determine their identification on the basis of practices they would be undertaking as members of an identifiable Islamic sect. This Islamic sect was identified from evidence of Islam derived from Western scholarship on Islam.

Chapters 4 and 5 analyse the application of the community model to study the dispute among the Vallabhacharya Vaishnavas in Bombay in 1862. In the early part of the nineteenth century, critics advocated changes in ritual and other practices of the Vallabhacharya sampradaya. They urged these reforms not as reform of religion but as reform of caste behaviour. Chapter 4 studies the conditions in which the court held that the efforts by caste authorities to effect or prevent changes in religious beliefs were illegitimate. This chapter examines under what circumstances the nexus of caste and religious authorities as organizing religious behaviour and beliefs was displaced. Chapter 5 looks at how the religious belief of the Pushtimargis was examined neither by reference to actual practices nor through a discussion of their faith, but by reliance on its convergence with or divergence from 'true' Hinduism, which was ascertained from the evidence of experts and by the application of the yardstick of morality.

The analysis of the two cases demonstrates that discourses of 'truth' replaced internal definitions of the religious groups based on their historical practices. An idea that socio-religious polities (the Khojas and Pushtimargis) were based on changing beliefs and faith determined for them in a large part by debates and disputes between social and religious authorities was replaced by a new one. This new idea was that the religious 'community' had fixed beliefs determined at the time of its origins and which were discoverable by an inquiry of objective experts. Membership in such a religious community was determined even for male members or religious authorities by reference to symbols and signs of convergence with the original religion. The legal definition of the disputing group by discovering its origins meant that the socio-religious authorities of that polity had no role to play in re-defining the community in contemporary or historical circumstances. Thus the means by which the socio-religious polity debated its current faith and practice, governed itself, and maintained religious coherence were displaced onto those with the knowledge of origins (Orientalists) and the authority to act on that knowledge (the courts).

In the Aga Khan Case the religion of the Khojas was represented as Muslim and in the Maharaj Libel Case the religion of the Pushtimargis was represented as Hindu. Both the Khojas and the Pushtimargis were described as marginal within Islam and Hinduism. Instead of being considered independent polities of Muslims and Hindus who could constitute their own idea of the religious tradition (Muslim and Hindu) to which they belonged, true Islam and Hinduism were examined in terms created in Western and westernized scholarship. The legal developments outlined occurred in the circumstances of the jurisdictions of the colonial court combined with the indigenous movements for reform and change in the nineteenth century. I examine very briefly some of the political and social history of the period in question, the mid-nineteenth century.

POLITICAL AND GOVERNMENTAL CONTEXT

The nineteenth century has been described as one which brought major changes to the Bombay Presidency as it did to other parts of South Asia because it saw the formation of modern modes of governance. From 1803 to 1827 through treaties with the Gaikwad and the defeat of the Peshwa, the territories of the Bombay Presidency expanded considerably. The amalgamation of the Peshwa's Deccan territories led to a major reorganization in legal and judicial administration. Mountstuart Elphinstone presided over this early organization of Company administration, first as Commissioner of the Deccan (1818-1819) and then as Governor of Bombay Presidency (1819-1827).

Until the reorganizations effected by Elphinstone, Bombay city had a Recorder's court (established by king's charter) which was replaced by a Supreme Court in 1823. The mofussil had the Sadar Diwani Adalat under which there was a judge in every district who was assisted by a register [*sic*] and an assistant register who were all covenanted servants of the East India Company.[4] Elphinstone, influenced by Bentham, was of the opinion that the features of the Bengal administration would not work in Bombay and that he should develop something better and something different. To this end he set up the Regulation Committee which formulated the Bombay Regulation Code also known as the Elphinstone Code which came into effect in 1827. By this Regulation Code Elphinstone established native commissioners who would try cases at the lowest level, above whom were assistant judges, then the District Diwani and Fauzdari Adalats, then the Sadar Diwani and Nizamat Adalat. Aspects of the jurisdictions of this court and the processes in formulating the Bombay Regulation Code of 1827 will be discussed in Chapter 2.

The order established in 1827 was entirely reworked by the crown's assumption of the government of India after the 1857 rebellion. The Government of India Act of 1858 reviewed and reformed almost every aspect of Indian administration. From 1858 to 1869 there were major changes in legislation with the codification of laws. This was the period when Henry Maine was member of the Governor-General's Legislative Council (1862-1869).[5] The system of courts was integrated in all the three presidencies of Bengal, Bombay, and Madras, with a high court in each one. Each Presidency also lost its autonomous functioning and was joined into a unified imperial rule. The features of the Company administration as they were developed in Bengal were made the basis for new forms of unified administration for all the three Presidencies. Thus, the Bombay Presidency's treatment of self-governing groups and its acceptance of customary law (discussed in Chapter 2) were given up. The Bengal legal practice of viewing all groups as possessing unified Hindu and Muslim laws was accepted for certain questions. On other questions, the new codifications provided a vastly expanded substantive law by which the local population could be tried. The codification undertaken in this period and the reorganization of the court system laid the foundations for the modern judiciary of India.[6]

Queen Victoria's Proclamation in 1858 promising equal protection of the law for all religions and the freedom of all her Indian subjects to practice their religion was an important statement.[7] The proclamation was often quoted by the local elite as a sign of her wise and just policies. The government was specifically prohibited from 'interfering' with the religious beliefs and practices of the subjects, as long as these religious practices did not disturb the public peace. However, the courts were forced to deal with numerous religious questions. The stand they took vis-à-vis religion varied according to the case, the context and even the predilections of the judges.[8]

Chapters 3, 4 and 5 look at the procedural effects of these changes by a detailed examination of the Khoja and the Vallabhacharya Vaishnava cases in the post–1858 phase of colonial rule. Though the Maharaj Libel Case was tried by the Supreme Court, the charter of the High Court had already been granted in 1861, and the Supreme Court judges were appointed to be judges in the High Court too. Thus, what happened during the case, may well have happened if the court had been constituted as the High Court rather than the Supreme Court. The Khoja dispute was examined within the earlier Supreme Court of the Bombay Presidency (see Chapter 2) and then again in 1866 by the High Court of the Presidency (see Chapter 3). The difference between the two judgements may at least in part be attributed to the effect of the new and regularized judicial system along with all the particular circumstances of the debate.

SOCIAL CONTEXT

The Khojas and the Pushtimargis were important groups within the commercial elite of Bombay. In Bombay the Pushti sampradaya was dominated by the castes of Bhatias (Halai and Kuchhi Bhatias) and banias (primarily Kapol Banias in Bombay). Besides these three groups, the Bombay commercial elite was made up of Maharashtrian brahmins, Pathare Prabhus, Parsis and Jews. These groups associated with the Khojas and Banias and Bhatias in many common tasks from commerce, to education, social reform and politics. An interesting survey of these groups has been carried out by Dobbin, who classifies Bombay's elite in the period 1840s to 1870s into two groups. One group was the commercial magnates—the *shethiyas* (whom Dobbin translates as merchant princes). The other group consisted of the professional men whom she calls the intelligentsia. There was a gap of two kinds between the two groups, in education and in political and commercial power. The political power of the shethiyas lay in their leadership in caste and community organizations and in the recognition from the British political establishment as members of the municipality, justices of the peace, and so on. The intelligentsia consisted primarily of men educated in the new Western mode.[9] As we shall show in the later chapters, this dichotomy between the two groups was overdrawn when the issue in question was the reform and change of society. In many cases, reforms were originated by the commercial elite, as in the Khoja and the Bhatia cases. I follow the classification, however, to give a brief introduction to the people involved in the disputes and controversies.

The Khojas were mainly merchants from Kutch and Kathiawar. They migrated to Bombay in the late eighteenth century to pursue trade. The *jamat* (association) was led by the shethiyas.[10] In 1847 Justice Perry described the Khojas in Bombay as largely uneducated and undertaking petty trading and shopkeeping. During the 1840s and 1850s merchants like Dhurremsey Poonjabhoy, Habib Ibrahim, Hemraj Jeya, Fazalbhoy Gulam Husen made their fortunes in the China, Muscat and Zanzibar trade.[11] They traded in opium, silk, sugar and rice. Along with other upper class merchants, they made up the reformist group of Khojas which was one party in the disputes. These men or their sons were considered leading representatives of the Khojas even after they had broken away from the mainstream. For example, when the Khoja Law Commission was established in 1878, Ahmedbhoy Habibbhoy (son of Habib Ibrahim), Jairazbhoy Peerbhoy and Rahimtulla Sayanee, all Sunni Khojas (the breakaway group), were appointed to the commission along with Aga Ali Shah and two European representatives.[12] In this period and later, many Khojas migrated and settled in different parts of eastern Africa and Muscat in the pursuit of trade.[13]

In 1847 the jamat in Bombay consisted of 2,000 members out of a total population of Bombay of around 500,000.[14] In 1872 when the total population of Bombay was 644,405, the Khojas were around 8,534 or 1.32 percent of the total population and approximately 6.2 percent of the total Muslim population[15] Other Gujarati Muslims, the Bohras and the Memons were approximately the same number, 7.8 percent and 6.4 percent respectively of the total Muslim population of Bombay.[16] The 1901 Census said there were 11,000 Khojas in Bombay; they were 1.4 percent of the total population of 776,006.[17] Their numbers were very similar to those of the other trading castes of Bombay, the Bhatias and the banias.

During the eighteenth and nineteenth centuries, the Bhatias and banias (especially of the Kapol division) had played an important part in the commercial development of Bombay. The Kapol banias came from Gogha and Surat in around the mid-eighteenth century. The Bhatias came to Bombay from Kathiawar and Kutch about the beginning of the nineteenth century. The Bhatias voyaged to Zanzibar, Muscat, China and Japan for trade, but were forbidden to journey to Europe and America by caste regulations.[18] According to the 1872 Census the total population of Bombay was 644,405 and Bhatias were 9,466, that is, 1.47 percent. In 1881 the Bhatia population in Bombay was 9,417 out of a total population of 773,196.[19]

In the mid-nineteenth century most banias were bankers, traders, and shopkeepers, participating in the coastal trade from Kutch to Kathiawar and Konkan. When the textile mill industry began, they along with Parsis, Bhatias and Khojas took a leading role in setting up the industry. Mangaldas Nathoobhoy (a Kapol bania shethiya) set up the United Spinning and Weaving Company in 1860. Habib Ibrahim was a shareholder in the first mill, Davar's in 1859.[20] Dhurremsey Poonjabhoy owned six mills in the 1870s, when there were only eighteen in Bombay.[21] Lakshmidas Khimji, a wealthy and conspicuous Bhatia caste leader, was a cotton merchant and agent to Wallace & Co, and became a millowner in the 1880s.[22]

Most of the commercial magnates studied at small private vernacular schools run by pandits or puntojees or non-official English and Portuguese, or with some of the same teachers at home.[23] The early laments of British administrators on the absence of the commercial elite in their institutions of education was well known.[24] Of the 152 students who had studied at the Elphinstone Institution between 1827 and 1842 there were no banias, Bhatias or Muslims.[25]

Besides the commercial magnates, the religious heads and acharyas were an important part of the local society. Not all the religious heads had the same powers, but some like the Aga Khan and the Pushtimarga maharajas exercised great power over their devotees. The first Vaishnava maharaj came to Bombay in 1801, but stayed only for a year or two. Then in 1810 or 1811 Gokulnathji Maharaj came to Bombay and in

1823 made an authoritative agreement with his devotees to set up a permanent temple in Bombay. By this agreement all the traders and bankers among his devotees agreed to pay a tax on their total turnover.[26] By the 1860s there were five to six maharajas in Bombay, the most important of whom was Jivanlalji Maharaj.

The Aga Khan I, Mohammed Hussein Husseini, popularly known as Imamshah Hasanali Shah Saheb, came to Bombay in 1845. He was an important nobleman at the Persian court of Shah Fateh Ali Shah and, after the latter's death, at the court of Mohammed Shah. In 1838 the Aga Khan seized control of Kerman, an Iranian province in the east. But he was unable to hold it on his own and was forced to retreat to Afghanistan.[27] In Kandahar he met the forces of General Nott, and fought alongside for the capture of Kabul, and then with Sir Charles Napier's forces in Sind up to 1845. By then the British had forged a treaty with the Shah of Iran who compelled them to restrain the Aga Khan from the battlefield. The Aga Khan came to Bombay first in 1845 and then was sent by the British to Calcutta. However, he returned to Bombay in 1848.[28] He was revered by the Khojas in this period and despite a dispute about the amount of tribute to be paid to him, the Khojas collectively contributed to his maintenance.[29]

THE REFORM PROJECT

The nineteenth century was a period of change and a time of increase in prosperity for the middle class men among the merchants, whom Dobbin calls the intelligentsia. These men, if they were not independent traders, worked as professionals in private trading firms, or for the government. Their interactions with different groups including the British largely remained at a professional level, maintaining the caste recommended distance. With growing prosperity many of these men could afford to hire help at home and at work and thus, many of their wives and daughters had greater leisure time. These women formed an important topic of reform. Even as they were crucial to the reform project, their presence in the public arena remained marginal. They were to be reformed to suit new notions of domesticity. Women's religious activities had to change to create this domestic angel. This change was frought with tension. Often the religious heads threatened the reformers with physical violence along with ostracism. The women often sided with the former. Since the book focuses on tracing the idea of religious group membership in law, it has left the question of gender and only religious 'community' inadequately addressed. It is present as 'interruptions', retained as marking how gendered the narrative on religious reform was and pointing a direction for future work on gender in the making of 'community'.

Many of the men involved in reform were middle class and upper caste men. They had studied in educational institutions established by the British. In the 1840s and 50s Western education was being popularized through the Elphinstone Institution, where the educators, Professor Green, Professor Wordsworth and others were liberal reformists. Sir Erskine Perry, President of the Board of Education (1842-1852), was deeply convinced by Bentham and Mill's work on the need to reform the law. While a young man in England in 1831, he formed the reform minded parliamentary candidate society to promote the return of 'fit and proper' members of Parliament, and Jeremy Bentham and Joseph Hume amongst others were its early members.[30] As President of the Board of Education, he wrote numerous reports and with the help of his friend John Stuart Mill obtained the services of some very vigorous teachers from England.[31] Students educated under such men were drawn to apply ideas of reform to the Indian situation.

Students of the Elphinstone Institution formed educational and literary societies. The most famous of these young men were Bhau Daji Lad, Dhirajram Dalpatram, Dadabhai Naoroji, Narmadshankar Lalshankar, Karsandas Mulji, Mahipatram Rupram and Nanabhai Rustomji Ranina, among numerous others. At these societies they read the contemporary European classics, studied scientific subjects and examined Indian social customs. A cursory scrutiny of reformist newspapers like *Rast Goftar*, *Jagat Premi*, *Gnan Vardhak* and collections of articles written in the 1850s and 1860s suggests that a large portion of the essays written by the reformers were on scientific subjects.[32] For example, on the earth being round, on comets, vaccination, on perfumes, on improved agriculture. Other articles were on self-improvement topics, virtues like loyalty were praised, the evils of anger, dependence, lethargy and superstition were deplored. Another set of articles addressed the need for the reform of native society. They criticized the wearing of excessive jewellery, advocated the education of women, re-marriage of high-caste and virgin widows, and the abolition of public festivities like Holi, superstitious practices, the singing of obscene songs at marriages, the 'nautch', and the practice of chest beating during mourning rituals. They commented on child rearing practices, on the behaviour of rich young men, addiction, and so on. The students also set up primary schools to educate younger children and women.

Just as the Khoja commercial magnates had joint commercial interests with other major commercial castes of Bombay, they also associated with each other in reform efforts. The editor of the *Khoja Dost*, a journal started by the reformists, was a Bhatia: Ramdas Bhanji.[33] The Khoja reformers gave a purse to Karsandas Mulji, the bania reformer, who challenged the maharaj and urged other reforms. Khojas introduced English education in their community's school and participated in the 'modern' public life of social meetings and clubs.

Christian missionaries provided an additional critique of indigenous practices. In Bombay, men like John Mitchell and John Wilson played a very important role in engaging the local elite in dialogue to critique traditional religious and social practices. These criticisms required a response and in formulating the response also, a considerable self-reformulation of native practices was undertaken. The missionaries in the 1820s and later periods marked caste as the sign of Hindu degradation.[34]

There was also a growing interest in the Sanskrit tradition sustained by the German romantics who were translating more and more of the Sanskrit classics. Simultaneously with liberal English education, translations from Sanskrit works were becoming available. The study of Sanskrit texts was also carried out by powerful members of native state governments, like Shyamaldas Gandhi, Diwan of Bhavanagar, Gokulji Jhala, Diwan of Junagadh and Manahsukhram Suryaram Tripathi, agent for Junagadh, then for Kutch, Idar and Bhavnagar.[35] They mostly read texts of the Advaita

Shankar Vedanta. Thus, classical Sanskrit literature was available to the Western-educated class without the mediation of traditional interpreters.

The indigenous sects offered another source of criticism of the current practices. For example, Bholanath Sarabhai was brought up by his mother and aunt who were both members of the Ramsanehi *panth* (sect) which replaced idol worship by recounting the name of Ram on a *japmala* or rosary. Founded by Baba Ramcharandas, this sect did not believe in Ram as an incarnation of Vishnu.[36] Bholanath Sarabhai was one of the foremost reformers and one of the founders of the Dharmasabha (religious assembly, 1858 or 1859) in Ahmedabad which eschewed idol worship, substituting prayers and assemblies. His father was a Shakta and it was this practice that he was reforming. The early teachings of his mother and aunt as much as any Western education or missionary chastisement must have encouraged his advocacy of changed ways of worship and belief.[37] The reformers in Bombay and Gujarat were also in touch with changes and reforms occurring in Bengal through visits of travellers both from and to Bengal and the transfer of news.

Discussing indigenous social life in the colonial period always gives rise to questions of whether the 'native' subjects had any independent agency outside the education and influence of the rulers. It would be extremely difficult to show any aspect of native life that was 'autonomous' or free of colonial influence/presence in nineteenth-century Bombay. The question of autonomy and independence is closely linked to a nationalist ethos. The relevance of colonial rule and European presence in India is not merely at the level of influence nor in the nature of a floating context but is crucial to the making of history itself.[38] This story of the nineteenth century could not be written without taking into consideration the concerns, ideas and actions of the local population. The story of those whose ideas succeeded is well known, perhaps. I want to look closely at the details of the same story to understand whose ideas and knowledges were denied and silenced. While the present history does not 'recover' these voices, it marks the silences to discover the creation of new dominant ideas and knowledges.

NOTES

'1. The guru was addressed as 'maharaj', and in the plural the word 'maharajas', usually associated with princely rulers, was accepted usage, for example, in the actual MLC and other writings in English on them. The implication was that the gurus were like rulers or kings to their followers. Thus this usage, that is, of 'maharaj' and 'maharajas' has been followed in this book.
2. Makrand Mehta, 'Maharaj Libel Case: A Study in Social Change in Western India in the Nineteenth Century.' *Indo-Asian Culture* 4, 19 (1970): 26-39; Charles Heimsath, *Indian Nationalism and Hindu Social Reform* (Princeton: Princeton University Press, 1964); R. L. Raval, *Socio-Religious Reform Movements in Gujarat during the Nineteenth Century* (New Delhi: Ess Ess Publications, 1987).
3. Christine Dobbin, *Urban Leadership in Western India : Politics and Communities in Bombay City 1840-1885* (Delhi: Oxford University Press, 1972): 118; James Masselos, 'The Khojas of Bombay: The Defining of Formal Membership Criteria during the Nineteenth Century.' In *Caste and Social Stratification among the Muslims*, edited by Imtiaz Ahmad (Delhi: Manohar, 1973).
4. Rama Jois, *Legal and Constitutional History of India* (Bombay: N. M. Tripathi, 1990): 139, 184.
5. During Maine's tenure 211 enactments were issued out of which perhaps thirty were major, according to G. C. Rankin, *Background to Indian Law* (Cambridge: Cambridge University Press, 1946): 74-75.
6. For a general review of this history refer to Jois, *Legal and Constitutional History*.
7. Quoted in Christine Dobbin, *Basic Documents in the Development of Modern India and Pakistan 1833-1947* (London: Van Nostrand Rheinhold, 1970).
8. Marc Galanter discusses this quality of judgements in various papers on the Indian judicial practice in the post-independence era: see his discussion of Justice Gajendragadkar's judgement of a temple entry dispute in 'Hinduism, Secularism and the Indian Judiciary.' In *Law and Society in Modern India*, edited by Rajeev Dhavan (Delhi: Oxford University Press, 1989).
9. Dobbin, *Urban Leadership in Western India:* Chapters 1, 2.
10. This association of the jamat and the jnati will be discussed in Chapter 1.
11. Jaffer Rahimtoola, *Khoja komano itihas* (Mumbai: Sanj Vartman Press, 1905): 256-274.

12. There was much protest later regarding this representation of the Khoja Ismaili community. C. Gonne, Secretary, Judicial Department, to Secretary, to the Government, in Judicial Department, letter, 29 April 1878, vol 36, 1878, Maharashtra State Archives. Also, Abdoola Allaruckia, petition of objections, 12 Jan 1880, Judicial Department, vol 31, 1880: 207, Maharashtra State Archives.
13. See Masselos, 'The Khojas of Bombay' for a detailed recounting of individual histories of many of the Khojas involved in the mid-century dispute. Many of them had lived in Muscat and Zanzibar for as long as 14 years and others for shorter periods of two years.
14. Estimates of Bombay's population in the 1840s range between 200,000 in 1842, according to Von Orlich's estimate; 566,119 in 1846 according to Murray's *Hand-book of India,* part 2; the population was 500,000 in the Census Report, 1849 quoted in *Life in Bombay* (1852). See *The Gazetteer of Bombay City and Island*, vol 1 (Poona: Government Press, 1909, repr. 1977): 162-163.
15. My calculation, on the basis of Dobbin, *Urban Leadership in Western India*: 153, quoting the figures of total population and percentages of the Muslim population and of the Khojas within the Muslim population.
16. *Gazetteer of Bombay City and Island*: 164; Dobbin, *Urban Leadership in Western India*: 153.
17. *Gazetteer of Bombay City and Island:* 167, 177.
18. Ibid: 168
19. Ibid: 164-165.
20. Dobbin, *Urban Leadership in Western India*: 3, 20.
21. Jaffer Rahimtoola, *Khoja komano itihas*: 257.
22. Ratanji Framji Vachha, *Mumbaino bahar* (Bombay: Union Press, 1874): 114.
23. Tribhovandas Mangaldas Nathoobhai, *Lectures on Hindu Castes, Ceremonies, Customs and Inheritance*: *Includes Life Sketch of Mangaldas Nathoobhai* (Bombay: Education Steam Press, 1896); Navrojajee Sorabjee Bengalee, *Life of Sorabjee Shapurjee Bengalee* (Bombay: Navrojajee Sorabjee Bengalee): 12; Vachha, *Mumbaino bahar:* 86, describes Murphy and Mainwaring as the expert tutors of English with whom Jagannath Shankarsheth and others studied.
24. *Report of the Board of Education, 1842,* a survey of indigenous education, suggested that many more students were receiving education in indigenous schools than in government-run institutions.

Collectorates	Male children in indigenous schools	Male children in government schools	Total male children between ages 5-10
Poona	3,195	2,460	31,979
Surat	3,002	630	16,373
Kaira	3,460	466	28,823
Ahmedabad	6,674	413	25,174

25. Dobbin, *Urban Leadership in Western India*, quoting *General Department, 1843* and *Report of the Board of Education, 1842:* 31.
26. Vachha, *Mumbaino Bahar:* 133.
27. Editor of the *Imperial and Asiatic Quarterly Review, The Biographies (with portraits) of Their Highnesses, the Present and the Two Preceding Aga Sahibs of Bombay, the Chiefs of the Khojas and Other Ismailians: The History of the Dynasty and the Organisation of the Khojas* (Woking: England: Oriental University Institute, 1894).
28. Judgement in the Aga Khan Case 12 *Bombay High Court Reports* (BHR): 341-342.
29. The early dispute between the Aga Khan and the elite Bombay Khojas is most easily accessible in Masselos, 'The Khojas of Bombay'.
30. Sir Thomas Erskine Perry [repr. from the *Biograph,* Feb 1880] (London: E. W. Allen, n.d.): 5.
31. Ibid: 9.
32. *Gnan Prasharak: etalej elam tatha honarano felavo karnar chopaniyun* (Bombay: Gnan Prasarak Mandali, 1849-1851); *The journal of the Students' Scientific and Literary Society*, vols 1-3 (1849-1851); Karsandas Mulji, *Nibandhamala*: *samsar sambandhi vishayo*, vol 1 (Bombay: Union Press, 1870).
33. Dobbin, *Urban Leadershipin Western India*: 116, quoting evidence of Ramdas Bhanjee quoted in *Times of India,* 22 Feb 1862.
34. William Ward, *A View of the History, Literature and Mythology of the Hindoos*, 3 vols (London: Kingsbury, Parbury and Allen, 1822); John Wilson, *Indian Caste*, 2 vols (Bombay: Times of India, 1877) (published posthumously, but the first draft was written in 1857; foreword). See Bernard Cohn's discussion of missionary writing on caste in 'The Study of Indian Society and Culture.' In *Structure and Change in Indian Society* (Chicago: Aldine, 1968): 9.

35. Harilal Savailal, *Shamaldas parmanandas* (Bombay: B. H. Shinde, Tata Vivechaka Press, 1912); Manahsukhram Suryaram Tripathi, *Sujna gokulji jhala: eonun patracitra sahit jivanacharitra tatha vedanta* (Bombay: Nirnayasagar Press, 1902); Hiralal Tribhuvandas Parekh, *Granth ane granthakar*, vol 8 (Ahmedabad: Gujarat Vernacular Society, 1937): 144.
36. Bholanath Sarabhai's son wrote a biography of his father: Krishnarao Bholanath Divetia, *Bholanath sarabhainun jivancharitra* (Mumbai: Nirnayasagar Press, 1888): 131.
37. This is the estimate of Krishnarao Bholanath Divetia, ibid: 131.
38. Michel de. Certeau, *The Writing of History,* Tom Conley (New York: Columbia University Press, 1988).

CHAPTER 1

Framing the Question of Community

'COMMUNITY' IS A much used and very slippery term. Scholars and lay people have employed it at different times and in different contexts to conceptualize collective behaviour. I want to focus on the way it is used to refer to a collective which maintains 'internal' order without any self-defined authorities and by reference to ancient traditions. This aspect of the term 'community' is contained in the predominant conceptualization of community. The colonial court's treatment of religious groups of Khojas and Vaishnavas as Muslim and Hindu sects may be described within the episteme of community.[1]

I use the term 'community' advisedly because it encapsulates the idea of the social and religious collective as it develops in the case proceedings of the nineteenth century and also as it is employed today to refer to Hindus and Muslims. Modern re-workings of this conceptualization of community in India need to be critically examined with reference to the context of the early and mid-nineteenth century and in the episteme of polities. The contrast between these two views of group life—as communities and as polities—marks the settlement of mid-nineteenth century disputes within the Khojas and the Pushtimarga Vaishnavas in the colonial court with tension.

DOMINANT MODE OF UNDERSTANDING COMMUNITY

One of the earliest legal scholars of community in India, Henry Maine, described two kinds of social organizations—

the ancient and the modern.[2] As Inden analyses it, such an 'ancient' communal entity had kinship (status) as its essence as opposed to a modern entity—the individual—which had contract (association) as its essence. India was made up of communities of the ancient type. Men, in this situation, were regarded and treated, not as individuals, but always as members of a particular group.[3] Maine thus employs the term 'community' to refer to a group which had kinship as the essence of the internal relations of its members. As a collective based on kinship, community existed independently of outside structures. Its members were not related to each other out of 'individual interest' but out of a communal empathy. Thus the relationship between them was considered organic : created by the very act of belonging.

It is useful to discuss the work of Ferdinand Tönnies briefly as providing the most succinct definition of the prevailing episteme about community in most modern scholarly and popular work. According to him, community is *Gemeinschaft:* that group where relations are based on bonds of empathy and kinship, and the sentiment of belonging to a group. A community is contrasted with society: *Gesellschaft.* Society is defined as civic life where relations between individual members are contractual and based on notions of self-interest. Thus, while communal relations are organic, societal relations are legal. In the first group, or those subject to *Gemeinshaft,* the organically grown rules, that is, mores, customs or 'folk-ways', organize relations. In the second—the *Gesellschaft*—all relations are embodied in a constitution and administered through law, a product of policy. Tönnies suggests that the state as a lawful form of association is the opposite of community as the organic form of association. In this vision, law and 'legality' are outside the community. Tönnies draws upon Henry Maine's work to locate community in an evolutionary scale.[4] He postulates that with progress and the passage of time, *Gesellschaft* (society or association) tends to replace *Gemeinschaft* (community). The evolutionary path from community to society will lead to the development of a political collectivity of self-interested individuals.

Community, thus contrasted with society, refers to a pre-political social form. Following this understanding, many scholars and commentators on society referred to communities as primordial, implying something that exists from the beginning—fundamental or original. Community, in this formulation, is an ancient entity and is occluded from history. Individual members of such communities have no role in constructing such a community. There is no question of change occurring within the community through the volition or agency of its members.

DISCOURSES ON INDIA: POLITICAL REPRESENTATION AND RELIGIOUS 'COMMUNITIES'

From Charles Metcalfe (1785-1846) onwards, British administrative discourse as well as that of anthropology described India as a land peopled by village communities.[5] Since independence, scholars, whether Indian sociologists or American cultural anthropologists, have viewed Indian social groups in structural-functional terms with outward and upward linkages and have discarded the image of the ungoverned, kinship-based, organic community to describe them.[6] The idea of community nonetheless continues to appear in other discussions of modern India. It is used ubiquitously to describe religious groups of Hindus and Muslims.

Politically this idea of India as peopled by communities is classically represented in the reforms suggested by the Lords Morley (secretary of state for India) and Minto (viceroy of India) in 1909. Lord Minto, when talking to a delegation of Muslims about reforms to the Indian Councils Act, said, 'Any electoral representation in India would be doomed to mischievous failure which aimed at granting a personal enfranchisement, regardless of the beliefs and traditions of the communities composing the population of this continent'.[7] This belief of Lord Minto was translated as policy in the Indian Councils Act of 1909. The act, however, replaced communities by the words 'the communities, classes and interests'. Under this rubric were covered Muslims, Sikhs, Depressed Classes as well as groups of Europeans, merchants, industrialists, and so on. While the term 'classes and interests' covered the latter groups, the religious adherents were covered by the term 'communities'.[8]

These reforms have been much studied as the first attempts by the British to divide a single native community and create two great divisions of Hindu and Muslim communities.[9] None, however, has examined the source of this construction of the two religious groups as communities. Thus in terms of representing the 'people' of India, we encounter a narrative of community: the community of religion. In contrast to the Tönnesian prediction that all communities would fade away with the evolution of modern social forms of the state and the law, it is found that the religious community persists within these associations.[10] This perceived persistence of 'communal' groups has forced scholars to argue that communities exist even in the modern world and in the context of the modern state. They argue that the ancient referents of modern communities (national or ethnic) are created in modern times and hence are not vestiges of an ancient period.[11] They suggest that an idea of a face-to-face, organic group is created through modern means of communication, primarily newspapers.[12] Others argue that 'communal' groups (national or religious) are constructs of the modern state and its governmental systems.[13] Thus they drop the Mainean notion of community as ancient. When one examines their work in more detail, their reworking of the idea of community retains the sense of a collective as an organic and pre-legal body.

RELIGIOUS COMMUNITY CONSTRUCTED BY THE ABSENCE OF STATE INTERVENTION

Sandria Freitag's work is one of the major studies of religious communities that adopts the insight that communities are historically constructed and applies it to examine community formation in modern India. Her study, dealing with the formation of large religious communities, suggests that such community formation occurred because of the failure of the state to organize and regulate public performances or rituals. She therefore suggests that while public performances created national communities in Europe, similar events mobilized religious communities in India. Freitag defines the primary aspect of community as the relation of empathy between its members. She therefore employs Tönnies' definition of *Gemeinschaft* to identify community, while dropping the evolutionary aspect of the argument for not being borne out by history. She says that community relates 'primarily to the ideological expressions of social organization'. Understanding community as an 'ideology' grants a cohesiveness and structure to the idea of community and a 'determination' to it even as she says that the ideology is a construction. It also invests community with a sense of being self-contained; the community as a whole then interacting with the state. She convincingly describes the creation of *communitas* at specific moments within the group and assumes that such moments of sharing allow the community to be maintained as a unity.[14]

Freitag assumes that various kinds of community exist whether they are maintained or re-created through structures or rituals. The effect of this assumption is most striking in the last section. Here she suggests that depending on the symbols selected, the corresponding 'community' is mobilized. If there is a recitation of *tabarra* the Shia community is mobilized. If the *char yari* is recited the Sunni community is mobilized or if the walking on fire ritual is performed the 'Indian' community is mobilized. This formulation assumes the automatic sharing of certain symbols by certain groups and not by others. She comes to this formulation even though she quotes the deposition of Syed Hyder Mehdi as saying, 'the recitation of tabarra is not an article of faith of the Shias . . . [today's] recitation of *tabarra* is in the nature of a defiance of the governmental order.'[15] If a reciter of the tabarra deposes that the recitation is not an article of faith for the Shia community then by what logic can we insist that if there is a recitation of tabarra the Shia community gets mobilized?

Her conclusion is logical only if one presumes the existence of a 'private' non-politicized community which can be mobilized with the use of 'its' symbols and rituals. Her conclusion suggests that the individual belongs naturally to a community and the public mobilization of community becomes inevitable given certain political conditions. The communal mind-set pre-exists as an ideology in individuals. Given certain conditions it 'enters' or 'emerges' or is 'mobilized' in the public arena. Freitag's study does not, thus, ultimately question the existence of 'communal' religious groups as 'ancient' status groups, it only questions their public mobilization.[16]

RELIGIOUS COMMUNITY CONSTRUCTED BY COLONIAL INTERVENTION

Other scholars follow Freitag in the same understanding of community formation in Europe, adding to it Foucault's insight that the knowledge through which those governing society understand their subjects is itself creative of reality.[17] Bernard Cohn and other scholars have pointed to the need to recognize the presence of the various ontologies within which colonial rulers viewed, understood and represented Indian society.[18]

Colonial administrators assumed the presence of different communities in India, and scholars have described its effects on colonial administration. Smith, Cohn and numerous others have suggested that colonial administrators in an attempt to rule in accordance with the 'character' of their subject communities, changed the very nature of collective organization. Scholars describe this change occurring in different areas of administration. Indian 'communities' were consolidated or objectified through colonial revenue collection, census operations, recruitment in services, maintenance of law and order or arrangements for orderly temple administration, processes of adjudication or social reform.[19] Cohn describes community in India as fluid in the non-colonial context, as opposed to being objectified and fixed in the colonial context.[20] Kaviraj describes the difference as being one between a 'fuzzy' community and an enumerated community.[21] Galanter describes group membership as varying between the pragmatic/empirical and the formal/fictional community.[22] In these studies, fluid, fuzzy or pragmatic communities consist of individuals whose membership is blurred and overlapping between groups, whereas, in the latter types of community—objectified, enumerated or formal—group membership is seen as exclusive and hierarchically compartmentalized.

Gyanendra Pandey's study of caste and religious communities is one of the most extensive and influential. How does he use the term 'community' in his treatment of collective structures and what implications does that have for individual membership in the group?[23] Like Freitag, Pandey examines 'communalism' (politicized religious community) in North India and like her he also begins with the premise that communities are constructed. They consider the 'creation' of community in the context of the state. Freitag suggests that the phenomenon of communalism was (and is) linked to the inadequate and stunted involvement of the state in defining activities in public arenas as national. Pandey, however, argues that where the state is actively involved in governance, religious identity replaces more local caste identities. He demonstrates clearly how the activity of the colonial state was crucially responsible for the emergence of communal identities. Thus, Freitag and Pandey are radically different from each other in the way they approach the state's role in defining communal identity.

Pandey's analysis suggests that colonial categorizing and recording practices created the notion of a single Julaha caste from the activities of numerous distinct weaver communities in the United Provinces. He carefully delineates how in the colonial writing of history different weaver communities are constituted as one Julaha caste and the account of the riots where different weaver communities were involved, gets transformed as the account of a single bigoted Julaha caste. He suggests that colonial sociology, which describes the Julaha as a bigot, draws upon the colonial writing of history.[24] Pandey handles the multiplicity of the individual's identities between caste, and religion very sensitively, and he pays a great deal of attention to the construction of local community identity as caste identity. He describes the rise of Hindu communalism and suggests that it occurs over the course of several processes, not the least being the suppression of local village or *qasba* (neighbourhood) communities. His account of Mubarakpur carefully delineates the numerous economic and social links forming the village community. Changes in the power structures within the village led to the occurrence of disputes and challenged neighbourhood traditions. He examines several such disputes, for example, one over a newly built Shivalaya (temple to Shiva) within Mubarakpur. The dispute ended with the Shivalaya being dismantled, described by him as the upholding of Mubarakpur's *local* tradition that no Shivalaya will bc built within the habitation area. He identifies the local traditions of Mubarakpur as Muslim and the dismantling of the Shivalayas as 'the Mubarakpur Muslims had their way'.[25] He does not, however, describe the links between the local tradition and Islam, nor why or how the local tradition and its opposition are now viewed as events of religious conflict.

Even when dealing with other challenges to local traditions Pandey does not examine the construction of the link identifying the local tradition with religion. He describes pig slaughter and playing music in front of the mosque as challenges to local tradition. But he also describes them as insults to Islam.[26] His study leaves unanswered the question, of how and why these 'local' traditions were understood in religious terms. Pandey recognizes this problem when he says, 'the larger question, which is here dealt with only *tangentially*, is that of the relationship in colonialist discourse between 'caste' and 'communalism'.[27] In this absence of a history of the narrative linking the local with the religious, religion is seen as providing a natural identification for individuals participating in local disputes.

A brief look at Pandey's description of the 'local/religious' dispute over the construction of the Shivalaya can give us some pointers to one of the locales of the creation of the link between local community and religious community. He says the dispute was settled after a *court case* that dragged on for months and the continuous efforts of district officials to arrange some sort of a compromise. He describes this intervention of the legal system, however, as a neutral creation of 'avenues' and the provision of 'new grounds of contention'. I would argue that an examination of this legal process would provide the story of how local collective dispute settlement practices were linked with the maintenance of 'religious' tradition.

As we have seen, Pandey assumes that historically more self-conscious 'enumerated' communities replaced local communities that were relational, developed through common residence, shared cultural activities and a recognition of the mutuality of interests of different segments of the local population.[28] This formulation about community persists despite evidence of disputes and antagonisms within the local community and their settlement through external governance. Pandey's analysis echoes one aspect of Tönnies' concept of community: that of community as a local sense of togetherness and tradition. It leads one to assume that the local relational community was maintained by 'natural' authority but not by any 'legal' forms of action. In this view of community the empathetic is opposed to the legal and it presumes that members are brought up in the community from childhood and thus are assumed to belong to it without dispute and without intervention by forms of external governance.

As seen in this critique of current studies of nineteenth-century perceptions of collective or group organization and behaviour, the scholars have missed important links between governance and group identification and behaviour. In Freitag's example there is a recitation of tabarra not as an article of faith, but as a defiance of a governmental order. In Pandey's work a long drawn out legal battle intervenes between the breaking of local traditions and a stand off between religiously defined communities. Neither scholar has examined the significance of these interventions in the governance of collective life, thus ignoring the importance of governance in the identification of the collectives as religious communities. They are still working within the notion of community we identified as the dominant mode of perceiving community—however modified—that is, they reject the idea that community is natural or ancient but still accept that it is empathetic and pre-legal. This dominant notion of community developed in the imperial context of British rule. In contrast to this imperial or colonial idea of community in the East are the early evidence and the vernacular understanding of collective life in India.

IDEAS OF CASTE AND RELIGIOUS COLLECTIVES

Caste Collectives

In Gujarati, castes were called *nat* or *jnati* or even *jamat* in the nineteenth century. At that time, the term *jamat* did not specify a Muslim identity to the group and was used for Hindu as well as Muslim groups.[29] A fine source to assess the meaning of this term is a dictionary compiled in the early part of this century in Gondal, a small principality of Saurashtra. It was painstakingly compiled in nine volumes, and great attention was paid to the origins and the historic as well as modern usage of the words. The *Bhagavadagomandala* dictionary defines *jamat* as deriving from Arabic *jama'a* (collected), synonymous with *nat*, meaning that collective (*mandal*) that has come together for the purpose of doing *vyavahar* (social business), those who eat together, intermarry, share the same religion. This dictionary defines *nat* as synonymous to *nyat*, deriving from Sanskrit *jnati*. It says the nat is that small or large *samudaya* (collective) of family, compound (*vado*) or class formed because of differences of custom, religion, and so on, which is created to maintain the business of life (*samsar vyavahar*) of people who share similar living habits of village or country. It also says that nat is a collective of people who share relationships of eating together and inter-marriage (i.e. commensal and endogamous). *Jnati* is defined as the name deriving from the occupation, region and so forth, by which one is known.[30]

Alexander Forbes (1821-1864), a British administrator of the romantic school, travelled extensively in Gujarat and compiled its history from traditional sources. He described caste as a small collective, local to village, which makes its laws (*kayada*) and enforces correct behaviour.[31] Kavi Dalpatram Dahyabhai (1820-1879) of Ahmedabad, who straddled the old and the new, was a reformer and a foremost interpreter of Gujarati literature and culture. He described how castes break up and come together. In case sufficient numbers of individuals disagreed with each other, they could break away from the caste even as they might continue to maintain certain affinities with the group.[32] He suggested that caste members could decide, for instance, that the caste had become too unwieldy in size and, in order to maintain economy at the time of collective meals and other rituals, break up. Also the 1911 *Census of India* shows a concise list of numerous caste groups which were known to have broken up.[33] Caste histories also record instances of differences and splits within the caste.[34] These descriptions show how castes and their boundaries were not seen in any sense as permanently fixed and were in fact negotiated from time to time.

These early references have not been followed up in scholarly studies of castes. Indeed there is very little information on how castes governed themselves or were governed.[35] Hocart, early on, and, later, Hutton are some of the very few sociologists to note the role of the political authority in controlling castes. Cohn mentions that in the pre-British period castes were supported by political authorities. Hiroshi Fukazawa has described briefly, but very significantly how the Peshwa governed caste affairs.[36]

The 1911 *Census of India* report on caste stated that under native rule the raja was the final authority in all caste matters. It cites the example of the maharajas of Krishnanagar, Nepal, Kushalgarh, Marwar, Rajpipla, Cochin, and so on, who exercised authority by punishing offences against caste and appointing the presidents of the various caste panchayats. In its early days the East India Company itself instituted 'caste cutcherries' for hearing and deciding cases relating to caste matters. This cutcherry was presided over by an officer appointed by the British Governor.[37] A Parsi panchayat's petition, as late as 1838, requested the Governor-General's support to regulate the community's members.[38] Derrett views this request as a demand for granting legal jurisdiction to castes. He comments that if this petition had been granted and if Hindu panchayats had also been granted legal jurisdiction, it would have led to collisions between these indigenous courts and the Supreme Court, which would have been similar to the collisions between spiritual and temporal courts in England. The Parsi panchayat request was denied by the Supreme Court.

Thus, as the early record reveals, the political governance of caste was a recognized affair and the political authorities were directly involved in it. In this context, how did the, Khojas, Bhatias, and Kapols regulate their affairs? The evidence the British themselves collected clearly points to the partially contractual nature of these groups. Adult Khoja men of a particular village or town came together to form a jamat which met regularly in the *jamatkhana* (meeting hall):

> Generally the wealthier and more respectable members manage the affairs and customarily elect Mookee [treasurer] and Camaria [accountant]. The election would be annual at a general meeting of the caste, at the jamatkhana where the most influential people would confer, propose the names which were elected by voice of assembly.[39]

The women, children and the poorer members of the Khojas obviously had little or no participation in the collective. The Aga Khan was revered as a *pir* and his opinion on Khoja practices and beliefs mattered, though he probably had little to do with the day-to-day management of the jamat.

In A.H. 1250 in a dispute between a Khoja leader Umed Ali in Kutch and his fellow Khojas, Aga Khan I was asked to intercede and remove Umed Ali from managing the jamat's affairs. When the Aga Khan was unable to do so directly he approached the British Agency in Kutch who forced Bava Umed Ali to hand over the jamat books to other members.[40]

The adult Bhatia and Kapol men were organized in village or town jnatis and they held meetings at least four times a month, that were attended by most of the adult men of the caste. Each meeting would be announced by the caste's *thanai* (crier) whose job was to inform each member about the meeting. In case of a dispute, both disputants would be informed of the matter and both sides would have to remain present. The leaders would read a statement and members could vote on it by a show of hands which would be counted or by a voice vote. Sometimes *vakils* (advocates) would also be used by both sides.[41] Castes were supposed to regulate most aspects of their members' lives. They accepted the influence and the power of the maharajas—the hereditary Vaishnava priests—to instruct them on some affairs. They also went with disputes either to the maharaj or to the local politically constituted authority. These inter-linkages will be discussed in Chapter 4 in more detail.

As groups that had membership by birth, jamats and jnatis were *Gemeinschaft,* though each was differentiated. Some of its members—like women and children, and, to a lesser extent, poorer men—were governed through their assemblies by wealthy and influential men. To the extent, however, that each was organized through different locii and centres of authority, and made laws and changed them, each came under *Gesellschaft* or Society. Collingwood's term 'polity' is most appropriately used to characterize such groups.[42] These were numerous and shifting, and were an integral and governed part of larger polities. Their jurisdictions were multiple and overlapping; while caste leaders governed their members, they in turn were governed by greater political and religious authorities.

In spite of this considerable evidence regarding the governed nature of caste groups, as Cohn has remarked, few anthropologists and sociologists have bothered to ask how exactly the political rulers settled caste disputes.[43] Did they refer a dispute back to the group or was it settled by some criteria independent of the group? This is a question that has to be traced historically. In 1838 the Supreme Court of Bombay Presidency examined this question and made an interesting suggestion: if the court was to be the final authority to determine caste questions, and if collisions between the caste panchayat and the Supreme Court were to be avoided, a lawyer would have to be appointed as assessor to the caste panchayat. However, as we shall see later (Chapter 2), this manner of treating castes was not considered within the structures of colonial governance in Bombay.

Religious Collective as Sampradaya

The local population in Bombay in the nineteenth century employed another model of religious collectives. The Khojas, as discussed earlier, formed a religious jamat within Islam. The Pushtimarga too were part of a religious organization placed within Hinduism. Instead of conceiving the religious tradition as centred on a church, the indigenous model recognized '*astika*' or believers, and among them they recognized different sampradayas. The Vallabhacharya Vaishnavas described themselves as following a sampradaya. Pandit Sukhalalji explains what a sampradaya is very lucidly and clearly when he quotes the *Amarakosha's* definition that says it is 'the teachings that have been passed on through a line of teachers'.

Sampradaya (often translated as 'sect') refers to specific teachings and religious organization, but is not defined in opposition to some other church or more established tradition. The identity of the sampradaya is to be defined in its own terms and does not need recognition of another tradition. In the *Kusumanjali*, sampradaya is defined as Veda.[44] This is a recognition of the sampradaya as an original teaching. By quoting the Shastra or previous authoritative thinkers, the founder of a sampradaya or the guru claims continuity with some recognized authority. There may, however, be several original works that he could choose from and he may be different from other thinkers commenting on the same text, who are also considered to have originated religious traditions. While the author of these interpretations may have to justify himself, this justification itself determines the legitimacy of the faith.

A dispute about sampradaya and its authority would result in a *shastrartha*, where judges, perhaps at the ruler's court, are to be convinced by the disputing parties as to the true meaning of the authoritative religious texts. For example, one dispute within Vaishnava groups was settled by a gathering of Bengali, Oriya and Kasi pandits, an account of which is given in the official record of a Muslim kingdom. Because it was officially recorded, it suggests that the discussion took place in a political venue, which could enforce the settlement of the dispute.[45] The meaning of the authoritative text is determined during the dispute, and the decision is not made on the grounds of some external determination of what the truth is. The shastrartha is intended to convince the political authority of the disputants' faith or belief in the Vedas and to the truth of their own interpretation of the text. It was also the occasion for determining the grounds or texts on which truth could be based. It was not meant to evaluate the concordance of faith with some outside understanding of truth but to demonstrate the truth of their own interpretation of the agreed upon authoritative texts. Thus, Narmad describing his shastrartha with Jadunath Maharaj on widow remarriage says, 'Jadunath and I had not thought to dispute the question of remarriage that day, but to determine the grounds [*rupak* lit. metaphor] of the dispute.'[46] Pollock's study indicates that what constitutes authoritative religious texts or Shastra is defined and redefined over time through such disputes.[47] During a shastrartha, regardless of whether it involves the redefinition of what constitutes the body of religious texts or interpretation of that body, the views of both debating parties are admissible. This question of establishing the truth of a sampradaya is raised among exponents of the religious texts.[48]

Sampradayik debates were encouraged by pre-British and non-British secular authorities to settle legal questions. Sampradaya*s* and gurus, as mentioned earlier, were governed by secular authorities, usually rajas and caste authorities, in the nineteenth century. Religious heads employed caste authorities to achieve their ends, for example, revenue collection and compliance with religious rules. Religious authorities could earn privileges and exemptions for their adherents from the political authorities.[49] As discussed earlier, in the event of a dispute between members of a sampradaya, which required a settlement of the dispute, the political authority or the caste concerned could hold a shastrartha. For example, the Nagar Baniya jnati of Surat had a dispute whether foreign travel was allowed by the religious. authorities. The caste authorities arranged for experts on the shastra to assemble in Surat and debate the issue and arrange a settlement (*bandobast),* which would be enforced by the political and caste authorities.[50]

Thus the sampradaya was linked with the caste and with political rulers as much as it was associated with religious preceptors, when it came to organizing its following and members. An individual became a member of a sampradaya by birth (*Gemeinschaft*). As we saw, however, the sampradaya was governed not merely by the sole authority of a whimsical guru but through a combination of religious texts and experts who accepted the laws and customs of political rulers as well as the social elite (*Gesellschaft*). The character of this group of which she or he was a member changed with different definitions of beliefs and practices by its governing elite: wealthy and influential men, religious preceptors, political authorities. The sampradaya can be called a polity—an association with governance. Again, it is important to recognize that the religious polity was not isolated or independent but was a part of other political and social polities.

Church and Sect

The British understood organized religious life as constituted in the Church of England. According to this model there was the established Church of England which was headed by the crown. Anglican religious disputes were tried by ecclesiastical courts which were set up by the crown, and presided over by bishops and laymen, over whom the final authority was the judicial committee of the Privy Council.

Those that differed from the established church were called sects. The term 'sect' is derived from the Latin *sequi* (to follow) and it does not necessarily imply a schism. In the nineteenth century the term 'sect' was employed for all non-conformist groups in Britain, and was almost invariably used to describe a contrapuntal (but not necessarily contradictory) ideal type to the church.[51] A sect is described as a voluntary society of strict believers. Its foundation upon contracted or freely elected membership marks a sharp contrast with the church into which members were largely born. Sects expected near total uniformity from their membership.[52]

After the Act of Toleration 1689, certain sects were allowed to govern themselves. They were treated as voluntary associations that had come together consciously. Thus, they had their own laws, which formed the 'constitution' (or canon or covenant) of their churches. It was assumed that such a constitution was developed by consultation within the sectarian body. The Anglican church made its laws under the authority of the crown and enacted by acts of Parliament. As long as these sects did not do anything illegal they had the right to organize their internal affairs.

The British had worked out, through a long period of struggle over church-state relations, what questions did not fall under the purview of religious laws. In Common Law and Equity jurisdictions, a rule of non-interference in religion was laid down. These courts were, however, often faced with the question of religion in many civil disputes, for example, in disputes over religious property. In such cases, the court had to remain judicially ignorant of religion, and it could not examine religious information as to its meanings. Religious matters would be examined for procedure, and authorities from the church or chapel (or any voluntary association) in question would be brought in to testify on the subject. A question pertaining to the Anglican church, however, would be tried in the ecclesiastical courts. If there were a question on the change of doctrine in a sect, it would have to be tried by the sect in accordance with its own constitution. No change in such constitution could be argued in the civil court as it was assumed that fundamental articles of the constitution of a sect could not be changed unless there was unanimity regarding the change. Thus, new doctrines or new interpretations of old doctrines could be introduced through internal law-making process, to be then codified in new constitutions/canons.[53]

The different ideas about castes, sampradayas, jamats, churches and sects were in tension. British ideas and their understanding of Indian circumstances structured governance of the collectives. According to the early judicial administrators of India, Hastings, Colebrooke and Cornwallis, Indians were governed by the law of their own religions. Just as the British government at home administered or headed the administration of religious law with regard to persons on certain subjects, so too they administered religious laws to the Indians.[54] Indeed, Derrett says, 'the Supreme Court in India, applying Hindu law [and I may add Islamic law], did so as a combined temporal and spiritual court'.[55] 'Hindoos' and 'Mussalmans' were expected to be homogeneous as if they were single 'churches'.[56] Yet in the process of 'discovery' of Hinduism and Islam the colonial rulers claimed that the Hindus and Muslims had no church and while there were differences in practices these were guided by their definitive texts.[57] All religious law was said to be pre-existing as written in the *Smriti* or the Quran and simply inherited.[58] They assumed that there were no systems of contractual governance within these religious traditions which would permit at least some of the members to participate in their reinterpretation to suit contemporary historical contexts. The British could not accept shastrartha as a genuine way of organizing a sect. Nor could they adopt an entirely confident ecclesiastical role—replacing the shastris. (In the early period they did accept pandits and kazis in court to give *vyavasthas*; however, they were never entirely confident of these 'judicial practitioners'.) Thus, in Bengal under Hastings, Indian religious sects like Pushtimargis or Shaivites or Sunnis or Shias or Khojas were not treated as voluntary associations but as parts of a church-like religious body, which however had no authorities to determine church law. The British assumption that there were no organized structures of church authorities among the Hindus and the Muslims led to the representation of these traditions by anyone who knew the texts. The religious authority was thus usurped by the expert in religion. Whereas hitherto he who claimed to represent religious authority had presumably been a member of a congregation, during British rule this expert in religion did not need to be one. Indeed the British believed that organized 'congregation' did not exist and therefore the question of belonging could not arise. The effect of this replacement was that an individual member of the religious tradition would have to give an account of his actions that demonstrated his membership in accordance with the religious description given by the evidence of experts in the singular and universal traditions of Hinduism and Islam.

In contrast to the British administration's rule of not entertaining religious debates the political recognition of the sampradaya was established without recourse to the universal religious category of 'Hindu' or 'Islamic'. There was no need to demonstrate membership in the religious group by proving concordance with doctrines as in the case of the British model of judicial administration and separation of church and state matters. It is this treatment of religious groups by the colonial authorities which may be characterized within the episteme of 'community'. Thus polities were treated as communities. This transformation of group governance needs to be carefully studied and established, and we will examine the various ways in which the paradigms laid out on group governance clashed in the early to mid-nineteenth century. We shall see in detail how the Khojas and the Pushtimargis were transformed from polities that were self-governing as well as governed from outside to communities that were either self-regulating or totally regulated by the state.

CONSTRUCTION OF COMMUNITY IN GOVERNANCE

Scholars have suggested that colonial administration constructed universal religious (Hindu and Muslim) communities.[59] They are, however, still working within the concept of community. The identification of smaller groups with the universal religious community is not seriously examined. I would argue that an individual member of a local social and religious polity could not 'naturally' be identified in law or in the courts with an unmarked religious community. The colonial judiciary's *denial* of the polities' ability to govern and their simultaneous exclusive governance by the colonial state led to the establishment of an individual as a member of a pre-legal original community, defined by birth and status.

Caste and religious groups were recognized as polities in a limited sense by the setting up of the Bombay Presidency's judicial jurisdictions and laws (1819-1827). Two legal proceedings in the post-1858 period reveal how the socio-religious polities were treated as communities. In this later period the relative autonomy of the Bombay Presidency judicial administration was given up in favour of the establishment of a uniform Bengal-style judiciary in Bombay and Madras. This judicial change took place post-Mutiny when the British were increasingly nervous of upsetting the religious beliefs of the local population, which was the context in which the cases were examined.

The early self-governance of socio-religious groups suggests that there was no reason in the collective life of the Khojas and the Pushtimargis for the court to deal with them as primordial communities incapable of changing their constitution. On the contrary one may suggest that they were contractual/associational, partially self-governing groups that had jurisdiction over a vast but context-sensitive nature over their members. Although the polities did not allow equal participation of all members in governance, they did involve the participation of a large number of male members in dispute settlements so that the settlement or bandobast arrived at in each case suited the purposes and contemporary contexts (elitist as they were) of each group. Such a mode of dispute settlement recognized that the polities could change their actual practices and religious beliefs during a dispute.

There was a disjuncture between the post-1858 legal representation of caste and religious groups as 'natural' or 'self-existent' and organic during the case proceedings and the early-nineteenth century representation of practices of jnatis and sampradayas. This disjuncture of the ideas of caste and religious collectives and their relationships with the state poses questions to our legal representational practices. One must examine what it means for law to define an individual or individuals by his/her/their community. If the naturalness and apolitical organic character of 'a community' is not axiomatic what does it mean to recognize membership in a community as independent of the individual members' decision-making? What role does the state play in providing individuals with an opportunity to make an active choice as to the construction of their collective? If such a provision is not made how can the court or the law make a definition of community applicable to all its members by default?

The question raised is whether the treatment in colonial law of these polities created for their members greater freedoms as subjects of the British queen. This question is, however, addressed only tangentially. The court's treatment of religious groups of the Khojas and the Vaishnavas as sects, whose members did not participate in defining their current practices, may be described, as suggested earlier, within the episteme of community. As in the case of all explanatory terms employed to 'capture' reality, this usage too does not deny the treatment by the court of these groups in different ways. The court was too close to the group not to recognize the different authorities within the groups, different interpretive frameworks, the means to settle differences.

However, as we shall see, these different practices were either silenced or negated and made to fit into the narrative of religious community that the court constructed for the Khojas and Vaishnavas.

'Community' is such a widely used term that its use often confuses the reader and writer. I employ it to describe the court's denial of the 'political' character of the Vaishnavas and the Khojas because it resonates with the term 'community' used today to describe the religious groups of Hindus and Muslims. My concern is with the modern construction of 'communities' of 'Hindus' and 'Muslims' which consistently informs the writing of this book. In today's political context the question uppermost in my mind is how was it that the numerous and often antagonistic religious groups and separately organized collectives were represented in the single category of either Hindu or Muslim. I have examined the Aga Khan and the Pushtimarga Vaishnava cases where the court decided legitimate Hindu and Muslim behaviour to reflect on the proces of universalization of the categories.

The law represents itself as not having an interest in Hindu or Muslim dogma. It could have asked the Khojas and Vaishnavas to determine their practice outside the court, or if they had accepted the jurisdiction of an ecclesiastical nature, they could have tried each group's true faith on the grounds of faith. But the courts, considering that the Hindus and Muslims had no church authorities to make decisions for either group or assuming that such religious authority was too dispersed and in any case not trustworthy, treated the religious group as a community that possessed no ongoing legal authority and, because of its antiquity, no means to create such an authority, thus providing for the imposition of its Orientalist knowledge. However, if one were to merely concentrate on the success of the court's establishment of an orthodox and Orientalist Hinduism and Islam we would be limited to describing the reformers as nothing but Western creations. We would not see them as denying the need to hear the case in court or the activity of the judges as not involving anything new—retaining at the time the possibilities of doing something different. I will argue away the priority of Orientalist knowledge to suggest that while Orientalist discourses speak of History (Truth), they are already situated in history (Events). Let us now examine colonial juridical practice to see how the colonial court became involved in religious inquiry at all and study the mechanisms of the production of homogeneous religious categories within the court.

NOTES

1. The courts too used the term 'community' to define these groups—especially the Khojas—sometimes also using the terms 'tribe' and 'sectaries'.
2. Henry Sumner Maine, *Village Communities in the East and West* (1871) (London: J. Murray, 1907).
3. I draw upon Ronald Inden's analysis of Maine's writings to bring out clearly his meaning of community, *Imagining India* (London: Blackwell, 1990): 139.
4. Ferdinand Tönnies, *Community and Association,* tr C. P. Loomis (London: Routledge and Kegan Paul, 1955): 69, 74, 264.
5. Inden, *Imagining India:* 131-148.
6. Bernard S. Cohn, 'Notes on the History of the Study of Indian Society and Culture'. In *An Anthropologist among Historians* (Delhi: Oxford University Press, 1987); Inden, *Imagining India*: 151-154.
7. Lord Minto's address to the Muslim deputation led by the Aga Khan in 1906, quoted in Lady Minto's *Journal* in Christine Dobbin, *Basic Documents in the Development of Modern India and Pakistan 1835-1947* (London: Van Nostrand, 1970): 66.
8. A. R. Desai, *Social Background of Indian Nationalism*, 5th ed (Mumbai; Popular Prakashan, 1998): 368, 370.
9. A. Mehta, and A. Patwardhan, *The Communal Triangle in India,* 2nd ed (Allahabad: Kitabistan, 1942).
10. Partha Chatterjee talks about the suppressed narrative of the community in the ideologies of the state and describes how this suppression is a consequence of the capital-community encounter, see his 'Response to Taylor's Invocation of Civil Society'. In *Working Papers and Proceedings for Psychosocial Studies* 39 (Chicago: Centre for Psychosocial Studies, 1990).
11. To mention one important early work on the subject, Eric Hobsbawm and T. Ranger, eds, *The Invention of Tradition* (Cambridge: Cambridge University Press, 1983).
12. Benedict Anderson, *Imagined Communities: Reflections on the*

Origin and Spread of Nationalism (London: Verso, 1983).
13. Clifford Geertz, 'The Integrating Revolution: Primordial Sentiments and Civil Politics in the New States.' In Clifford Geertz, *Interpretation of Cultures* (London: Hutchinson, 1975); Manning Nash, *The Cauldron of Ethnicity in the Modern World* (Chicago: Chicago University Press, 1989); Sandria Freitag, *Collective Action and Community: Public Arenas and the Emergence of Communalism in North India* (Delhi: Oxford University Press, 1990).
14. Freitag, *Collective Action and Community*: 4, 5, 128-138.
15. Ibid: 249, 275.
16. See also Sumit Sarkar's review of her work 'Popular Culture, Community, Power: Three Studies of Modern Indian Social History', *Studies in History* 8, 2 ns (1992): 309-323.
17. Michel Foucault, *The History of Sexuality,* vol 1, tr Robert Hurley (New York: Vintage, 1980); Edward Said, *Orientalism* (New York: Pantheon, 1978).
18. Cohn, 'Notes on the History of the Study of Indian Society and Culture'; Lata Mani, 'Contentious Traditions: The Debate on Sati in Colonial India'. In *Recasting Women: Essays in Colonial History,* edited by Kumkum Sangari and Sudesh Vaid (New Delhi: Kali for Women, 1989).
19. R. Suarez-Smith, 'Rule-by-Records and Rule-by-Reports: Contemporary Aspects of the British Imperial Rule of Law.' *Contributions to Indian Sociology* ns 19 1, (1985) 153-196; Bernard S. Cohn, 'The Census, Social Structure and Objectification in South Asia.' In *An Anthropologist among Historians;* N. G. Barrier, ed, *The Census in British India: New Perspectives* (Delhi: Manohar, 1981); Gyanendra Pandey, *The Construction of Communalism in Colonial North India* (Delhi: Oxford University Press, 1990); R. Pant, 'The Cognitive Status of Caste in Colonial Ethnography: A Review of Some Literature on the North West Provinces and Oudh.' *IESHR* 24, 2 (1987): 145-162; Arjun Appadurai, *Worship and Conflict under Colonial Rule: A South Asian Case*. Cambridge South Asian Studies, vol 27 (Cambridge: Cambridge University Press, 1992); Marc Galanter, *Law and Society in Modern India* (Delhi: Oxford University Press, 1992); Minoti Kaul, 'Commons, Community and Courts in Colonial Punjab.' *IESHR* (Dec 1992) 29, 4 (1992): 393-436.
20. Bernard S. Cohn, 'The Census, Social Structure and Objectification in South Asia.' In *An Anthropologist among the Historians and Other Essays.*
21. Sudipta Kaviraj, 'Imagined Institution of India.' In *Subaltern Studies*, vol 7 (Delhi: Oxford University Press, 1992).

22. Galanter, 'Group Membership and Group Preferences in India.' In *Law and Society in Modern India.*
23. Pandey, *The Construction of Communalism.*
24. Ibid: 69; 94-107.
25. Ibid: 160.
26. Ibid: 148-157.
27. Ibid: 69.
28. Ibid: 151, 160.
29. See, for example, its use to describe the Dusa Shrimali Banias in H. Borradaile, *Reports of Civil Causes Adjudged by the Court of Sudder Dewanee Adawlut for the Presidency of Bombay from 1800-1824, Cases Decided in Surat* (Bombay: Educational Society Press, 1863), case no 18, p80.
30. Bhagvatsinhji, *Bhagavadagomandal* (1950) (Rajkot: Pravin Prakashan, 1986), vol 4: 3430; vol 5: 4964; vol 4: 3638.
31. Alexander Kinloch Forbes, *Rasmala: The Hindu Annals of the Province of Gujarat*, tr Ranchhodbhai Udayram, 3rd ed (Bombay: Pharbus Gujarati Sabha, 1927).
32. Dalpatram Dahyabhai, *Jnatinibandh* (1851), 4th ed (Ahmedabad: Gujarat Vernacular Society, V.S. 1943 [A.D. 1885]): 7.
33. E. A. Gait, *Census of India 1911: Reports,* vol 1, part 1 (Calcutta: Government of India, 1912).
34. See, eg, *Porvad: surati dasa porvad hitecchu sabhana jubilee mahotsavanum smarak pustak* (Mumbai: Sabhana Pustak Samiti, 1922); Manjula Kakatiya, *'Bhrihad mumbayini kapol vaishya jnati: ek samajashastriya anveshan.'* PhD diss, SNDT Women's University, 1978.
35. See Inden's survey of scholarship on castes, *Imagining India*: 49-84.
36. M. Hocart, *Caste, A Comparative Study* (London: Methuen, 1950); J. H. Hutton, *Caste in India: Its Nature, Function and Origins*, 3rd ed (London: Oxford University Press, 1961); Cohn, 'Anthropological Notes on Disputes and Law in India.' In *An Anthropologist among the Historians*: 605; Fukazawa Hiroshi, 'The State and the Caste System (Jati).' In *The Medieval Deccan: Peasants, Social Systems and States Sixteenth to Eighteenth Centuries* (Delhi: Oxford University Press, 1991).
37. Gait, the author of the report, was also a member of the Royal Asiatic Society; Gait, *Census of India 1911,* vol 1: 393; he quotes the report of O'Malley, the provincial superintendent of the Census for Bengal, Bihar and Orissa: 394.
38. Petition to Lord Auckland dated 21 Nov 1838, quoted in Dobbins, *Urban Leadership*: 99; J. D. M. Derrett, *Religion, Law and*

the State in India (London: Faber, 1968): 234, refers to this petition and comments that if it had been granted and if Hindu panchayats had also been granted legal jurisdiction, it would have led to collisions between these indigenous courts and the Supreme Court, similar to the collisions between spiritual and temporal courts in England.

39. Plaint filed on 21 Feb 1850 by Dhurrmsey Poojabhoy and others, see *Bombay Times and Journal of Commerce,* 21 July 1851.
40. Chunara Vazirmohammad Janmahommmad, *Nurammobin* (1936), 4th ed (Bombay: Ismailia Association for India, 1961).
41. *Sri mumbayina halai bhatia mahajana hisab: sam 1917-1918* [A.D. 1860-1861] *to sam 1940* [A.D. 1883] (Mumbai: Lakshmidas Khimjina Hukamathi Metaji Chaturbhuj Balaji, annual reports 1863-1883); see especially the use of vakils in 1872 vol: 37-46.
42. R. G. Collingwood, *The New Leviathan, or Man, Society, Civilisation, Barbarism* (Oxford: Clarendon, 1944); Inden, *Imagining India,* for a discussion of the notion of plural sovereignties and dispersed polities.
43. Cohn, 'Notes on Disputes and Law in India.'
44. '*Sampradayah: guru paramparagate sadupadeshe, upacharat tadupadesayute jane cha.*' His Gujarati translation: '*guruparamparathi chalyo avato sadupadesha.*' Pandit Sukhalalji, *Darsan ane chintan: pandit sukhalaljina gujarati lekhono samagraha.* (Ahmedabad: Gujarat Vidyasabha, 1957): 1107.
45. Quoted in D. K. Shastri, '*Agiyaramathi solama shatakana vaishnavabhaktinum prthakkarana*', in *Aitihasika samshodhana*, 2nd ed (Ahmedabad: Gujarati Sahitya Parishad, 1977), which refers to Sen, *Typical Selections from Old Bengali*, part 2, p 16: 187 (Sen's first name not given). I am indebted to Achut Yajnik for this reference.
46. Narmadshankar Lalshankar, *Mari hakikat ane anya atmakathaniya lakhano*, edited by Dhirubhai Thakar (Ahmedabad: Gurjar Grantharatna Karyalaya 1983), p73. Narmad says '*maro ne jadunathno vichar te dahade punarvivah sambandhi vad karvano nahin pan te vadanun rupak bandhavano*' (my translation) I have translated 'metaphor' as 'grounds', for the first question debated was their agreement on the canon (Shastra) to be employed. See also Mahipatram's *Uttam kapol karsandal mulji* for an account of the meeting.
47. Sheldon Pollock, 'The Idea of Shastra in Traditional India.' In *Shastric Traditions in the Indian Arts*, edited by Anna Libera Dallapiccola et al. Contributions to South Asian Studies no 125 (Stuttgart: Steiner, 1989): 17-26.

48. Some events of shastrartha in the nineteenth century: *(i)* in Pune on the question of widow remarriage; *(ii)* in Surat in 1870, on the question of foreign travel. *Rast Goftar and Satya Prakasha* (*RGSP*) (8 May 1870): 303.
49. I am grateful to Achyut Yajnik for sharing his interpretation of the relations between the maharaj and the Delhi rulers as evidenced by the grants received by the maharajas. These grants have been studied by Edwin Allen Richardson, 'Mughal and Rajput Patronage of the Bhakti Sect of the Maharajas, the Vallabha Sampradaya, A.D. 1640-1760.' PhD diss, University of Arizona, 1979, microfilm; Rajendra Jindel, *Culture of a Sacred Town: A Sociological Study of Nathdwara* (Mumbai: Popular Prakashan, 1976).
50. *Rast Goftar and Satya Prakasha,* 8 May 1870: 303; see also n48.
51. A. J. Maclean, 'Law (Christian, Anglican)', *Encyclopaedia of Religion and Ethics,* vol 7, edited by James Hastings (New York: Scribner's, 1915): 840-846; Michael Hill, 'Sects', *Encyclopaedia of Religion and Ethics,* vol 13, edited by M. Eliade (New York: Macmillan, 1987): 157; Thomas O'Dea, 'Sects', *International Encyclopaedia of the Social Sciences,* vol 14, edited by David Sills (New York: Macmillan, 1968): 130-136.
52. O'Dea, 'Sects': 137.
53. Maclean, 'Law (Christian, Anglican)': 841, says 'a constitution was very much the same as a "canon", and so it is in the titles of the English and Irish codes of canons'; he adds, 'the civil courts do not protect the churches . . . from the influx of new doctrines, it only ensures that there is not an abandonment of the principles of the church': 845.
54. According to English legal theory, religion governs personal interactions like marriage, succession, adoption, and so on, hence disputes relating to these issues were settled in accordance with religious laws. English ecclesiastical courts tried these disputes for church members.
55. J. D. M. Derrett, *Religion, Law and the State in India*: 234.
56. The colonial administrators assumed that a single set of religious laws, one each for the Hindus and the Muslims could be produced. They also assumed that any fair and impartial student could extract the true original religious precepts. Many scholars have examined in detail the processes and contents or characteristics of this discovery of the canon: the main tradition in Hinduism and Islam. Among others, Lucy Carroll, 'Law, Custom, and Statutory Social Reforms: The Hindu Widows' Remarriage Act of 1856.' In *Women in Colonial India: Essays on*

Survival, Work and State, edited by J. Krishnamurthy (Delhi: Oxford University Press, 1989); Bernard S. Cohn, 'Law and the Colonial State in India'. Paper presented at the International Symposium on Ethnohistorical Models for the Evolution of Law in Specific Societies, Bellagio, Italy, 1985; Derrett, *Religion, Law and the State*; Asaf Ali Asghar Fyzee, *Outlines of Muhammadan Law*, 3rd ed (Oxford: Oxford University Press, 1964); Gregory C. Kozlowski, *Muslim Endowments and Society in British India* (Cambridge: Cambridge University Press, 1985); P. J. Marshall, *The British Discovery of Hinduism in the Eighteenth Century* (Cambridge: Cambridge University Press, 1970).

57. Inden, describing various colonial and Orientalist views of Hinduism says they assumed that Hinduism was deficient in the capacity to form voluntary associations and carry out joint activities. That is why the religion of the Brahman philosopher had no church and was not congregational, requiring no organization, *Imagining India*: 128. Similarly for Islam, Kozlowski and Wilson describe how a singularly Quran-based Islam was constructed in the judicial system.
58. This view of Hindu and Muslim religious law is described in the two essays one on Hindu law and the other on Muhammadan law in *Encyclopaedia of Religion and Ethics*, vol 7, edited by James Hastings; T. W. Juynboll on 'Law (Muhammadan): 858-883; and J. Jolly on 'Law (Hindu): 850-853.
59. Pandey, *The Construction of Communalism,* discussed earlier, has been one of the most important works to make this argument.

CHAPTER 2

Colonial Representation of 'Caste' as Self-Governing Community, 1819-1827

IT HAS LONG been recognized that the Bombay Regulations possessed a different understanding of local laws (i.e. customary rule of the country) from the other presidencies. In the separately administered province of Punjab there was a much stronger recognition of customary laws than in the Bombay Presidency.[1] It has, however, not been understood exactly how the customary local rule would be ascertained and furthermore what would be the likely consequences of representing 'natives' in law. I suggest that recognition of customary rule meant a recognition of castes and religious groups. The indigenous authorities that governed this internal sphere were recognized within the colonial 'rule of law' and consulted in court as partners in dispute settlement and to that extent the groups were treated as self-governing 'polities'. Their self-governance was circumscribed to jurisdiction over 'internal' affairs; however, the definition of 'internal' meant different things at different times.

Scholars have in general studied the rule of law for India in two ways. One kind of study examines the history of the substantive law.[2] These works examine how law was compiled, with various kinds of help from 'native specialists' and varying degrees of employment of 'native tradition', whether textual or customary. Derrett and Rocher describe how the British compiled a code of Hindu law. Similarly, Fyzee, Wilson and others have studied how the Anglo-Mohammedan law was set up in India.

The second type of studies are very few and these examine the British administration of law. Some describe this administration as growing straightforwardly from a small beginning, setting up courts, and then expanding their jurisdiction.[3] Others indicate some of the ways that the judiciary has been responsible for the creation of new social definitions.[4] There are also studies that indicate how the courts maintained certain areas of independence in which they refused to adjudicate: areas which they felt were best ruled by the natives themselves.[5]

British administrators in different parts of India employed different models of law and governance to determine which law should be employed in their courts to settle disputes between natives.[6] In Bengal, where the colonial judicial administration of disputes between natives was the oldest, the Roman model of law, distinguishing between personal law, which would govern personal or family issues, and civil law that would govern other issues, was employed. William Jones, who came out to Bengal as a judge, saw himself as the Indian Justinian, guaranteeing to his subjects their law as Justinian guaranteed his Roman and Greek subjects their own law.[7] In Christian Europe this distinction was between civil law and canon law.

Following this model, administrators in India like Lord Hastings, William Jones and others assumed that Indian subjects already possessed their law of marriage, inheritance and other practised custom in their *religious* texts. Hastings and Jones felt that, once these texts were made available to the British, they could rule 'directly'—without reliance on 'crooked, partisan and corrupt natives'. Thus, in Bengal, first William Halhed and then William Jones and T. E. Colebrooke compiled a digest of indigenous laws for Hindus based on Sanskrit texts.[8] Jones also compiled a detailed code of Mohammedan laws regarding inheritance.[9] Charles Hamilton in 1791 under Lord Hastings' directions compiled a detailed code of Mohammedan laws, based on his own English translation of the Persian translation of the Arabic *Hedaya* (Guide) of Al Marghianini.[10]

On questions other than inheritance (marriage and so on), justice, equity and good conscience were to be applied by the judge. The question of what constituted 'justice, equity and good conscience' in terms of substantive law has been discussed in various studies of Indian legal history.[11] Most of these studies provide details of this route by which English law was applied in the Indian courts.

The Bombay Presidency Regulations of the same period especially the 1799 Regulation did not follow the legal scheme that was devised by Hastings in Bengal. In Bombay, the English distinction between the king's law and common law, rather than that between civil law and canon law, was applied. The common law notion was that all law is based on customs of place, deriving its moral force from having developed with the people in a place from time immemorial. British legal theorists held that rules, to be recognized as custom, must have 'the express or tacit sanction of the collective will or common consent of the people among whom they prevail'. 'The binding force of a custom derives from the common consent of a community that originates a custom and this *obliges* every individual to observe and obey it.'[12] This understanding of the legitimacy of customary law drove the English kings to recognize and administer customary law.

This understanding of law can be seen in the Channel Islands. These islands remained loyal to the English crown though Normandy was lost to France in 1204. The customary law of the Channel Islands was Norman law and English judges appointed to local courts applied Norman customs. The king retained judicial authority and assumed appellate jurisdiction through the king's council in 1495, and later, through the Privy Council. This model of law was closest to the judicial situation in the Bombay Presidency.[13]

The Bombay Regulation IV of 1799 under John Duncan, which set up the judiciary in the Bombay Presidency, specified the importance of local customary law. Section 14 of Regulation IV required judges to ascertain the customary rule of the district or any particular family usage or if there was an unwritten yet ascertained common law (called *ralje* [*sic*; *rivaj*?] *al-moolk* or 'customary rule of the country'). If this law was not opposed to equity then it was to operate to the exclusion of the written and formal code of the Hindu law books. Native laws were not reserved for the few subject matters mentioned in the Bengal Regulation but were to be applied to all sorts of disputes between parties.[14] Customary law, rules or usage to be acceptable to Anglo-Indian judiciary, had to be 'communal' or deriving from a collective will. It was the task of the administrator and judge to locate this communal body and derive from it the indigenous law.

ELPHINSTONE'S ADMINISTRATION

The British considerably expanded their rule in Gujarat and the Deccan in the first two decades of the nineteenth century, defeating the peshwa in various battles. Lord Mountstuart Elphinstone was the British resident at the peshwa's court (1810-1818), then commissioner of the Deccan Territories (1818-1819) and later governor of Bombay Presidency (1819-1827) when the territories conquered from the peshwa were finally incorporated into the Presidency. With the establishment of the Deccan Commissionership in 1818, Elphinstone, a Scotsman, and Orientalist of the 'old school,' began directly to replace the administration of the Marathas.[15]

Though a Whig all his life, as a boy in Edinburgh, Elphinstone had admired the French Republicans. According to the report of his friend Sir Robert Houston to Mr. Erskine, Elphinstone's home used to overlook the grounds where the French prisoners were allowed to walk, and he was fond of talking to them and listening to their revolutionary songs. Robert Houston says that some of Elphinstone's friends sent him a red night cap and a tricolor cockade, addressed to 'The Hon. M.E., alias Tom Paine', in the early part of his Indian career.[16]

Perhaps these populist leanings and the recognition of the life of the people as separate from the activities of the state led Elphinstone to propound a doctrine that required officials to inquire in as detailed a manner as possible into the laws used in practice by the people. In his early reports, such as the *Report on the Territories Conquered from the Peshwa,* he described the strong native tradition of justice that was not textual. He felt that employing this tradition would be the best way to govern the territories.[17] He said, 'No law seems ever to be referred to, except in cases connected with religion, where Shastris were sometimes consulted. The only rule seems to have been the custom of the country . . . The Hindu law was quite disused, probably owing to its absurdity.' In fact he goes so far as to say, 'We ought not to be guided by Hindu law, *which is a new introduction of our own*'.[18] This early opinion was codified in Elphinstone's Minute of 22 July 1823. He said,

> The Dhurm Shaster, it is understood, is a collection of ancient treatises neither clear nor consistent in themselves, and now buried under a heap of more modern commentaries; the whole beyond the knowledge of perhaps the most learned pandits, and every part wholly unknown to the people who live under it. Its place is supplied in many cases by known customs founded indeed on the Dhurm Shaster but modified by the convenience of different castes and communities, and no longer deriving authority from any written text . . .[19]

Thus, in the judicial system as set up then, following Duncan's earlier resolution and Elphinstone's expressed opinion, law was to be ascertained in each case by consulting either 'private opinion' or that of the Pandit or the Kazi. However, this mode of establishing the law was not comfortable. As Elphinstone said, native law was so vague that 'different pandits who know the tradition give different opinions for similar cases and two different pandits might give different opinions for the same case!' Even as regards private opinion consulted to ascertain the law, Elphinstone's minute stated that 'the chances of corruption, faction favour, and other sources of partiality' made such reliance untrustworthy. Overall the 'situation regarding law was intolerable'.[20]

It was deemed necessary to make the judges independent of the native law officers—the Pandit and the Kazi—and private opinion. The Bengal administrators earlier had felt a similar need and had relied on a codification of religious law. Elphinstone and others felt that a codification of common law was essential to guide the European judges in their administration of the native law to the natives. This 'common' law had to be based on the customary practices of the people rather than religious textual practices.

THE COMPILATION OF INDIAN COMMON LAW

The need for a common law thus derived from a desire to preserve for the natives their way of ruling combined with the unwillingness to allow them to manage their own rule. This attempt to discover the law by which the natives governed themselves in the Bombay Presidency set into motion the collection of exhaustive information on castes. The view of caste as the sole source and administrator of law was neither immediate nor pre-determined. Elphinstone's Report on the Maratha administration of law describes the involvement of the peshwa, the brahmins, the jagirdars, the kazis and so on. Caste was not mentioned as the sole source of law even when the task of collecting customary law was defined.

By 1822 Elphinstone set up a Regulation Committee to oversee the formation of the code of Indian common law.[21] He became the president of the committee and Arthur Steele was the secretary. In a letter to the Court of Directors Elphinstone said

> the project when completed shall be framed into a concise digest by the Sadar Diwani Adalat or a committee hereafter to be appointed. It will be first circulated as information though not of authority, it should ultimately be improved by decisions of all doubtful questions, the removal of all glaring blemishes, and the filling up of all great deficiencies until it forms a complete code of laws sanctioned by government and accessible in their vernacular language to all classes of its subjects.[22]

Two of Elphinstone's Minutes to the Regulation Committee (26 March 1823 and 22 July 1823) define the task of preparing the code. He suggested that it would be best to compile a complete and consistent code. Such a code was to be formed in three ways. Firstly, by ascertaining in each district whether there was any book of acknowledged authority either for the whole or any branch of the law. Secondly, by ascertaining whether there were exceptions to the written authorities and the type of customs and traditions that existed independent of them. This was to be accomplished by reference to oral testimony of the natives—shastris, heads of castes and others knowledgeable about law—at a time when it was not influenced by any existing controversy. The collection of opinion regarding the general rule in the absence of any particular controversy was expected to provide an unbiased standard law which could be referred to in all cases of dispute. Thirdly, a common code was to be formed by extracting the law from the information already obtained in the course of judicial investigation. He suggested that since the second procedure would require considerable exertion from a 'numerous body of natives' it would be desirable to pursue the third option—that is, reporting on cases—as the first one. These Minutes did not envision that castes alone would be examined to establish indigenous law.

While hoping to identify the 'native' custom and law exhaustively, Elphinstone's Minute denied the need to examine Muslim law for the Presidency. It said 'the number of Mussalmans under this Presidency is comparatively small and their code is little liable to local variation [and therefore] the same rules as found in Bengal will be applicable all over India.'[23] Yet, in the administration of justice, as I shall show, Muslim communities were treated as self-governing communities autonomous to a certain extent from orthodox Islamic laws.

The task for compiling the laws was begun in the two areas of the Deccan and Gujarat simultaneously. In the Deccan, under the guidance of Arthur Steele, the secretary to the Regulation Committee, the collectors of each district were asked to ascertain the law by identifying the Shastras used, by questioning the shastris, heads of castes, and other persons likely to be acquainted with the law.[24] In Gujarat, where the British courts had functioned for a longer period, the first task was to examine the records of the court and extract the information already obtained on the subject of native law during judicial investigation. The other task of questioning authorities on local custom was to begin later. In July 1823 Harry Borradaile was appointed for the job of collecting cases from the records of the courts of justice.

Borradaile was the register to the collector at Poona. Registers were appointed in 1822 to undertake the work of supervising panchayats under each collector. Borradaile received high recommendation from the collector Robertson at Poona for his 'enthusiasm, cooperation and patient mildness with the natives.' Borradaile came to India through his uncle, a merchant and shipowner in London who leased his ships to the East India Company.[25] His personal file is tentative about the beginning of his career. It says he was a writer of the season of 1818 and 'probably' came to Bombay in the early part of 1819. From September of that year he worked as second assistant to the criminal judge in the southern Konkan. His career progressed steadily in the judicial administration so that in February 1822 he was made the register to the collector. He remained at the middle level of the company's administrative system, married an 'Indian' woman, that is, a woman of British descent who was born and brought up in India.[26] This particular history of Borradaile might explain the earnestness with which he undertook his task and the attention he paid to detail. Within the year he produced the first volume of the courts' case reports from the years 1800-1820, in the second year he produced the second volume of cases from 1820 to 1824.

Other officials in the judicial administration did not see the need of Borradaile's work. The judges of the Sadar Diwani Adalat (Upper Civil Court) were against reporting cases. On 19 May 1823 the register of the Sadar Adalat, E. Grant, wrote that no report of cases should be expected from the court and a reporter should be appointed for the job.[27] Because of this opposition from the established judiciary in Surat, Borradaile—'an outsider' had to be appointed to the courts as a reporter.

As a useful reference that would help him in his task, Borradaile was given the Minute by Macnaghten that laid the guidelines for a similar task in Bengal, directing the officers to circumvent the shastris and extract a body of law from the working of the European courts. Macnaghten produced *The Principles and Precedents of Hindu Law* in 1827. Here he referred directly to the Jones and Colebrooke Hindu code and other Sanskrit texts and commentaries for a statement of the law and illustrated the statement with case law. The cases were treated only as illustrations of how the textual law was treated in the European courts. Macnaghten's case reports are not full reports of cases, nor did he examine the *bebasthas* (*vyavasthas* would be the term in Western India; statements of law) given by the pandits during the case. The case reports are a compilation of decrees issued by the European officers of the appellate court though based on the bebasthas and *fatwas* of native law officers. He recorded only those questions of law which had actually been adjudicated in British courts, not all available indigenous laws.[28] Borradaile was perhaps to do something similar— to provide a clear and concise description of the general principles of law and see how the European court dealt with these issues. He produced something different and far more comprehensive on the native law. He provided reports of cases extensive enough to be used as precedents, with special references to the native law officer's opinions—bebasthas.

In the preface, Borradaile described his reports of cases 'as collected for the purpose of forming a body of information regarding the laws and usages in force among the natives, providing a ground work of a rational and consistent digest for the guidance of the courts of justice.' He says he tried to make the reports as general as possible—covering as many subjects as possible in order to provide a wide range of precedents and to prevent the possibility of having contrary decisions made on the same point. He recorded the cases in the fullest possible detail, including all opinions of the court expressed as well as all the evidence presented.[29] He recorded the vyavasthas for the cases cited and even printed the passages from the relevant Sanskrit law books as illustrations of the vyavasthas. These passages were selected by a pandit at Borradaile's behest and then verified with the original and the English translations of Jones and Colebrooke. In his *Reports of Cases,* he referred to the Sanskrit legal texts used by the shastris to give decisions and recommended that authoritative copies of these texts be provided to the courts and to the judges to prevent deception by the shastris who made up new ones to show their extensive reading and intelligence. Thus the compilation of cases was seen by him not as providing a guidance to the law but as reports providing precedents for the guidance of the courts.

From the beginning caste was not identified as the primary source of law. This can be seen in Elphinstone's early descriptions of indigenous systems of the administration of justice, and his definition of the task of the compilation of local customary law for the courts, and in Borradaile's work in collecting Adalat cases. Caste became important in the second stage of the compilation of customary law, that is, in the process of extraction of rules from the local population directly. In common law, custom in order to be accepted as the rule of decision, must be practised by a community.

When it came to collecting local customary law, the earlier observed multiplicity of administrators of justice, the jagirdars, patils (village headman), kulkarnis (village accountant), shastris (experts in the Dharmashastra), was ignored, and castes were privileged as the source of law. There was a considerable shifting from 'common people', 'those knowledgeable about the law', to 'heads of castes'. These terms were used again and again, side by side, as in Elphinstone's Minute of 22 July 1823, and even as substitutes for each other. Still, the local group that was identified as possessing customary law was identified as the caste. As we shall see in the discussion, castes were seen as self-governed polities. The colonial administrators determined their laws by reference to actual practices at the time (not by some original constitution). In the Minute of 26 March 1823, Elphinstone said that the judges of the zillah courts were to examine the 'heads of the castes' in the district. This questioning was to be done with the aim of establishing the code of law. This motive was to be 'kept secret as it might [upset] a people so adverse to any interference with their customs'.[30] It was assumed that groups that largely enforced their own laws, would not look kindly to the British usurping their powers.

In the Deccan, this task was pursued by Arthur Steele. He questioned the shastris in order to obtain a statement of indigenous law, he examined customs and the compliance with the injunction of the Shastra in actual practice. When Steele began questioning the castes in Poona, it was feared that the government was going to tax salt, marriages and funerals, and there was great disturbance among the local populace.[31] Data about the customs of the Poona collectorate was compiled from the replies of castes and traders, as well as from cases selected from the *daftar* of the *nyayadhish* of Poona.

Information from the other collectorates of the Deccan was obtained from their respective collectors. These collectors reported on the customs they found based on cases from the register's files, from awards by panchayats of native arbitrators, and also from replies to queries put to individuals of different castes.[32] The information from all the collectorates was presented briefly and in a consolidated fashion in Steele's report on the Deccan customary law.

The task, of compiling customary law by reference to the local populace, in Gujarat was entrusted to Borradaile. It was pursued in a more systematic manner, extracting more detail. Borradaile recorded opinion not of individuals from castes, but from the entire caste, assembled together. He recorded their answers separately and did not collate them together. Also he preserved the various caveats and differing opinions given by each caste.

Borradaile began his caste survey in Surat district after he finished his task of reporting on cases from the Sadar Adalat. In December 1827 the Surat caste rules were completely collected and transmitted to the zillah judges. Then similar work was done for Broach district (published 1887) and also Ahmedabad and Kaira districts.[33]

Borradaile set out with a staff of ten—writers, translators, *purvoees* (copyists who made 'fair' English copies) and peons—to record the caste laws. He collected *sabhas* and sat with caste leaders and encouraged them to reply to his queries in writing, taking signatures of caste members on copies of these replies. The manner in which Borradaile categorized and understood caste is also interesting. He did not employ the *varna* notion of classical Sanskrit and Orientalist texts which divided all castes, that is, *jatis* into brahmin, kshatriya, vaishya and sudra. He divided all the castes into three categories on the basis of presumed social advancement. This division was made to enable questioning of the castes. Slightly varying questions were put to the different groups supposedly in accordance with their practices. The most 'advanced' group was supposed to follow the Shastras most closely and its members were considered eligible for *sams-*

karas (canonical rites). This group was made up of only three brahmin castes: the Nagar, Modh and Audich. The second group was not considered eligible for the samskaras, was said to allow adoption, had special caste observances, and so on. This group was made up of the castes even today considered *savarna*—upper castes—all brahmins and *vaniya* or trading castes. The third group was considered similar to the second group and was asked all the same questions with one addition, on *natra* (remarriage for women). This group was made up of kanbis or agriculturist castes and all other *lok* or people. The term *lok* suggests that these castes constituted, in Borradaile's scheme, one undistinguished mass.[34] The kshatriyas are also included in this lok category, thus indicating their position in the local hierarchy.

Borradaile treated the castes as having real organizational and political power and not as a part of a religious textual system. He determined caste groups by ascertaining the local hierarchies and the ritual and textual practices of the particular groups. His interest in the *jnati*s may remind one of the 'empiricist' treatment of caste in the works of the British Indian census collectors, examined by Inden. Yet, Borradaile did not employ racialist ideology to classify and understand caste, as done by 'classical' empiricists like Risley and others. He did, however, reduce sources of law from the numerous local and state authorities to the castes. In doing this, he seems to begin the administrative empiricist project of treating castes as the manageable units of local government. Perhaps he is following Mill's influential reading of Indian society and polity as governed by caste, and Mill's treatment of castes as corporate citizens of the Indian polity.[35] Yet, he radically differs from Mill's paradigm of caste being governed by a priestly hierarchy, for he assumes that caste authority rests not in any one caste but in each caste individually.

Borradaile's work with castes contradicts Dirks attempts to periodize the romantic and empiricist readings of caste by the colonial administrators.[36] Dirks says that in the early colonial period caste was viewed as a textual and religious category and denuded of its political or regulatory meaning. He comes to this conclusion from reading the 'hegemonic' historical texts produced by the early colonial administrators and missionaries like Abbé Dubois, James Mill, Alexander Dow, Mountstuart Elphinstone and John Malcolm who represent the Orientalist textual and ritualized reading of caste. He suggests that the empirical, political and sociological reading of caste came later, with the work of Thurston and the various censuses. He places the beginning of this empiricism in 1872.

In the Bombay Presidency under Elphinstone, a much earlier empirical reading of castes was undertaken and their institutional provenance and importance for governance was established. Castes were constructed as the sole source of law in the officers' search for identifying custom from 'the native community'. The latter were seen as most approachable and manageable when organized in castes. Judicial officers themselves were opposed to the codification of laws. E. Grant, the register of Surat, abstracted a letter from the chief justice of the Sadar Adalat objecting to the need for the code of laws. The chief justice said that the 'natives' were never unanimous upon the tenor of their law; that the variation from the Dharmashastra was very limited; of the variations, few were reduced to writing; and the oral testimony was never unanimous as to the extent of variation from the Shastra. The Chief Justice also suggested that 'the enactment of distinct and separate laws . . . can run the risk of not being exactly applicable'. For, in its regular procedure, the court 'collected for consideration all the facts relating to each particular case and thereon determined whether the bye-law pleaded [by the disputants] or that of the Dhurum Shaster [*sic*] shall govern the question before the court'.[37] He said that since the number of cases was small and a full and particular investigation of each individual case was possible, there was hardly any necessity to have distinct and separate laws. As mentioned by the judge, what the rule of the caste was and what modification was to be introduced to meet the need of the circumstances were contested. Borradaile also received several caveats when he was taking down the laws.

One of the caveats was from the brahmin Bhargav Visa Surti caste. Its signatories were all those who had signed the official collection of the caste rules. They noted down their objections to the reduction of their customs to writing. They said that while they had written out their regulations, their caste tradition was to collect at a place and make the right arrangement/settlement (*bandobast*) suited to the particular case and they would continue to do so. They said that 'one type of settlement does not apply to all cases, the behaviour and situation of the plaintiff of every case, its time and contemporaneous context *(vartman)* are considered when the caste decides, and the necessary adjustments *(kumbesh,* ie, increase-decrease) are made. Thus, the written rules, which they had submitted, were not really binding on them.[38] Their affirmation directly challenges Borradaile's instructions to them before he questioned them. These instructions clearly stated that the very purpose of collecting the rules was to fix them and to provide a uniform guide to settlement of disputes.

In December 1827, the Court of Directors ordered the 'discontinuance of Borradaile's appointment' on the ground that as

> reference must ultimately be made to usage, which being a matter of fact can only be determined by the examination of witnesses, or such evidence as the case may admit of, and that any other mode of ascertaining the Hindoo law must be arbitrary or unsatisfactory.[39]

One needs to mark here the reasons for the discontinuation of the work. It was not that the law could be ascertained by reference to some external body of texts or some original constitution, but because each usage was determined by the evidence ascertained in that particular case.

The Bombay government did not immediately stop the collection of caste rules. Six months after the decision had been taken, the Board said that Borradaile had discontinued the publication of reports of cases decided in the Sadar Adalat. Later, in October 1828, they wrote to the Home office that they did not discontinue his work with the caste rules for the work 'was amazingly complete—persuading the natives to declare their rules in writing to be ascribed to the zeal, perseverance, judgement and ability of this distinguished public officer'. They wrote that they had kept him in Surat by appointing him acting collector of sea customs and hoped that this did not contravene orders but by doing this they had 'acceded to Mr. Borradaile's earnest wishes to be allowed to continue his caste investigations and the simultaneous publication of standard translations of the Sanskrit legal texts being used in Surat and other areas'.[40]

The Court of Directors censured the conduct of the government on this matter and directed the immediate abandonment of the work.[41] Thus, the work of ascertaining caste law in the Bombay Presidency continued in a semi-official manner.

Stopping the collection of rules from castes was not seen as a denial of caste as a source of law. Caste continued to be seen as an important source of law by the Bombay courts. Borradaile's rules were used by the Courts, both district courts and the Sadar courts, as attested to by the publication of these caste rules in 1884 and 1886 in two volumes almost sixty-five years after the compilation.

THE NATIVE ADMINISTRATION OF LAW UNDER THE BRITISH

The compilation of a native common law was simultaneous with Elphinstone's innovations in the administration of justice in the Deccan. The system of judicial administration through the Adalat as established by Lord Cornwallis in Bengal was anathema to Elphinstone who would often tell the following story. During one of Lord Lake's campaigns someone met a group of people in flight and asked, 'Is Lord Lake coming?' 'No,' they replied, 'The Adawlut is coming, which is ten times worse.'[42]

Elphinstone's report on the judicial administration of the Deccan describes various modes of local administration of justice. He mentioned jahagirdars [*sic*] as administering justice in their own lands. Some towns had judicial officers of the peshwa called nyayadhish (judge). Local town officials like patels (headmen), mamlatadars, and kulkarnis (accountants) also settled disputes. He said if the patel couldn't bring a resolution he would assemble a panchayat of inhabitants of the village who inquired into the matter with little form and these inhabitants decided as they thought best.

In the same report Elphinstone described the kind of people who made up the panchayat: 'the members were people of the same situation in life as the parties, or people likely to understand the subject in discussion as bankers in a matter of accounts, *Deshmukhs* [police and revenue authority at district level—superintendent of village headmen] and *Deshpandes* [revenue authority at district level—superintendent of village accountants] when the suit was about land.' Further, 'disputes about caste were settled by the caste, unless a complaint of unjust expulsion took place when government ordered a panchayat of respectable persons of the caste from an unprejudiced part of the country.'[43] Thus even caste panchayats would be ordered and supervised by the government.[44]

Elphinstone felt that the most immediate level of dispute settlement in the Deccan was the panchayat. As he said in his *Report on the Territories Conquered from the Peshwa,* 'The panchayat may . . . be considered as the great instrument in the administration of justice.' After weighing the pros and cons of the Adalat system and the panchayat at length, he concluded, 'I propose, therefore, that the native system should still be preserved . . . Such a course will be more welcome to the natives than any entire change, and, if it should fail entirely, it is never too late to introduce the Adalat.'[45] He saw the advantages of the panchayats: their immediate accessibility to the local population, their being understandable to them, following familiar principles of justice and being cheap and efficient. He therefore asked the collectors to conduct all civil judicial business through panchayats in all the Deccan collectorates.

He laid down rules according to which the panchayat was to be assembled and its decisions were to be effected. The collectors were given the responsibility of calling the panchayat, being present during the hearings and ascertaining that an acceptable settlement had been reached. They were to modify the rulings of the natives to accord with their own notions of fairness as and when it was necessary.

In the first two years of the Deccan Commission, reports from all the collectors except Pottinger in Ahmednagar were positive. However, as the business of the collectors increased, panchayats were found to be more difficult to manage. The collectors did not have the time to provide the panchayats with the necessary supervision. Thus, in February 1822, registers were appointed to aid the collectors of Poona, Ahmednagar and Dharwar where panchayats were more regularly used. Yet, many difficulties were experienced with panchayat administration, the primary being a lack of eligible people volunteering to sit on the panchayat and very poor attendance of the panchayat so that there were delays in the trial of the case, and confusion as to the nature of arguments.[46]

It was soon felt, especially under Chaplin, Elphinstone's successor to the Deccan Commission, that panchayats would not have a very bright future. There was consistent mistrust of the people who turned up for the panchayats. Moreover, the delays and the irregularities in the system irritated the European administrators who felt they were losing control. As Elphinstone admitted to Strachey, his friend in the Judicial Department at India House, 'The panchayats were peculiarly difficult for a European to supervise, as the want of regularity in the proceedings of panchayats makes them difficult to revise. Their decisions being founded on traditional maxims are not easily understood by a foreigner.'[47] Thus, several changes were made in the panchayat administration. Native officers—sub-judges, that is, amins and munsiffs were appointed to try many cases parallel to the panchayat, though they were not to supersede the panchayats altogether. With the recognition that the Adalats were not entirely bad, numerous innovations were made in Elphinstone's judicial system and panchayats slowly became irrelevant in the Deccan as a means of settling local disputes.[48]

THE MAPPING OF COLONIAL JUDICIAL ADMINISTRATION

The two main projects of judicial administration outlined by Elphinstone were to define the native laws and to arrange for the native administration of justice. The subjects considered relevant for a native judicial administration remained consistent or constant in both the projects. The Regulation Committee appointed by Elphinstone to oversee the formulation of the native code decided the subjects on which caste rules were to be found. They said that the one subject on which caste rules were framed and which should be left out was the one which they claimed was 'usually perverted to the injury of public prosperity, the destruction of private rights and seldom calculated to answer any conceivable intention whatever, we allude, to *rules for carrying on trades and manufactures.*'[49] The committee described caste rules on the subject of trade and manufactures as enactments which, though directed by the Shastra, were to be supported by the constituted authority and were, in principle as well as in practice of native governments, liable to be overruled when they became preposterous and injurious.

The fact that such an abrogation of native practice was permitted only when the rules had become preposterous and injurious is not explicitly addressed. The colonial administrators did not demonstrate that the rules then existing in the Deccan or Gujarat were perverted and injurious. Thus, trade rules were to be determined by the ruling authority, that is, the Company. The implications of a government with such a vested interest in trade is encapsulated in the popular Gujarati saying—'*jeno raja vepari, teni praja bhikhari*' (where the king is a trader, the subjects are beggars).

The set of categories deemed appropriate by the Regulation Committee for a compilation of native laws were:

(i) framing and formation of caste rules;
(ii) marriage;
(iii) divorce;
(iv) inheritance;
(v) wills and gifts;
(vi) adoption;
(vii) funerals.

Steele compiled for the Deccan a whole section on contracts and rules of traders as well. Borradaile divided the questions slightly differently:

(i) betrothal;
(ii) *palla* (gifts given by groom to the bride);
(iii) marriage;
(iv) separation and divorce;
(v) maintenance;
(vi) after death ceremonies;
(vii) samskara (Sanskritic rituals);

(viii) inheritance;
(ix) partition;
(x) funerals;
(xi) caste observations;
(xii) adoption;
(xiii) natra (remarriage for women);
(xiv) miscellaneous questions.[50]

Each question was further divided into fifteen to twenty-five other questions. Steele examined questions of contracts and rules of traders for the Deccan. Borradaile did not examine the caste laws on contracts or, if he did, these were not published in 1884.

Perhaps what was operating was the conception of 'personal law' which was well known from the administration of Bengal. Personal law was justified in terms of religious law (parallel to civil and canon law in Roman administration) and also in terms of customary laws.

These limitations on the issues on which caste laws were collected, preserved the right of castes to regulate family and home. Any other sphere would have to be governed in a public way by the 'rule of law' as established by the colonial court. The court sought a reference to leaders of the caste and its representatives only for questions of family. This constructed caste as a community of people related to each other, which should govern their personal matters. Thus, the jurisdiction within which the castes could be self-governing was limited and circumscribed to an interior kinship based space. As such they were considered *Gemeinschaft*, however, to the extent that their current decisions regarding such practices were respected, they were also *Gesellschaft* or determined by their own law.

When panchayats were first administered by British collectors, they were employed to solve all kinds of civil disputes including those of castes, in some places both criminal and civil disputes. Decisions arrived at within the panchayat could not be appealed in any arena, unless proven to have been guilty of gross corruption, or partiality or gross injustice.[51] When the panchayats came into disfavour, as under Chaplin from 1822 onwards, their role was limited.

Harry Borradaile, then register of Poona and in charge of panchayats there, suggested in an 'able' Memorandum that the jurisdiction of the panchayats be limited to certain types of suits. He had, says Ballhatchet, approached this question by assuming that the importance of panchayats lay in their superior knowledge of the particular matter at issue. He suggested that they deal with only those types of suits where this advantage was most relevant.

Borradaile listed among other things trade and caste disputes as falling within panchayat jurisdiction. Elphinstone accepted the principle in general, but his list was significantly different. The customs of trade were dropped and reserved for the Company administration. Caste questions were also dropped from the jurisdiction of the panchayat. Castes were separately empowered to look after their own disputes outside the panchayats regulated by the British administration. This is a change from the practice noted by Elphinstone in his early *Report on the Territories Conquered from the Peshwa* where he mentioned caste disputes were solved by panchayats presided over by the peshwa's administrators.[52] By omitting castes from the jurisdiction of the panchayats colonial administrators positioned castes as groups that had no external governance. Thus, caste disputes were treated as internal matters of a self-governing polity that was not to be interfered with, by any external figure.

The list of subjects falling within panchayat jurisdiction, though neither formalized nor exact, did however, enumerate matters supposedly internal to the local village community and as a result, outlined the limits of local jurisdiction. As these lists were made up, Elphinstone made a determined attempt to ensure that the munsiffs (the subordinate judges), the instruments of colonial rule, would not try suits falling within panchayat jurisdiction. He specifically asked for this limitation of the munsiff's power to protect the panchayat's area of operation.[53] This area was to be the area of local independence. This was a change from Maratha practice, where the panchayat ruling could be appealed and reviewed by the peshwa's officers like the sarsubedars, mamlatdars (revenue and judicial head of several villages: taluka) and others.[54] In an effort to make panchayats more popular Elphinstone suggested that appeals be allowed from panchayats to colonial authorities.[55] This suggestion was modified so that only appeals from town panchayats were allowed not from village panchayats. However, on the whole the circumscription of panchayat justice and the growth of the parallel colonial judiciary slowly made the panchayat unimportant in the system of colonial judicial administration.

THE BOMBAY CODE OF 1827 AND JURIDICAL RIGHTS

In 1827 Elphinstone formalized the information and experience generated from these efforts into the Bombay Regulations of 1827. Two Regulations determined the two distinct views of the local judicial situation.

The Bombay Regulation II Section 21, Clause 1 defining the court's jurisdiction said,

> The jurisdiction of the civil court shall extend to . . . complaints between Natives and other not British-born subjects, respecting . . . all suits and complaints of a civil nature; it being understood that *no interference on the part of the Court in caste questions is hereby warranted,* beyond the admission and trial of any suit . . . for recovery of damages on account of an alleged injury to the caste and character of the plaintiff.[56]

This was the only clause out of the whole Regulation II of this code which was *not* repealed by the various Bombay Acts.[57] However, as the idea of caste and religion changed, the specific effect of excluding the 'caste question' varied considerably. Mulla says the earliest definition of the term 'caste question' is to be found in the judgement delivered in the case of Bhima *vs.* Vitta Ram in 1857:

> [It] includes all those questions of a *religious* nature which affect a man solely in his relations to his tribe, community or sect to which he belongs, and which are governed entirely by the traditional rules and usages which obtain in the particular tribe, community or sect.[58]

In 1857, when this definition was laid out, restricting the caste question to issues of a 'religious nature' meant the exclusion of the castes' jurisdiction over trades and manufactures and other such questions of a political and economic nature. This exclusion had become so naturalized in the seventy-odd years of the application of the Bombay Code that Mulla in 1901 comments that there was no need to define the question as being religious. In Mulla's understanding, the idea of caste itself had become 'religious'. The other point to be made about the early definition of the caste question was that this area of indigenous jurisdiction was extended beyond notions of caste to cover tribe and religious groups. We shall elaborate the extension of the definition of caste to other groups later. Here let it suffice to know that the court jurisdiction defined by the word 'caste' did not exclude other indigenous polities. Justice Ranade in 1899 defined a caste question as 'a question relating to matters which affect the internal autonomy of caste and its social relations.'[59] Thus, by the turn of the century, caste autonomy was well mapped on to an 'interior' space and the outlines of this interior did not need to be specified.

THE BOMBAY REGULATION IV

This regulation of 1827 laid down the legal system by which the Bombay Presidency was to be governed. It provided that after:

(i) acts of the British Parliament;
(ii) regulations of governor in council;
(iii) the custom and usage of the place where the case arose were employed to decide the case, only after these were found to be unavailable;
(iv) the personal law of the defendant;
(v) justice, equity and good conscience would prevail as law.[60]

The compilations of Borradaile and Steele continued to provide the law under areas *(iii)* and *(iv)*, that is, laws of place and law of the defendant. A copy of Borradaile's caste rules was sent to all the zillah judges (subordinates to the Sadar

Diwani Adalat). The circular said that the caste rules must be certified and made available to all who inquire for them.[61] The circular then quoted Regulation IV,

> It is clear [by this regulation] that the usage of the country has precedence over the law of the defendant and consequently in all disputes between parties who have given in caste rules [i.e. those whose caste rules are recorded in the court], these only shall be referred to by Judicial authorities and taken as a guide unless rescinded by any subsequent set of rules.[62]

Judge Kentish of the Surat court of Sadar Diwani Adalat immediately wrote back questioning whether the rules deposited by Borradaile were to be held conclusive under all circumstances as to the law and usage of any particular caste.[63] Glass replied positively that '[they] are to be held conclusive under all circumstances.' He said, 'The courts of judicature are by the arrangement relieved from the very doubtful mode hitherto in practice of fixing custom by parole evidence, which is not infrequently [*sic*] conflicting in its nature as much from the private interests involved in the matter as from party spirit rendering it difficult to come to a correct decision on points of vast importance to individuals.[64]

THE EFFECT OF THE BOMBAY CODE OF 1827

According to the Code, the caste could regulate matters relating to its members as long as the civil rights of the individual were not violated. One of the most important rights that the colonial state guaranteed its subjects was the right to property. Without it, the moral, material and political progress of India was thought to be impossible. Questions of property distribution, division and disposal occupied the courts most frequently. The court decided a number of suits relating to the *use* of caste property such as cooking utensils and so on, by caste members. The court held that within the Regulation of 1827 that was *not* a caste question.[65] As stated by the court, 'A suit for possession of caste property can be entertained because such a suit is clearly of a civil nature and the jurisdiction of the court is not excluded by the mere circumstance that the court has to determine a caste question in order to adjudicate on the question of possession'.[66] The decision was based on the simple principle that the members of the caste are *prima facie* entitled to the use of caste property for caste purposes. Since the state must safeguard the civil rights of individuals—especially rights in property—it must 'interfere' in the polity.

Other cases of dispute over caste property, however, had been dismissed by the Bombay courts. In the case of Nemchand *vs.* Savaichand in 1855 it was held that if factions of a caste split up and one section had to recover caste property from the other, this was a caste question. The decision was that 'caste alone could adjudicate respecting the disposal of caste property and that none of the caste had any individual right in it.'[67] Thus, a caste must collectively determine rival claims to common property. The civil courts would not solve these disputes in 1855.

What was the difference between the case cited earlier where the court entertained a dispute over the rights of caste members to use the common property and the one cited later where the court did not entertain dispute over the caste property? In the latter case, groups of caste members were seeking absolute rights to the property, whereas in the latter case, the dispute revolved around the use of the property. Thus, while individuals had a civil right in the use of caste property, they had no joint rights to the 'possession', disposal and division of such property. The ownership of caste property remained with the caste as a whole.

As a corporate body caste was self-constituted and was granted a limited autonomy. In case of differences, the caste would govern by majority. As judged in a variety of cases reported in Borradaile's *Reports of Civil Causes Adjudged by the Court of Sudder Adawlut,* the majority of the caste must control the minority. Mulla says that the court at this time held that '[Since] there is an absence of a written or proved customary constitution, there would be no way to administer the affairs of a caste if the decision of the majority were not held binding on the minority.'[68] The absence of written or proved custom was accepted as natural.

Following the Regulation IV, the Sadar Diwani Adalat and the Supreme Court, when deciding on questions affecting persons and castes, called upon the caste to assemble in court and give its law. For example, in a case regarding who should collect the caste dues,

> The court called up the whole of the cast [*sic*], and taking the vote of every individual member upon the question, found a majority against. The court decided thereupon that it was neither consistent with justice, nor within its province to make the majority of a cast [*sic*] conform to the wishes of the few, and dismissed the suit recommending the parties to arrange matters . . .[69]

The caste thus retained the right to come to court and determine their laws for themselves and retained the confidence that the court would accept and support this right, as in the case just mentioned. Later, when the absence of written caste rules became problematic (as discussed later in Chapters 3 and 5), castes could no longer rule by majority. They had to demonstrate and prove their 'constitution'—literally, their coming into being. Once this deed/act of origination was confirmed, every action of the caste had to be carried out in accordance with it and the court was enabled to verify that the caste actions were in accordance with this original purpose. Thus, a caste would no longer be consulted to determine its contemporary opinion as to the correct rule, the court could determine it independently.

APPLICATION OF CUSTOMARY LAW IN DISPUTES BETWEEN MUSLIMS

Allowing castes a limited jurisdiction was meant to be applicable only to 'Hindus'. Elphinstone's early Minute of 23 July 1823 specifically denies Muslim communities the exercise of their customary laws. This was because Elphinstone imagined that the Muslims of the Bombay Presidency were the same as all the Muslims of Hindustan and all of them were expected to follow Shariat law.[70] This legislative construction of Muslims, however, was not adhered to in the judicial practice of the Bombay courts. Justice Thomas Erskine Perry emphatically denied this sameness of all Muslims of India when he was called upon to decide on the question of inheritance among the Khojas and Memons of Bombay. These oft-quoted and described disputes were precedent-setting, allowing Muslim polities to be ruled by non-orthodox 'local' customs, outside the established Anglo-Mohammadan law.

The Khoja case over inheritance rights of women was reported in Perry's *Cases Illustrative of the Oriental Life* as the *Khoja and Memon's Case.* Perry tried the case in 1848. One party to the case pleaded a Khoja daughter's right to succession to property according to Shariat law; the other party pleaded a Khoja wife's right to succession according to Khoja caste custom. Justice Perry glossed the clause of the court's charter which enjoins the court to apply 'Mohammedan laws to the Mohammedans', with a principle strictly adhered to in the Bombay Presidency: 'to retain to the whole people lately conquered their ancient usages and laws.'[71] He justified his gloss of the clause of the charter thus:

> I think it is quite clear that the clause in question was framed solely with political views and without any reference to orthodoxy or the purity of any particular religious belief.
>
> It was believed erroneously that the population of India might be classified under the two great heads of Mohammedan and Gentoo and the use of the latter term as a *nomen generalissimum,* which is unknown, by the bye, in Eastern tongue or even in colloquial use . . . shews that the main object was to retain to the people . . . their ancient usages and laws, on the principle of *uti possidetis.*[72]

Thus Perry ruled on Khoja succession according to the Khoja custom rather than according to *Shariat* law. He employed a principle of English law to demonstrate how custom was a source of law and could override textual law: 'if the custom has been proved to exist from time whereof the memory of man runneth not to the contrary, if it is not injurious to the public interest and if it does not conflict with any express law of the ruling power, such custom is entitled to receive the sanction of a court of law.'[73] According to this principle of

English law, Khoja custom, in order to be sanctioned and enforced, would have to be examined by the court in its material content. The court would have to demonstrate that the particular custom was not contrary to the public good.

The custom which sought to be upheld was the denial of the daughter's right to inherit from her father. Perry said that during the case,

> It has been stoutly argued, that this Hindu custom of disinheriting daughters, which has been adopted by these Mohammedan sectarians, is most unreasonable, and that public policy would dictate the adoption of the wiser rule laid down in the Koran, by which daughters are allowed a defined share in the succession. A contrast is then drawn between the relative positions which females hold in the Hindu and Mussulman systems and it is argued that the policy of the latter is so much more enlarged and beneficial, and it is the duty of the court to give it effect when the two come in collision.[74]

Justice Perry ruled on the question of public duty against the arguments made for recognizing daughters rights that 'a custom for females to take no share in the inheritance is not unreasonable in the eyes of the English law'.[75] Thus the court refused to try the case on the grounds that the woman's right to property was a valid civil right to be enforced by the state, even though the justice or fairness of this right was specifically argued in the case.

The content of the customary law had as much to do with its acceptance as its source in collective practice. There was a provision in the law to override custom when it was injurious to public interest. When exactly this provision was invoked was arbitrary and left to the sanction of the court. In a case where women's right to inherit was under question—the reasonableness of disinheriting women allowed the court to accept the custom of the Khojas as rule.

This allowance of a non-Shariat practice did not threaten the identification of Khojas as Mahommedan. Customary provisions were not seen as threatening religious identity. After this case, all parties to the dispute including the Aga Khan who had supported the daughter's right to inherit, agreed that customary practices of (dis)inheritance must be allowed to continue.[76]

Another typical dispute that the courts had to deal with was over the possession of collective property. Such a dispute occurred among the Khojas in 1848; it has been described in the Information filed in the Aga Khan Case of 1866. The dispute was over the use of *jamat* vessels and other property by the different parties of the Khojas. At the time, the Aga Khan's party had padlocked the *jamatkhana* (assembly hall) godowns and refused to allow the other party access to the vessels. This action of the Aga Khan's party was challenged as trespass. When the action came up before the Supreme Court in November 1848, Justice Perry made a general reference for settlement of the dispute within the jamat, with the help of the attorneys Howard and Dickinson.[77] This recognition of collective authority and its power as a collective decision-making body by calling on it to assemble was a common practice with the Sadar Diwani Adalat as well.[78] Here the Khoja dispute was seen as an internal matter to be settled without recourse to the court.

The arbitration did not work and a complaint was lodged with the Supreme Court of Bombay in 1850. The case came up for trial in 1851 before Justice Erskine Perry. In the 1851 decree Justice Perry accepted the court's jurisdiction over settling a 'caste' matter in court since it concerned a substantial question of property.[79] However, recognizing the collective nature of the Khojas and explicitly calling them a caste he directed the Khojas to retain to all members the right to use of the caste property and the right to decide collectively on how to dispose off the property. He pronounced what he called a 'declaration of rights' and expressed a hope that the Khojas, by its aid, would 'be able to elect a mukhi [treasurer] and kamaria [accountant] and manage their caste affairs among themselves, without rendering any further application to the court necessary'.

The court used its weight to enforce the rule of the majority and even attempted to facilitate the creation of the majority opinion in the caste. The only reason why Justice Perry failed to draw up his order, regarding the settlement of the dispute within the caste, as a formal decree was that the

Khojas agreed to settle their dispute. If he had, however, drawn up the decree, his judgement would have been considered a precedent and would have been seen as the enforcement of the majority caste opinion on the minority.[80] In this case (and in other cases reported from the Sadar Diwani Adalat) the polity—caste or jamat would be assembled in court to give its opinions and so on. The rule of majority would work. If the courts had codified the law of the castes, the caste's internal functioning could have been regularized and a transparency in its functioning (with written rules and so on) could have been created.

In the period after 1858, the effect of Regulations II and IV was considerably diluted. The assumption of government by the crown saw a regularization of the powers of the governments of the Presidencies. The judiciary of all the provinces was uniform and brought into a single system from 1861. Enormous codification work was undertaken by the Legislative Council from 1862 to 1869 during the tenure of Henry Maine. The Penal Code (1858) the Codes of Civil and Criminal Procedure, the Indian Succession Act (1861), were passed during this period, along with 211 other enactments. Regulation IV was framed in a residual manner so as to provide for the application of usage in cases for which there was no specific parliamentary provisions or government regulations. The new body of laws left a small and shrinking residual sphere of usage where no state law was available and customary law could be applied. The effect of Regulation II also varied as we saw with the changing meaning of caste matters. After 1858 and Queen Victoria's Proclamation assuring freedom of religion to all her subjects, sects and religious groups in theory at least were to be unregulated. Religious boundaries were more defined and the wide application of the term 'caste' to refer to tribe and sect was restricted. Sectarian groups that were considered within this jurisdiction earlier, were dealt with outside it.

CONCLUSION

Early British judicial practice in Bombay Presidency, before Henry Maine's codification of laws (1862-1869), treated castes and religious groups (as castes, eg, the Khojas) as the polity through which the local population was to be governed. The British represented these castes and small religious groups as self-governing collectives. Even when their laws were to be codified and administered by the court, they had retained the right to modify their laws. Borradaile instructed castes whom he questioned when compiling the laws, to inform the government of the changes they may make in the future. Thus castes continued to report changes they made in their rules and regulations. For example, a deposition was made on 2 March 1865 by the Ghanchi Modh Ahmedabadi caste on an eight-rupee stamp paper to register the bandobast they had recently made and was signed by 250 signatories.[81]

Caste and socio-religious polities ruled by majority decision (majority of adult male members). Individuals having any opposition to the polity's decision could challenge them in a court of law, but the polity would be tried for procedure rather than the facts of the case or the substance of the law.[82] When a case came before court concerning an issue for which no state law was formulated, the court would obtain the law from the caste or the local polity. In such a case, the content of the law was to be determined by what the majority said the law was. There was no attempt to find out what the origin of the polity was, what its original laws were and so on. This allowed a freedom to the local social and religious polities not possible once they were treated as parts of a religious community with known religious laws.

As governed polities the castes and the small religious groups determined their laws and regulations. Later in the period when caste ties or religious groups treated as castes were being questioned and seen as marking out Indians and natives as backward, caste as a self-constituted entity ruled by a majority of its adult male members was no longer acceptable (see Chapter 3). The court either would dismiss the case if it fell within the definition of the 'caste question' or it required a definition of the group as 'community' against which the individual could press claims. For example, in disputes over similar questions of joint use of collectively held property, the attachment of the individual to the group had to be proven. The group to which the individual demonstrated attachment was assumed to have existed from ancient times in an original form, not as one constituted by the majority decision of the time. Once the court recognized such an original community and the definition of the individual within that, collective rights were absolutely enforced. This treatment of enforcing the collective rights permitted *no* dispute as to the nature of the polity from within.

NOTES

1. G. C. Rankin, *Background to Indian Law* (Cambridge: Cambridge University Press, 1946), quoting Sir Courtenay Ilbert, p15.
2. Among others, Lucy Carroll, 'Law, Custom and Statutory Social Reforms: The Hindu Widows' Remarriage Act of 1856.' In *Women in Colonial India,. Essays on Survival, Work and the State,* edited by J. Krishnamurthy (Delhi: Oxford University Press, 1989); Bernard S. Cohn, 'Law and the Colonial State in India,' paper presented at 'International Symposium on Ethnohistorical Models for the Evolution of Law in Specific Societies'. Bellagio, Italy 1985; J. D. M. Derrett, *Religion, Law and the State in India* (London: Faber, 1968); Asaf Ali Asghar Fyzee, *Outlines of Muhammadan Law,* 3rd ed (London: Oxford University Press, 1964); Gregory C. Kozlowski, *Muslim Endowments and Society in British India* (Cambridge University Press, 1985); P. J. Marshall, *The British Discovery of Hinduism in the Eighteenth Century* (Cambridge: Cambridge University Press, 1970); see also Ludo Rocher, 'Schools of Hindu law.' In *India Major*, edited by J. Ensink and P. Gaffke (Leiden: Brill, 1972): 167-176.
3. Rama Jois, Legal and Constitutional History of India, vols 1, 2 (Mumbai: Tripathi, 1984).
4. Lucy Carroll, 'Law, Custom and Statutory Social Reforms'; Marc Galanter, 'Hinduism, Secularism and the Indian Judiciary.' In *Law and Society in Modern India,* edited by Rajeev Dhavan (Delhi: Oxford University Press, 1989).
5. Catherine S. Meschievitz, 'Panchayat Justice: State Sponsored Informal Courts in Nineteenth-Century India.' Disputes Processing Research Program Working Papers series 8, University of Wisconsin–Madison Law School, 1987; and D. F. Mulla, *Jurisdiction of Courts in Matters Relating to the Rights and Powers*

of Castes (Bombay: Caxton Printing Works, 1901); L. T. Kikani, *Caste in Courts or Rights and Powers of Castes in Social and Religious Matters as Recognized by Indian Courts* (Rajkot: Ganatra Printing Works, 1912).

6. The discussion on the law to be enforced in the Company's courts and its common law model would be made more meaningful if there was a clearer understanding of the meaning of the Company being both *nawab bahadur* as well as charter holder from the British crown. However, this combined aspect of the Company has been inadequately explored in the Indian histories of the period. Unfortunately an analysis of the Company state lies beyond the scope of this study.
7. Cohn discusses this model of law to develop the 'religious' textual Hindu and Islamic laws, 'Law and the Colonial State in India: 19-20.
8. Carroll, 'Law, Custom and Statutory Social Reforms', for a discussion of the particularly damaging effect to women and tribal people of the application of textual law. Derrett, *Religion, Law and the State in India*; Rocher, Schools of Hindu Law'. Others have studied the codification of Hindu law in Bengal and held it to be descriptive of the situation for all of India. Their analysis is applicable to the extent that Jones and Colebrooke set up the archive of Sanskrit Dharmashastra texts which was duplicated in later colonial studies of Sanskritic tradition in the rest of the country.
9. Sir William Jones translated the *Al Sirajiyyah* or the Muhammedan law of inheritance.
10. This text was used as the only authority till Baillie published his *Digest of Mohammedan Law* in 1860. Even today, Hamilton's *Hedaya* is used as a textbook in law schools in India and Pakistan. The 1962 edition of Hamilton's *The Hedaya or Guide: A Commentary on the Mussulman Laws* (Delhi: Islamic Book Trust) is a reprint of Standish Grove Grady's 1870 edition and bears witness to its importance: it includes the advertisement to Grady's edition, describing the importance of the work as a textbook of law for those qualifying for the Indian Bar. Kozlowski, *Muslim Endowments and Society in British India,* describes how Hamilton's work established the Hanafi Shariat as the only source of Muslim law in India and how that was destructive of private rights in property through the administration of *waqfs*.
11. Rankin, *Background to Indian Common Law*; Jois, *Legal and Constitutional History of India*.
12. For a more detailed description see Sripati Roy, *Customs and*

Customary Law in British India, Tagore Lectures, 12 (Calcutta: Hare's Press, 1912); quoting Anton Friedrich Thibaut (1772-1840) *System des Pendektenrechts* [1855, in English]. Justice Perry quotes the same authority for the force of custom in Erskine Perry, *Cases Illustrative of Oriental Life and That Application of English Law to India Decided in Her Majesty's Supreme Court in Bombay* (London: 1853); See also p12 where Roy again follows Thibaut in explaining the binding forces of custom.

13. This was to provide a model for the distant dominions; J. H. Baker, *An Introduction to English Legal History*, 3rd ed (London: Butterworth, 1990): 35.
14. Rankin, *Background to Indian Law:* 14; also see Jois, *Legal and Constitution History of India*, vol 5:38-39.
15. T. E. Colebrooke, *Life of the Honourable Mountstuart Elphinstone*, 2 vols (London: 1884); C. J. R Radcliffe, *Mountstuart Elphinstone*, The Romanes Lectures delivered in the Examination Schools, 15 May 1962 (Oxford: Clarendon, 1962); Sushma Varma, *Mountstuart Elphinstone in Maharashtra 1800-1827: A Study of the Territories Conquered from the Peshwas* (Calcutta: K. P. Bagchi, 1981).
16. Colebrooke, *Life of the Honourable Mountstuart Elphinstone*: 7.
17. Mountstuart Elphinstone, *Report on the Territories Conquered from the Peshwa* (Calcutta: Government of India, 1821).
18. George W. Forrest, *Selections from the Minutes and Other Official Writings of Mountstuart Elphinstone* (London: Richard Bentley and Son, 1884); 310; 330, emphasis added.
19. Arthur Steele, *The Hindu Castes: Their Law, Religion and Customs* (K. M. Mittal, 1986): iii-iv. Varma, *Mountstuart Elphinstone in Maharashtra*: 216.
20. Mountstuart Elphinstone, Minute of 22 July 1823, quoted in preface to Arthur Steele's *Hindu Castes*, and in the Board' Collection, India Office Records, nos 25950-26035, vol 926, 1827-1828.
21. Varma, *Mountstuart Elphinstone in Maharashtra:* 216.
22. Letter from Government of Bombay, detailing the plans of the Regulation Committee as described by the committee's president, Elphinstone. dated 4 May, 1825, India Office Records, Board's Collection, vol. 926.
23. Ibid, quoting Minute of 22 July 1823 and Minute of 26 March 1823; the Minute refutes the general understanding that customary law was privileged for all races and religions in the Bombay Presidency, see Rankin, Jois, n14.

24. Steele, *The Hindu Castes, Their Law, Religion and Customs:* v.
25. India Office Records, 0/6/20 Personal Records; Arthur Frederick Borradaile, *A Sketch of the Borradailes of Cumberland* (London: Maclure and Macdonald, 1881).
26. His wife was Alexandrina née Davidson, daughter of a woman who came out to India to keep house for her brother and married a British merchant and shipowner in Calcutta. Ibid: 31.
27. Board's Collection, vol. 926.
28. This Minute was prepared in August 1822 by William Hay Macnaghten (1793-1841), a judge and a magistrate in the Bengal District judiciary, who started his task before Borradaile and published his compilations of Muhammedan law in 1825 and of Hindu law in 1827, which were consolidated in: *Principles of Mohammedan and Hindu Law,* edited by H. H. Wilson, 9th ed (London: Norgate, 1885): 8.
29. H. Borradaile, *Reports of Civil Causes Adjudged by the Court of Sudder Dewanee Adawlut for the Presidency of Bombay from 1800-1824,* vol.1 (up to 1821, cases decided in Bombay); vol.2 (1821-1824, cases decided in Surat) (Bombay: Educational Society Press, 1863): 1-3
30. Unreadable in Board's Collection, vol 926.
31. R. D. Choksey, *Mountstuart Elphinstone, The Indian Years 1796-1827* (Bombay: Popular Prakashan, 1971): 426.
32. Steele, *Hindu Castes: Their Law, Religion and Customs*: xiv-xv;. p. xv-xvi.
33. It is not clear whether the latter two districts were covered by Borradaile's investigation. In 1886 Nana Moroji, the editor and compiler of *Gujarat Caste Rules,* believed them to have been completed, but he did not find them in the courts. I did not find them either during my research at the Bombay and Surat courts during 1990-1992. An extract from Judicial Consultation of 11 February 1829 in the Personal Records O/6/20 suggests that Borradaile's caste rules would be completed for all of Gujarat 'in a short time'. Yet, the work may have been stopped under the orders of the Home government before its completion.
34. It is a curious word used here in the singular: one mass. The plural *loko* means people. The term *lok varna* is used as a term of contempt in Gujarati to refer to all the lower castes or even specifically the dalit castes.
35. Inden, *Imagining India*; 56-66; 167
36. Nick Dirks, 'Castes of Mind', *Representations* 37 (Winter 1992): 56-80.
37. Letter, 19 May 1825 in Board's Collection, vol. 926.

38. One section of Borradaile's rules as published in the 1880s is devoted to addenda he received that commented on the replies he had officially collected from the castes. Harry Borradaile, *Gujarat Caste Rules Published from the Original Answers of the Castes* (Bombay: Mangaldass Nathoobhoy, 1887) vol. 2: 535. Memorial dated 11 June 1827, my translation from the Gujarati.
39. India Office Records, 0/6/20 Personal Records.
40. Ibid, letter, June 1828; Personal Records O/6/20, extracts from judicial letters and consultations from Bombay, February, May and June 1829.
41. Despatch of 5 June 1833, Personal Records, O/6/20.
42. Varma, *Elphinstone in Maharashtra:*. 215; Radcliffe, *Mountstuart Elphinstone:* 25.
43. Forrest, *Selections from the Minutes:* 336 and Elphinstone, Report of the Territories Conquered *from the Peshwa;* Forrest, *Selections from the Minutes*: 338, 342.
44. See *Census of India,* vol 1, 1911, Report by E. A. Gait on caste for extensive information about how the political authority was the final decision-maker on all caste matters. I am grateful to Achyut Yajnik for bringing this reference to my notice.
45. Forrest, *Selections from the Minutes,*: 337, 359.
46. Ballhatchet, *Social Policy and Social Change:* 195.
47. Varma quoting Elphinstone to Strachey, letter of 21 April 1821, *Elphinstone in Maharashtra*: 209. A similar sentiment in Elphinstone's Minute dated 14 January 1923, quoted by Ballhatchet, *Social Policy and Social Change*: 196.
48. See Ballhatchet, *Social Policy and Social Change*: 193-205, for discussion of the 'Deccan System' on how the panchayats were superseded by the Adalat system and they never became the chief instrument of civil justice in the Deccan.
49. Letter from the Regulation Committee to the governor, 16 May 1823, signed by I Bernard and others. Board's Collection vol. 926, *emphasis mine.*
50. Borradaile, *Report of Civil Causes:* p iii (preface).
51. Ballhatchet, *Social Policy and Social Change:* 194.
52. Ibid: 197, n1, quoting Borradaile, 'Note upon Panchayats.
53. Ibid: 197, n2.
54. V. T. Gune, *The Judicial System of the Marathas,* Deccan College Dissertation Series, 12 (Pune: Deccan College Post Graduate and Research Institute, 1953): 48.
55. Suggested in 1825, quoted in Ballhatchet, *Social Policy and Social Change:* 198.
56. Government of India, Legislative Department, *The Bombay*

Code, vol 1, 4th ed (Calcutta: Superintendent Government Printing, 1924): 1-2. *emphasis added.*

57. Government of India, *Chronological Tables of Indian Statutes* (Calcutta: Government Printing Press, 1909), specifically mentions the continuation of this article in the Presidency. It was not repealed even by the Government of India Act of 1920, Section 17. According to Galanter it continues in Section 9 of the Civil Procedure Code of independent India, see his 'Changing Legal Conceptions of Caste': 174.
58. Mulla, *Jurisdiction of Courts in Matters Relating to Castes,* quoting from 4 Bom SDA 118: 123, *emphasis added.* Also, in this judgement quoted by Mulla the term 'caste' is glossed by the terms 'tribe, sect and community'. Community here must refer to caste groups and tribes and sects are seen to be similar to caste groups to the extent that they are also said to be governed by their own rules and usage.
59. The case of Appaya *vs.* Padappa 1899 23 Bom 122: 130.
60. Jois, Rama, *The Legal and Constitutional History of India:* 38-39; Rankin, *Background to Indian Law:* 195.
61. Circular no. 29, 24 Dec 1827 from H. H. Glass and Bedarkar (registrar and acting registrar [not 'register' used hitherto]), Surat Sadar Diwani Adalat), reproduced in Borradaile, *Gujarat Caste Rules: Based on the Original Answers of the Castes*, vol 1: 5-7.
62. Ibid: 6; Regulation IV of 1827, Section 26, Chapter 6.
63. Borradaile, *Gujarat Caste Rules*: 7 Judge Kentish to H.H. Glass, registrar, Sadar Diwani Adalat, Surat. Letter, 31 Dec. 1827.
64. Ibid: 7, Glass and Bedarkar to Kentish, 2 Jan 1828.
65. Mulla, *Jurisdiction of Courts in Matters Relating to Castes*: 68, decision in Dulabh *vs.* Narayan 1867 4 Bom HC AC 110. The suit was to adjudicate the use of cooking utensils between the two factions of a caste.
66. Ibid: 64, decisions in Pragji *vs.* Govind 1887 11 Bom 534 and Mehta Jethalal *vs.* Jamiatram 1888, 12 Bom 225.
67. Ibid: 29-30, Bom SDA suit 591 of 1855.
68. Ibid: 47.
69. Borradaile, *Reports of Civil Causes Adjudged by the Court of Sudder Dewanee Adawlut:* 108, no. 26.
70. Elphinstone's Minute of 22 July 1823, Board's Collection, v. 926.
71. Perry, *Cases Illustrative of the Oriental Life:* 124.
72. Ibid: 123-124.
73. Ibid: 121.
74. Ibid: 120.

75. Ibid.
76. Under the Shariat Act,1937, when customary practice was seen as threatening an Islamic identity, the Khoja rule of not granting daughters a right to inheritance was given up and the Islamic law of inheritance was made applicable to Khojas. See A. A. A. Fyzee, *Outlines of Muhammadan Law:* 68; however, this women's right to inherit was granted not because it was a question of fairness to women, but because it was a question of 'true' practice.
77. Bill of Complaint filed on 2 June 1862 before the Bombay Supreme court, Equity side, quoting the bill filed in 1850 before the same court. Supreme Court Records, 18/248 of 1866.; see also p4.
78. Numerous instances in Borradaile, *Reports of Civil Causes Adjudged by the Court of Sudder Dewanee Adawlut.*
79. Bombay Times and Journal of Commerce, 10 Oct 1851, report of the judgement of Justice Perry in the Khoja Case.
80. Justice Arnould judgement in the Agā Khan case, where he did not hold Perry's decree as binding precedent and treated the caste as a sect, whose rights were to be determined according to different principles. See also Chapter 3, this volume.
81. Borradaile, *Gujarat Caste Rules,* vol. 2: 531-532.
82. Galanter, 'Changing Legal Conceptions of Caste': 152, says of a later period, when the jurisdiction on caste questions was still applicable that the courts had 'set up a standard of judgement that emphasized procedural rather than substantive supervision'. This regulation of caste procedure is also mentioned in Roy, *Customs and Customary Law in British India:* 104-105.

CHAPTER 3

The Aga Khan Case : The Religious Community in the Bombay Law Courts

CASTE AND RELIGIOUS groups were treated as self-governing and their conflicts were settled in court in accordance with laws determined by castes (sects and tribes) themselves. Subsequent to 1858, codified British regulations narrowed the areas in which customary laws were employed in court and, furthermore, colonial courts had no jurisdiction over religious questions. In the aftermath of the 1857 rebellion, there was a growing fear of upsetting the religious beliefs of the local populations. It was in this politico-legal context that the courts attempted to settle the religious disputes of the Khojas in court. Though the civil courts had no jurisdiction to interfere in religious questions and interpretations, as we shall see in this and the other case, the courts actively defined religion. Thus the legal paradigm which held the civil law and religion to be entirely separated and as having an uncomplicated relationship needs to be questioned.

Legal disputation during the Aga Khan case represented the Khoja polity within an episteme which we may call 'community' (see Chapter 1). As a 'community' its true religious beliefs were represented not as based on practice, or determined by consultation between believers, but as determined at an original moment which could be discovered by the objective study of experts. Individual Khojas claimed membership in their religion—Islam—and were not subject to any confusion that they were part Hindu. This later contention was introduced by those who studied Khoja Islam and found that it did not fit the classic Arabic Islam. This discovery of Khoja religion by reference to an externally defined Islam represented them as unable to determine their own interpretation of their religion.

In a dispute of 1851, Justice Perry referred back to the Khojas for settlement (see Chapter 2). This decision of the judge characterized the Khojas as a polity possessing law and dispute-solving mechanisms. His decision attempted to strengthen and support these mechanisms. Perry's settlement lasted for a period of ten years. Around 1861 a group of reformist Khoja leaders (including some who had opposed the Aga Khan earlier, their sons and others) tried to break away from the Aga Khan. Their dispute again centred on the question of the right to use their collective property. It could not be solved internally and came to court in 1862.[1] The case was heard in 1866 and came to be known as the Aga Khan Case. The court, which in an earlier instance with the same people, and in a similar dispute, had consulted the polity and set the parameters within which the polity could settle its dispute, now decided to settle the dispute itself. This decision led to an absence of consultation with the polity in adjudicating a dispute within it. This meant that the knowledge and logic of the polity which hitherto structured the resolution of disputes were replaced by those of the common law.

The judgement went in favour of the Aga Khan in 1866. It ruled that the Khojas were his followers and the reformers who had argued against him had changed their religion. Moreover, it defined the Khojas as a *sect* belonging to the Shia Imami Ismaili persuasion, thus creating another group of Khojas: a sect belonging to the Sunni persuasion. But as the judgement of Justice Arnould said,

> In order to enjoy the full privilege of membership in the, Khoja community, a person must be one of that sect whose ancestors were originally Hindus, which was converted to, and has throughout abided in the faith of, the Shia Imami Ismailis, and which has always been and still is bound by ties of spiritual allegiance to the hereditary Imams of the Ismailis [the Aga Khan].[2]

In most pre-nineteenth century accounts the Khojas are not mentioned separately but identified with other more prominent Gujarati Muslim 'sects' such as the Bohras and the Memons. There are also references to Khoja pirs where they are identified as Sunni sufis. For example, Nanji cites Abdal Haq Dihlavi (d. 1642) as referring to Hasan Kabiruddin (*c* sixteenth century, who followed Pir Sadruddin as one of the most important pirs of the Khojas), as a Suhrawardi saint, that is, a Sunni Sufi.[3] This does not mean that in the pre-nineteenth century period the Khojas did not know who they were, or that there were no categories with which to describe well-defined groups. Rather it is to suggest that they were not defined as an unchanging religious group that had heavily marked and defined boundaries.

The Aga Khan case is cited as a precedent in subsequent cases as defining the Khojas, their history and their status in the eyes of British law. It is cited in scholarly as well as popular works for a similar purpose. Indeed it was so definitive a pronouncement that the Aga Khan III cites it extensively in his autobiography to describe the history of conversion, the relations maintained by the Khojas of India with the Aga Khans as well as the history of his grandfather before he came to Bombay.[4] Obviously one recognizes that it was not because he had no other source to tell him about the Khojas but because the judgement in this case was considered to be the most authoritative and succinct statement available of the Aga Khan's claim.

The definition given during the case also seems to have set the terms for the academic discourse. Scholars like Ivanow begin a Khoja history by discussing this case. Khoja practices were seen as deviant and deformed by those scholars who approved of orthodoxies. On the other hand, they were seen as signs of the 'syncretic,' popular will that accommodated all orthodox behaviours by those who found orthodox behaviour constraining. Yet both these positions silence another possibility: this was a different tradition that did not fall into any simple symmetry with any orthodoxy or any authority figure. As Mallison suggests, Khoja practices may have been more a reflection of local innovation in Islam rather than popular syncretism of an Islamic and Hindu orthodoxy. Devji briefly critiques the academic discourse which talks about the Khojas and their incomplete conversion to Islam, for discussing Khoja beliefs only from the point of view of an Islamic teleology.[5]

The Aga Khan case was fought in 1866 in the Bombay High Court under Justice Arnould. This litigation required a necessary transformation of the dispute within the polity in order to enable the court to settle it. In this process the Khojas, who were actively organizing a socio-religious collective in their dispute, were reduced to being passive subjects—'witnesses'—who must demonstrate but not 'make' their collective life, a *Gemeinschaft* or community. The identity or cohesiveness was determined in the court by reference to a sameness—'identity' of the Khojas with something else. This identity, both a sameness to something and cohesiveness within the polity, was created in the judgement by checking or testing Khoja behaviour and practices against a master historical narrative centred on the identification of the Shiah Imami Ismaili and on the identification of the Imam of the Ismailis. These latter terms were not derived from an interrogation of the Khojas themselves, for the expression of Khoja faith could not be entertained in a court of law. The term 'Shiah Imami Ismaili' had to be understood as 'matter of fact' grounded not in the historically grounded self-estimate of the group but was learnt from textual or expert authorities in a context necessarily separated from the Khojas. The acceptance of such prepared definitions without consulting practices and behaviours of Khojas, was to produce for them a straightjacket of historical identity (sameness) that allowed neither contestation nor change from within and privileged homogeneity and orthodoxy.

The case was instituted by several rich and important Bombay Khoja businessmen: Habib Ibrahim, Hemraj Jeya, Daya Muhammad, Muhammad Saya, Pir Muhammad Kasambhai, Fazalbhai Gulam Husen, among others. They have been characterized in later as well as contemporary literature as 'reformists'. They were suing for the removal of the treasurer and the accountant of the Khoja *jamatkhana* or association in Bombay and for an accounting of all the property. They also asked for restraining the Aga Khan from 'interfering in the management of the property and affairs of the Khoja community . . . from excommunicating any members of the community, from celebrating marriages, and from demanding or receiving any offering.'[6]

The Aga Khan Mehelatee or Mahommad Hussein Husseini (popularly known in Gujarati sectarian literature as Imamshah Hasanali Shah Saheb) had first come to Bombay in 1845 and then was sent by the British to Calcutta, from where he returned to Bombay in 1848. He had been welcomed by the Khojas on his arrival with receptions and so on.[7] As their pir the Aga Khan began to insist upon changes in several Khoja practices. In 1847 he supported a change in the Khoja's customary rules for the inheritance of daughters. He supported the daughter's right to inherit a share in her father's property in opposition to accepted Khoja practice whereby daughters were not granted any share in their father's property.[8]

He also introduced new religious practices. In 1851 several Khoja reformers mentioned in their court plea against the Aga Khan that 'the Aga also considers many of their practices heretical'.[9] Aga Jehangir Shah, one of the sons of the Aga Khan, remembers his father as being very strict about memorizing Shia prayers, even though few Khojas actually knew them. Jehangir Shah describes a journey with his father. On the way to Pune they stopped at Luni village and the Aga Khan collected all his attendants around him and questioned them about their religious beliefs and most could not answer well. He then entrusted them to Shahrukh Khan to be educated. Hasanali Shah Saheb also insisted that the *namaz e jamayat* was read in a mosque and so on.[10] Greater effort at participation by the Khojas was expected at Mohurrum, the *majlis* (gathering), and the *matam* (lamentation) normally led by the Aga Khan's mother, who until then did not do these things.[11] The newspaper *Rast Goftar* said that these religious practices earned the Khojas the opprobium of being Ismaili rather than Muslim and for this and other reasons a section of the Khojas separated from the Aga Khan.[12] The Aga Khan's financial needs—feeding Persian supporters, funding his racehorses, and so on—were extensive. He needed to spend almost one lakh rupees in a year according to the estimates submitted during the case.[13] The contributions required by the Aga Khan were repeatedly under dispute. Many of the leading Khojas resented the Aga Khan's authority and tried to restrain him from managing the Khoja properties and funds as well as changing practices such as inheritance. This obviously led to furious conflicts and many elite Khojas challenged the Aga Khan's authority in court.

Among the educated upper classes in Bombay there was considerable reformist effort, and many Khoja shethiyas (rich men who were leaders) were involved. The reformist journal for women *Stri-Bodh* (Women's Advisor) carried articles on Khoja women's appearance and behaviour. The specific targets of criticism were their 'pre-modern' selves—the immense amounts of heavy jewellery they wore—especially the thick *vitas* (nose rings), *kadas* (anklets/bracelets) and so on. Their lack of education and 'imperfect' Gujarati was also criticized.[14] The Khoja shethiyas tried to start a school (by subscription) for providing 'English' education, which the Aga Khan opposed, and the reformist newspaper described him as the cruel guru who refused to change and modernize.[15]

During this period the position of pir/imam/guru vis-à-vis the devotee was seriously criticized as degrading to the latter by critics of Indian religions—both elite Hindu reformist men and Christian missionaries.[16] The guru or imam as a path to God was questioned. The imam/guru as having the right to participate in the private family life of the devotee, advising on questions of marriage, property, inheritance, and so on, was also criticized as unnecessarily interfering in the life of the individual. The levy collected by the caste or the religious preceptor on income, goods and services, marriages, births and deaths was severely censured by the courts as an illegal exaction. Indeed in 1829 when the Aga Khan had put in a claim in the Sudder Court against certain Khojas for nonpayment of dues, he was advised to withdraw it because of the illegality of such a prosecution. Thus the collections had to be called voluntary donations. They were illegal because the only legal contract for compulsory taxes was between the state and the individual, not between the individual and any other authority. The British criticized and tried to abolish these charges as levying multiple and uneconomic burdens on the economy.[17]

The payment of *jamat* (assembly) dues was an important issue in the dispute within the Khojas. Masselos discusses this aspect of the longstanding dispute between the Khoja shethiyas and the Aga Khan from 1829 onwards. At one point the Aga Khan's party laid down three conditions by which they would accept all the dissenting members. Two related to consenting to rules of the jamat and one was about agreement to pay outstanding dues and the assurance of future payment.[18]

Over a period of ten to fifteen years, there were numerous differences between the Aga Khan and the reforming party. The differences could not be settled either by arbitration or by violence. During the Ramzan of 1863, the pesh imam of the Khoja masjid since the time of its establishment in 1822 was Ghoolam Rasool, a Sunni, and the Bangi (the crier of the call to prayer) was also a Sunni. In 1863 during Ramzan, the Shia party called on a Shia pesh imam to occupy the place of the imam in the mosque during the maghrib namaz (evening prayer). The next day at the same time they placed a dead body in the middle of the prayer area of the mosque so that prayers could not be held there. The day after that they barred the Bangi from calling the Sunni bang. On the fourth day they had their own bangi deliver the call to prayer. The occupation of the mosque consisted in occupying the places of the pesh imam and the bangi, who determined the nature of the prayers followed by the Khoja devotees. The spaces occupied, the timing, and the people involved in the conflict suggest that these were specific religious claims and they expressed a profession of faith.

Another set of disputes took place when the reformist Khojas wanted to use the jamatkhana for funerals or during Mohurrum. Again, the timing and places claimed suggest religious claims and aggressive professions of faith. Through the claims the disputes could be seen as organizing and constructing a collectivity. These disputes led to disturbances of peace and public order. Both groups were equally powerful and thus they had to invite the state to keep the peace. From February 1861 to 1866 when the court ruled on the rights of the Khoja 'community', both parties paid for a police patrol to man the gates of the jamatkhana. Since both parties requested the same rights from the police and the same exclusion of the other's rights, the police, too, had to defer to judicial authorities to decide on which group to support.[19]

Under the law the occupation of property was seen as a move to claim rights to property not as attempts to distinguish religious practice. The court treated these actions as disputes over unmarked 'common' property. The property was not seen as a ground for displaying religious behaviour, but as an important possession. For the court the identity of the Khojas would secure them their right to property. This identity of the Khojas had to be determined independently of their claims to customary use or occupation of property. This method of treatment required that the Khojas first describe who they were and how they collectively owned property not how the use of their property was itself a way of organizing collective practices and inculcating beliefs. Thus, the use of the property was not merely a fight for property rights, but crucially important in making or constituting the group.

In 1866 when Justice Arnould tried the case, he treated the Khojas as a sect, and the property as vested in the trust. Following this argument, the dispute over right to sectarian property was tried and judged by the court under its equity jurisdiction over charitable trusts. The court dealt with a charity according to English law.[20] According to English practice, the right over such charitable trust or association was established on the basis of the group's closeness to the original charitable and religious purpose for which it was dedicated.

> The Court, in exercise of its charitable jurisdiction, is called upon to adjudicate between conflicting claims of dissident parties in a community distinguished by some religious profession, [then] the rights of the litigants will be regulated by reference to the religious tenets held by the community *in its origins* in fact a minority holding those tenets will prevail against a majority which has receded from them.[21]

The right over property was therefore to be granted to the group which held those original religious beliefs. Indeed religion was privileged not in terms of the faith and belief 'at present', but faith and belief 'in the origin'. Thus the *origin* was given primacy over present practice.

Following the logic of this law the defendants' first attorney, Anstey, very popular with his Indian clients but a thorn in the flesh for the judges and his colleagues at the bar, opened his argument with the claim,

> If the Khojas are proved in their origin to have been Sunis [*sic*], the relators and plaintiffs must succeed: if they are proved to have been originally Shias or Shia Imami Ismailis, or in any way non-Sunis [*sic*], then the defendants must succeed.[22]

This is a shift from the earlier legal descriptions of Khojas as a caste to Khojas as a sect. The claim to describing the Khoja collective as a caste formulated the right to property quite differently. In both instances the right to property is framed within the legal framework of property being an unmarked possession, while the nature of the group is described differently. Both descriptions of Khojas as sect and as caste were present in the 1862 judicial proceedings. While in their opening arguments and their plaint the Khojas describe themselves as a sect, towards the end of the argumentation they return to a description of the Khojas as a caste. In the letter of plaint the Khoja reformers claimed that their present complaint was in continuity with their 1851 complaint. In 1851 they had argued that they had a right to the jamatkhana, durgah, the burial grounds, and so on. They based their claim to these properties on the fact that the property had always been held in their names on the books of the collector of land revenue and their money or contributions had paid for it. The property was held in individual names, for example, a house in Bhindi Bazaar was listed in the collector's book under the name of Allaruckia Soomar, a garden in the name of Allaruckia Soomar and Khakhi Pudumsey, a mosque and burial ground in the name of Ebrahim Cassum, a jamatkhana with buildings and other property in the name of

Premjee Jewraj, Dhurremsey Poonjah and so on.[23]

These owners, most of whom were of the reformist group recognized that this was not private property. As they said in 1851, 'Every Khojah [*sic*] had a right to use the above property and be buried in the grounds, though wealthier members (responsible for collecting the funds) exercised a larger influence.'[24] In 1851 Justice Perry and the defendants (i.e. the Aga Khan party) themselves accepted this argument that ownership of the property was vested in the Khoja caste. Thus collective property was said to belong to the whole group who used it currently and they were all empowered to use it. Scoble, the attorney for the reformists, returned to this argument later in the case, and said that all the Khojas should be entitled to the use of the property regardless of the religious faith of the group. He said that the chief criteria of being a Khoja was birth.[25] Here he seems to argue that the Khojas were *Gemeinschaft* or a natural 'community', which, as discussed earlier, did not and should not have processes of governance.

However, when the suit was first filed in 1862, the plaintiffs maintained that this property was a 'trust estate . . . maintained for the exclusive benefit of the said Khoja sect'. In the 1862 plaint the personal ownership was represented as being held in trust on behalf of the religious and charitable group. The defendants themselves use the term 'trust estate' to describe their ownership of the property. They couldn't make a *waqf* (charitable trust) argument as there was no founding *trust* deed for any of the property.[26]

In the arguments presented to the court, two different ways were maintained for describing the collective property. The plaintiffs claimed a right to use the property on the one hand based on the fact that they had helped to create this property, and on the other hand, based on the fact of their membership in the sect of the Khojas. The court once convinced that the property was sectarian property was unwilling to entertain grounds such as birth. One would assume that such an unwillingness to examine the *Gemeinschaft* nature of the religious polity would create possibilities for the Khojas to determine who should belong to their group.

The reformist Khojas also preferred the sectarian identification. In their Bill of Complaint of 2 June 1862 from the sixth paragraph onwards the term 'sect' is consistently used to describe the Khojas. The dispute of 1862 and their complaint followed a considerable erosion of the sense of 'natural collectivity' of the Khojas. Many events contributed to this erosion. There were serious disputes over the occupation of the mosque, the Khoja schools, several death threats, deaths at the Mahim dargah which was also a disputed property, the trial of the murderers, the celebration of the conviction of the murderers by the Aga Khan's party as martyrdom, publication of newspapers and even comments by other elite reformers about the Aga Khan. The *Rast Goftar* exhorted the leading Khoja reformers to set up a separate jamat, to give up the Aga Khan, and it suggested that reform could not be achieved by wrangling over property.[27] Thus it exhorted the Khojas to separate from the Aga Khan in the same way that they exhorted the Pushtimargis (Vallabhacharya Vaishnav sect, see Chapters 4 and 5) to give up their maharajas and their temples. This kind of similarity drawn between the Aga Khan and the Vaishnav maharaj, also presumed that just as the maharaj owned the Vaishnav temples, the Aga Khan owned the Khoja jamatkhana and mosques. Yet the collective consciousness of the Khojas and their collective creation and use of jamat property would not let the Khoja reformers give in to this easy identification. They had to contest the Aga Khan's right to the collective property. Their claim to rights in property was not based on their customary use of the property till much later in the case. When the case was first put to the court the claim to property was a religious claim, that the property belonged rightfully to those who profess a certain faith. They introduced themselves as a sect, 'Hindoos, converted to Mahomedanism by a Mahomedan teacher of Soonee persuasion'.[28]

Why this change in nomenclature? Why this decision to treat the Khojas as a sect rather than a caste? If we examine the history of the Khojas in the period between 1850 and 1860 we find their growing engagement in the nineteenth-century reform project. They shared the same platforms with the other reformers of Bombay: men like Karsandas Mulji, Narmadshankar Lalshankar, Bhau Daji and others. These other reformers criticized caste bonds in Hindu society, and the restrictions these placed on social movement and intercourse within the society at large. The Paramahansa Mandali—a society where caste taboos were deliberately broken—had been established somewhere around 1854 or 1855. The Khojas too perhaps made serious attempts to devalue caste ties and definitions.

The understanding of Islam as rejecting caste was also established in 'modern' Knowledge. In fact, when witnesses referred to the Khoja caste, the judge interrupted and asked for a clarification from the interpreter.

> The Judge: When he says he would allow his children to marry Syuds of another 'caste' what does he, a Mussulman, mean?
>
> The Witness: All I can pretend to say is, we would not intermarry with any other caste . . .
>
> The learned Judge [to the interpreter]: How is it the word 'caste' is used?
>
> The Interpreter: 'Tribe' is meant, my Lord.[29]

Thus, the very construction of the Khojas as Muslims in European knowledge would ensure that *caste* was not insisted upon. In this case caste was translated as tribe, but the Khojas preferred to identify themselves as a sect within Islam rather than as a tribe or caste.

This is not to suggest that after this period of reform the representation of sect completely replaced the Khojas' representation of themselves as a caste. During the case the judge suggests the possibility of a different argument for the plaintiffs: an identity of Khojahood—neither Shia nor Sunni. At that point, the Aga Khan's lawyer contradicts him: 'They had committed themselves to a most uncompromising statement of their Sunnism, and if they chose to take a false foundation for their case they must stand the consequences.'[30] Thus the logic of legal argumentation pushed forward the discussion towards the establishment of a doctrinal character of the Khojas.

Towards the end of the case, the reformers suggested that

even if they were proved to have changed their religion they must receive the protection of the Act 21 of 1850, which guaranteed an interest in caste property to members who changed their religion. Their attorney Scoble pleaded that even if it was proved that the Sunni Khojas had changed their religion, they would not be deprived of their interest in caste property. The judge squashed this by saying that the plea was a case of failed proof, and that their first argument, that the Khojas are Sunni in their origins and thus all those who are Sunni should maintain their rights in the property, was the most correct assessment of the situation.[31]

Once the Khojas were defined as a sect the judge was compelled to 'find' on it, that is, to discover whether they were such a sect through the evidence presented and collected in the court. As a sectarian group, the court could treat the Khojas as an organized body that determined its doctrine through covenants. It could examine evidence regarding Khoja beliefs by reference to Khoja experts themselves. But the court did not avail of this possibility. The court's character as a civil court re-formulated the religious question. This was done by the parties to the case as well as by the court. Before the case could proceed the defendants, that is, the Aga Khan party, argued that the court had no jurisdiction to try the case. This objection had to be overcome by the plaintiff. The Aga Khan party's objection was that the relationship between the Aga Khan and the Khojas was similar to one between an abbot and his monks. The court, not being a religious court, could not come between them. The only logic that could invoke the court's interference in sectarian affairs would have been a perceived violation of 'public' concern. Anstey, the first prosecuting attorney, tried very hard to build a case that opposition to the Aga Khan was a matter of morality, which was a public concern. In this he was explicitly following the Maharaj Libel Case (see Chapter 4), where this proposition was explicitly upheld. He castigated the Aga Khan as a harsh dictator, interested only in collecting money from the Khojas, using the money to finance racing and gambling and womanizing. Anstey called the declaration of Shia faith that the Aga Khan circulated a 'slavery bond' (see Chapters 4 and 5). He argued that the Aga Khan was immoral because he was a Shia and all Shias permitted 'temporary' marriages.

Anstey could not make the charges of personal immorality of the Aga Khan stick. The defendants were able to show that the charitable character of the Khoja jamats was not changed by the Aga Khan. Poor Khojas were helped from the funds collected in his name, that the various jamats all around the country used the funds collected in this manner. Horse racing was portrayed as a pastime in the most noble Persian tradition, of which the Aga Khan was heir. His personal life, number of wives, and so on, were classified as a private matter, not of concern to the court. The payments to the Aga Khan were demonstrated to be traditional, by describing the method of transmitting the money to the *Moula Salamat* (the Aga Khan) through *jowlies* (small cloth bags), by showing entries—in the jamat books credited in the name of Pir Salamat (the Aga Khan of the time), dating to 1776, and by letters from the Aga Khan and his father to the Bombay jamat and to other jamats dating from 1793 to 1836 relating chiefly to remittances of money.[32] The remittances of money were described as being voluntary and being a criteria of membership in a group and, therefore, not coercive. The threat of excommunication for non-payment was considered justified by the judge as a way of maintaining the group.

The acceptance of temporary marriage was justified by an appeal to the commonly shared male culture. The lawyer said temporary marriage arose out of the Shiah's concern for the Prophet's injunction against concubinage. He argued that the Shiahs wished to follow this injunction and therefore they arranged a law that would make temporary sexual relationships legal. He suggested that Sunnis who completely forbid such temporary sexual relationships, would probably have more concubinage. Thus, the common sense assumption about the 'natural' male sexual urge and the consequent universal presence of concubinage was called upon to show how temporary marriages were a pious attempt to legalize male sexuality.

Thus the charge of immorality, which had operated in the maharaj case, was successfully refuted in the Khoja case. The reformist claim of the Sunni Khojas could not be sustained as directed against a tyrannical guru. The Aga Khan and his authority within the Khojas was considered as not to be of concern to the court. As the judge said at the end of the case in court, 'I may think—and probably do think—that the Kojahs [*sic*] have been very ill-advised in paying these moneys to Aga Khan, but that is not the question I have to decide.'

Anstey's other plank for argumentation and means of dismissing the Aga Khan's claim on the Khojas was by trying to show that the Aga Khan and the Ismailis were heterodox in their faith. He described how their practice of temporary marriage was non-Islamic. Anstey even attempted to show how the Ismailis were distant from the Shias as well and persecuted by Shias and Sunnis alike. He went about associating all possible heresies—the Mahabadian, Kharejite and others with the Ismailis and the Aga Khan. He used the *Desatir,* a pre-Islamic Persian text, included in the *Dabistan*, translated by David Shea and Anthony Troyer in 1845, to show how the Ismailis were the Mahabadians, a Zoroastrian sect—thus conclusively assigning them a non-Muslim status.

The secularism of the court, its expressed inability to deal with religion and religious beliefs, helped it dismiss Anstey's arguments of the Aga Khan's unacceptable heterodoxy out of court. As Mr. Howard, the attorney for the defence argued, '[there had been an attempt] to prove that the Sheas [*sic*] were not Mussalmans on the ground of their heterodoxy with reference to the Koran, but I do not think that could be made an argument which His Lordship would attend to.'

> His lordship: 'No I think not.'
>
> Mr. Howard: 'I do not think we can here bandy texts from the Koran.'
>
> His Lordship: 'No, I am not here to decide as to the orthodoxy of the Kojahs.'[33]

Howard, then, in spite of saying that one couldn't prove the heterodoxy or otherwise of the Shias, went on to argue against Anstey's construction of Shias as heterodox. He based himself on all the same authorities used by Anstey, primarily

Sale, De Sacy, Hamilton, Muir and others. Quoting Sale's *Preliminary Discourse to the Koran* he said how Shias and Sunnis were like Christians and Jews, the Shias adopting the feminine and softer aspects of life by revering Fatima, just as the Christians revered Mary.[34] Thus, the question of morality and of religious heterodoxy—the two planks on which Anstey had built his arguments to discredit the Aga Khan—were completely destroyed by his rival.

How did the judge make the decision in the case on the basis of identifying the religion of the Khojas? If the Khojas were a sect, would it not favour their legal representation as a self-determined polity whose members determine their religion on the basis of their faith and practice? In a civil court, the judge could not admit a debate regarding religious faith in court. He could only determine the nature of the faith by evidence or proof regarding the faith. Within the court's model of church and sect, sectarian faith would have to be presented in court in the form a covenant unanimously agreed upon by the sect in its moment of foundation. The court determined that within the court, religion was to be defined not in terms of the contemporary faith and belief of the Khojas but faith and belief 'in the origin'.

Indeed, the primacy of origins was made even stronger in the law. The law said, 'a minority holding those religious tenets . . . will prevail against a majority which has receded from them'. How strange that in a legal system that placed so much emphasis on the principle of majority, religious belief 'in the origin' was held more important than majority belief of the present! This insistence, arising from the aggressive application of English law in India, contrasts starkly with the earlier practices of the Company courts in the Bombay Presidency. These courts in the same situation assembled the polity in the court and presided over the settling of the dispute by a majority of assembled members. The Aga Khan party asserted this earlier practice. They said, 'if there is no evidence of what the religion was in the origin, then the opinion of the majority must prevail'.[35]

However the court constantly stressed the notion of origins as the 'true'. The origins were important in law because it was assumed that they were closest to the spontaneous, the uncrafted inspiration. Any subsequent development was supposed to be false and less important, a result of 'crafty humans'. For a government supposed to be 'humanist', this was surely a strange view of humanity! By assuming that the collective was determined in its origins the court denied that this collective was made in contemporary circumstances by its current practitioners. As such the group that it discovered was a 'community' of the ancient type, that did not change or debate its circumstances. Thus, the believer 'at present'—the ordinary Khoja—was effectively silenced and fixed in some ancient 'community'.

How were the origins uncovered? In a situation where there was a church, the original covenant would be discovered. In the absence of such a statement of faith, the discovery of the origins required a historical investigation. The witnesses and both parties of the case represented themselves as originally converted from Hinduism. Almost all witnesses along with the plaintiffs and defendants, claimed Hindu origins and indicated their current use of numerous 'Hindu' practices, clothes, names, and so on. They, however, definitely saw themselves as Muslim. Yet, Justice Perry in an earlier case did not accept that claim. In his notes during the Khoja and Memon inheritance case of 1847 he said,

> their dress, appearance, manners [are] for the most part Hindu . . . these facts do not warrant the conclusion being drawn, . . . that the Khojas were originally Hindus for such is the influence of Hindu manners and opinions on all castes and colors who come into close connection with them that they are gradually brought within its magic circle . . . it [Hinduism] is like the black soil of Deccan which converts all foreign material into its own material.[36]

The colonial image of India—as a land of mystery and fascination, with magical powers to absorb and convert—is asserted in the judge's statement. It is this kind of understanding of India that would prevent the judge from recognizing the possibility of a dissenting tradition arising in India. Thus, at its moment of origin the religious group could not assert a separateness or change or a volition to change. It was seen as an unthinking 'material'. Even the idea of change and conversion which operates to describe religious beliefs invokes the episteme of a non-volitional 'community'.

The Khojas use the term 'converted' in English to describe their origins. In Gujarati they used the term *vatlayela*. The two terms have very different meanings. The Gujarati term is a reference to change, suggesting contamination. It is a transformation that is permanent but not necessarily to a pre-determined other. The English word refers to a change in religion and a complete acceptance of the faith to which the conversion is made. It is this Christian notion of proselytization or conversion that prevails in the examination of the case. As 'converts' the individuals converting had no role in determining their faith, it was determined when they were converted.

The Khojas would now have to identify that religion to which they were converted. When the judge and the attorneys heard from the Khojas that they were originally Hindu and had converted to Islam, they assumed fixed and fundamentalist ideas of Hindus and Muslims from which and to which they were converted. When they did not find the ideal convert—the one using classical texts and practices—they were very disturbed and could not explain or accept that behaviour as logical or reliable.

The religion to which the Khojas in 1866 were claiming to belong was Shia on the one hand and Sunni on the other. The judge and the law pushed these disputing claims of Shia or Sunni back to the period of origins, in order to recognize the authentic faith of the Khojas. The judge handled the large volume of evidence presented in the court by positing various questions to be decided in a sequential manner. The first two questions were,

> First: What are the Sunis as distinct from the Shias?
>
> Secondly: Who and what are the Shia Imami Ismailis?

The most inclusive categories were laid out first, as orthodox or classical categories, which could be understood as absolute categories without reference to any context. As the judge said,

> This question, 'Were the Khojas, in their origin . . . Suni or Shia Imami Ismaili' . . . is an historical question, to be decided by evidence as to matter of fact.[37]

To produce such 'matter of fact' truth, extensive evidence was laid out in the court. It was curious to see which authorities were consulted to learn who or what the Shias and Sunnis were. To discover the 'matter of fact' the judge could have referred to the facts of contemporary faith. This was how the words 'matter of fact' were used earlier in the legal opinion of the Court of Directors of the East India Company.[38] But the judge chose to discover the matter of fact from expert authorities on Islam. The list of these expert authorities is significant. He consulted Hamilton's *Hedaya*, Morley's *Administration of Justice in India*, Muir's *Life of Mahomed*, Sale's *Preliminary Discourse to the Koran*, De Sacy's *Exposé de la religion des Druzes*, D' Herbelot's *Bibliotheque orientale*, Von Hammer's *History of the Assasins*, Gibbon's *Decline and Fall of the Roman Empire*, Milman's *Notes*, and so on, a list of thirty texts in all. By insisting on a *factual* account of the religion, the judge privileged the writing of history. As can be seen in some of the titles quoted, this truth or history came from personal travel accounts and studies of the Europeans as 'impartial students' of the past. Historians were seen as 'truth-tellers'. The position of the expert, as opposed to the position of the believer, was privileged by seeing the question as one of fact and history. During the hearing the plaintiffs brought a Sunni Kazi to give evidence as to Shiism. The judge wanted to check his testimony regarding the Shias against the description of Shias in Von Hammer's *History of the Assassins*![39]

Once the categories of Sunni and Shia were constructed, the Khojas were as it turned out, studied in the manner in which they fitted these categories. All the witnesses who were examined had to demonstrate Khojahood as Shia or Sunni. Arguments outside central framework could be dismissed as meaningless and unacceptable. When the rigours of the sectarian argument, constructed by the elite Khoja leadership, their lawyers and the court were applied in the court, there was a complete breakdown of meaning between the court and the Khoja witnesses.

For example, during his examination, Mohammed Dama said, 'I am a member of the Jumat of the Khojas . . . my religion is Shiah—no Sunni. I was twice married in the Sunni form that is the reason I have for knowing I am a Sunni.'[40] His statement was followed by laughter. The court could not accept this kind of identification of religion. In response to the laughter the witness then said, 'We say the *Kulma* and I have never followed any religion but the Sunni.' Thus, all behaviour must demonstrate a single identity, the representation of identity could not be multi-valent (both Sunni and Shia).

Such claims to multiple associations were made by different witnesses in a variety of cases. For example, in 1847, in a Khoja succession case tried before Justice Perry, the witness Hubib Ebrahim said, 'Some say we are Soonees, some, Sheas. Our religion is a separate religion, Aga Khan is esteemed as a great man amongst us. Since we keep beards we are Mahommedans, our religion is a different religion.'[41] Or in the evidence of another witness, 'The *Moula ka Kalam* is a simple book in which good moral precepts are recommended . . . It is neither a Suni [*sic*] book nor a Shia book. It is a good book.' Again there was laughter in the court.[42]

Attempts to describe Khoja texts and practices as something different from Sunni or Shia Islam were seen as meaningless and utterly unacceptable as definitions of 'Khojahood'. Khoja descriptions of their practices had to be a testimony to a fact that was defined by outsiders to their polity. We may characterize this representation of Khojas as 'community'. The categories Shia, Sunni and Khoja were supposed to be categories of belief and faith but the court could only accept demonstration of faith as proof of faith, not the affirmation of faith. It was in search of this demonstration that various Khoja practices were examined—the manner in which they held their hands in the mosque or the jamatkhana, whether they used the mosque or the jamatkhana to pray, whether they employed a Sunni Mullah (priest) or a Shia for their rituals, whether they prayed five times a day or three, whether they went on pilgrimages to Mecca or to Kerbala, or to the Durkhana (the temporary residence of the imam), whether they gave the money to the jamat in the name of the imam or not, and so on. The very manner of the person's being—clothes, practices, actions—became markers of identity.

In fact the only item containing some of the beliefs of the Khojas, cited in the court was the text of the *Dashavatar*. The *Dashavatar* referred to Vishnu's avatars and is an important Khoja *ginan* [Sanskrit *jnana* = knowledge, here text/ hymn]. In this text the tenth avatar of Vishnu is claimed to be Ali. The presence of Ali in a position of reverence was used to indicate the text's Shia's character. Yet in the 1847 case of Khoja succession which came up before Justice Perry, the judge said that the *Dashavatar* 'professes to give a history of the tenth incarnation in the person of their Saint, Sudr Din.'[43] The same claim is made in the information filed on behalf of the reformers in the 1851 case.[44] Other figures like Pir Shams are also described as avatars of Vishnu in other texts.[45] I do not quote this discrepancy to suggest that Perry's finding was more authentic, but to foreground the fact that the claim of who was the tenth and most respected avatar became a strategic and declaratory one. The figure of the tenth avatar, now Hazrat Ali, was reduced in the case to being a claim to a significant universe, that of the Shias.

Custom was of serious concern to the court when making decisions regarding such issues as inheritance laws. The court assumed that the social and religious polities governed themselves and determined their customary laws and practices for themselves and therefore these customs were important. In the matter of deciding on what religion was professed, the customs by which it was professed were not trusted or examined at all. The Khojas considered their customary professions of identity—the use of different *bangis*, or different ceremonies—important enough to fight over and change. However, the court did not think it relevant to consider their use over time important enough to determine what were the Khojas. Such practices were not seen as creating and making the religious polity. Even as these beliefs or practices were described in court, they were only important for matching evidence with definitions as to classical Shia or

Sunni. Thus, the customs by which religion was professed was not to be trusted or examined at all. There seemed to be no need to examine the history of customs such as *jamatkhanas,* their prayers, and so on.

In spite of the fact that many Khoja affirmations of difference from Shia or Sunni practices were laughed out of court as meaningless, these remained a problematic presence in their incompatibility with the classical Shia or Sunni categories that were set up by the court. The judge said that he arrived at the conclusion that Khojas were Shia Imami Ismaili in explaining some undeniably Khoja practices. These practices were primarily: *(i)* reading the *Dashavatar* and other *ginans;* and *(ii)* employing a Sunni Kazi for solemnizing marriage, following Sunni funeral rituals, Sunni styles of prayer; and *(iii)* not visiting Pir Saduddin's tomb but venerating the Aga Khan and his ancestors.[46] The judge examined all three Khoja characteristics from the point of view of determining which of the two groups—Shia or Sunni—was more likely to undertake all these practices which all Khojas admittedly shared. He concluded that the Shia Ismailis were most likely to undertake all these practices.

The arguments by which these practices were placed squarely in the middle of Shiism were not natural or self-evident. They were slowly constructed as the case progressed. For example, at the beginning of the case, the ginan literature was consistently denied by both parties. The *Dashavatar* was consistently denied or represented as a book used only by the ignorant, only at the end of their lives and so on. In fact till the middle of the case it was often referred to as the *Desatir*—a pre-Islamic Persian text.[47] The *Dashavatar*, describing Ali or Sadruddin as the tenth avatar of Vishnu, was not accepted as an important text and yet none could deny its existence. Its very presence was disturbing and problematic. The defendant, that is, the Aga Khan's party, was the one to develop a strategy to deal with it, about halfway through the argumentation, during the statement of Karim Khan, the Aga Khan's secretary. His strategy was to call it the instrument of conversion: the conversion begun by the dais sent to Sindh and Gujarat from Persia. The presence of the *Dashavatar* and other 'Hindu' practices were by this strategy, included within Shiism as a tool of conversion.

In the earlier 1851 case, the *Dashavatar* text and the ceremony were merely described as either Hindu influence or Hindu remnants. This strategy of calling certain practices 'Hindu' was not always seen as natural, obvious or a common mode of critiquing Indian Muslim practices as it seems to us now. Surveying literature from Sirhindi to Shah Waliullah, Gaborieau suggests that while several Sufi practices or Mohurrum taziya were criticized as resembling Hindu practices, they were not described as survivals of Hindu practices or as Hindu influences. He suggests that the latter characterizations may have arisen with British ethnography.[48]

During the evidence taken from the witnesses, there was no indication that Khojas characterized any of their practices as Hindu. The *Dashavatar*, the *ghat pat* and other rituals were not classified as Hindu. The witnesses had no doubt that they were Muslims. The court, which was referring to a fixed essentialized understanding of Muslim and Hindu, had problems reconciling the self-representation of the members as Muslim while they clearly talked of the *Dashavatar* of Vishnu. Karim Khan stated during examination that the *Dashavatar* was a book made for the conversion of the Khojas by Pir Sudroodeen, the Khojas having originally been Hindus.[49] Howard, his attorney, in his statement, insisted that the *Desatir* [*sic*] was read over dying Khojas, notwithstanding all that the evidence denying the importance of the text. He brought forward a good deal of learned research to show that the text about ten incarnations bore evidence of having been written to smooth the conversion of Hindus to Islam, and that nine of these incarnations were of Hindu origin. At this juncture the judge remarked that

> the learned gentleman's point was to show that they could not have been composed by a Suni [*sic*], but might have been by a Shia.[50]

The judge made the necessary link showing that the texts composed for the conversion of Hindus to Islam were Shia. This link was essential in order to sustain the Aga Khan's claim that the Khojas were converted to Shiism. The fact that there was nothing essentially Shia about the use of local names, symbols, texts and rituals for conversion was later asserted by Kaba and other writers on Khoja history.[51] The judge in his judgement elaborated on the link he found between Ismailism/Shiism and the strategy of conversion. He cited Silvestre De Sacy, 'the great French Orientalist who created a standard corpus of critically edited texts for the European student'. The judge quoted from the introduction to De Sacy's *Religion des Druzes,* in which the author has described the instructions given to the Dai or the Ismaili missionary. The mission strategy was one where the missionary represents himself as a zealous partisan of the doctrine professed by the subject. Thus to a Shia he must pose as Shia, to a Sunni as Sunni, and so on. He must then posit the Ismaili doctrine as the necessary completion of that religious doctrine. De Sacy says, 'fixe son attention par une devotion affectée et hypocrite.'[52] In De Sacy's text this understanding of the strategy of conversion is a masterly reduction of his own earlier discussion of the nine stages of initiation into Ismaili doctrine, also discussed by Von Hammer's *The History of the Assassins*.

The initiation began with the raising of doubt and leading to full Ismaili knowledge. One could interpret the method of conversion as one where the missionary would first admit a premise of the religion of the prospective convert, then raise doubts, and then introduce Ismaili doctrine as the solution. Given de Sacy's prejudice against considering Ismailism as a valid religious system, all its teachings were considered false and fraudulent. Even the very method of transmission of knowledge was characterized as fraudulent and hypocritical. Conversion was thus seen as the moment of 'duping'.

The judge then had to explain why the Khojas accepted certain Sunni practices. The argument that provided this explanation was the one of *taqiyya* [Arabic = caution, mental reservation]. This argument was used by the Aga Khan side to disown the Sunni elements of ritual practice and consistent adherence to the Sunni Kazi and Mulla by the Khojas. Yet, taqiyya did not fully explain many practices of the Khojas. For example, many of these practices which were considered to be Khoja from the beginning, and adopted to preserve their true faith from fanatic Sunni rulers, were actually begun during the period of British rule in the Bombay Presidency. For example, the mosque at Chatree Sarang Street (where a Sunni pesh imam and bangi officiated), which was the object of such fierce dispute, was built only in 1822. Until then the Khojas had only used the jamatkhana. Also the Khojas had not adopted all Sunni public ceremonies. Thus, their attempt to simulate Sunni behaviour was obviously incomplete. For example, A. Soomar described a public ceremony of the Sunnis during marriages which the Khcjas did not perform.[53] It would seem from these instances that the Khojas did maintain difference from the Sunnis publicly, thus suggesting that the few instances of similarity with the Sunnis may have been a matter of considered decision rather than blind dissimulation.

However, this alternative understanding of Khoja practice was not convincing to the judge. Dissimulation was made out to be a necessity by quoting Orientalist accounts of Sunni fanaticism. In his judgement, Justice Arnould described the need for taqiyya by quoting several instances of alleged Sunni fanaticism, and said, 'the above passage breathes the full spirit of the Sunni bigot—the pharisee of Islam—narrow, and formal, and fierce'.[54]

In order that this use of caution be recognized as Shiism Mr. Howard even called upon the common male perception of women. He gave an example of taqiyya permitted by the Prophet. He said, when the wife asked for jewels, it was permitted for the husband to say he had no money. This example, by employing the common notion of women's greed and male helplessness before it, stepped in to make taqiyya appear to be a matter of everyday cheating that was necessary for domestic peace. The judge then concurred with this instance of dissimulation as a matter of necessity.

The two arguments, 'unfinished conversion' and 'dissimulation', are placed squarely in the very centre of Ismailism. So much so that numerous other practices that were put forward as positive evidence of non-Shia behaviour and belief could be elided and explained away. They were not acceptable to the court as convincing for they were now accounted for by an inner reason, discovered and demonstrated in the court, which guided these kinds of practices. This inner reason was constructed, as we have seen, by reference to a true Shiism and Shia practices.[55] Thus, a hierarchy was set up between the 'surface' practices and their inner, 'more serious', reasons known to the experts—Persian texts, as authenticated and presented to the West by their own scholars.

Yet, there was no rigorous attempt to test the explanatory power of the doctrine of taqiyya and conversion through dissimulation once they were set up as essentially and authoritatively Shia. Thus, while these arguments can explain why the Khojas pray in the mosque in the Sunni fashion, they cannot explain why the Khojas pray in the jamatkhanas sitting cross-legged, or why in fact they have jamatkhanas at all. Nor can they explain why they are organized as communities with officers like the Mukhi and Kamaria, since these institutions cannot be attributed to Sunni, Shia or Hindu practices. According to Farhad Daftary, Pir Sadruddin was supposed to have established the first jamatkhana at Kotri, Sind, and appointed the first Mukhi and Kamaria.[56]

Thus a history as teleology of the Khojas was set up at the end of which their full recognition of their own identity would be achieved when their conversion was completed and all history in between was erased. As it turned out, the court did not examine these as statements of the beliefs of the Khojas at the time of their origins. Instead, the judge examined the beliefs of the proselytizer, Pir Sadrudddin, to determine the nature of this founding moment. Thus he had to be convinced that Pir Sadruddin was a Shia and not Sunni, which he felt was conclusively proven by the fact that his tomb was not much visited by the Khojas. If Pir Sadruddin was a Sunni and he had converted the Khojas, then his tomb—his only relic on earth—would have been a very important figure. However, the fact that his tomb was overshadowed by the visits being paid to the Aga Khan and his ancestors proved that these latter were more important than the pir. This meant that Pir Sadruddin must have merely been an emissary of one of the Aga Khan's ancestors.[57]

Thus, the judge after setting out the first two questions on Shiism and Sunnism sets out his third, fourth and fifth questions to organize the evidence. These were regarding the Aga Khan and his relationship with the Khojas.[58] The only question concerning the Khojas, 'Who or what are the Khojas?', was posed with the qualification *independently* of their distinctive religious belief. The court in its magisterial distance from religion would have to examine religion on the basis of something other than religious belief. In the way the question was posed, the identity of the Khojas was seen as deriving from a single source—the Aga Khan or Pir Sadruddin. As the judge said, the beliefs of the Khojas could be derived more easily 'without bandying texts' or without reliance on witnesses that did not understand the question. The beliefs were to be ascertained through the identity of the proselytizer, a singularizing totalizing patriarchal identity, deriving from the father. Khojas were here represented as an organic or kinship 'community'.

The link made between the Aga Khan and the Khojas was a genealogical claim. In the 1840s and 1850s, in several representations, the Aga Khan claimed to be, and was described as, being a lineal descendant of the original converter of the Khojas, Pir Sadruddin. The Aga Khan described himself as such in his letters to the Governor-General Viscount Hardinge (22 Oct 1846) and to his successor, Lord Dalhousie (4 June 1849).[59] In the 1847 Khoja succession case proceedings and in the information filed in the Khoja case of 1851, the Aga Khan was described as a pir, a lineal descendant of the Pir Sadruddin who converted the Khojas to Islam. Thus the claim stated a direct and intimate connection between the pir and the Khojas. The image of father manifest in this claim was of one who was directly in touch with his children.

Justice Perry, while describing the 1851 Khoja case, quoted 'an instructive note' by Rawlinson on the Aga Khan, where it was stated that the Aga Khan was a lineal descendant not of Pir Sadruddin but of the sixth Imam, whom a large section of Mussalmans believed would again appear on earth. He then described the Ismailis as believing that each successive Imam from Ali to Ismail was an incarnation of the Divine essence, and further that the incarnation was hereditary in the direct male line; hence the Aga Khan was worshipped 'as a God' by all true Ismailis.[60]

Perry, by reference to the more authoritative Rawlinson, and on the assumption that if the Aga Khan was a descendant of the sixth Imam, held that he could not be the direct descendant of Pir Sadrudddin as claimed by the some of the Khojas and the Aga Khan himself. Justice Perry provided the explanation or strategy for linking the Aga Khan with the Pir. He said, 'it is probable that the Pir, who converted these Khojas, belonged to this Imamy[61] sect of Persia, and hence the reverence for the Aga Khan'.[62] Thus in 1851 itself, the Aga Khan's filial connection with Pir Sadruddin was denied, and he was linked in a different genealogy to Ali in which the father receded further, connected through agents rather than by actual personal presence.

This relationship between Sadruddin and the Aga Khan became an important area of academic interest for European scholarship.[63] European scholars took great pains to show that the link had to be proven to be true and historical. The project then spread even further to link all the known pirs of the Khojas—Pir Shams and Pir Nur Satgur primarily—to the different descendants in the Ismaili line. The history and activity of each Imam had to be identified.

The question was not that the link between the Pirs and the Imams was false and manipulative, but that it was in both instances, genealogical. The Khojas were linked to this Ur figure as children to a father. Yet, in the evidence presented during the case such a close link was not demonstrated. On the contrary, it was conclusively held that few people visited the dargah of Pir Sadruddin at Uchh, and equally few visited the Aga Khan at his residence in Iran. The Aga Khan and his ancestors were visited at their *darkhana* (residence of the current Imam) and money had been traditionally presented to them. A later attempt to explain the Khoja link to the Aga Khan denied a genealogical claim even as it accepted the importance of the Aga Khan as a pir.[64] Even during the case, it had been claimed that the Aga Khan was revered as an important person but not as a source of all faith. This alternative explanation of the reverence for the Aga Khan would be possible only if the Khojas were viewed as a self-determined polity. However, the court's understanding of the Khojas became the most authoritative statement of Khoja religious beliefs.

CONCLUSION

The Khoja religious dispute was settled in court in favour of the Aga Khan, who was then established as the final authority in the Khoja jamat. This religious dispute was examined in court only because it led to competing claims on collective property. The law regarding collectively held 'charitable' property required an examination of the origins of the Khojas. The law of charitable property was employed despite a different claim by the Khojas of their rights in their property. Their right was not a result of original endowment but was earned through contributions members had made to create collective resources like jamatkhana, burial ground, mosque and so on. The reformers who were breaking off did later make an argument about right in collective property which was thrown out of the court as a matter of failed proof. Thus the Khojas were constructed in the court as a sectarian 'community' of Muslims.

In the judicial proceedings of this case we see the setting up of a history as teleology for the Khojas. The judgement in the Aga Khan Case defined the Khojas as converted to Shiism. The Khojas were joined to an externally defined Islam and lost the power to define themselves as Muslim and to simultaneously define Muslim-ness by reference to their historically grounded religious practices. As the Khoja elites attempted to negotiate a recognition of their claim to power through the colonial state they removed the spaces where practices not generally considered as orthodox Islam could still be held to be valid Muslim practices.

In a slightly earlier colonial period (1848 and 1851), the court treated the Khojas as self-governing. The court recognized that their decisions regarding faith and collective rights were made by majority opinion of the group in conjunction with their religious and social leaders at the time and in that place. In contrast in 1866 the court sought to define the religion of the Khojas in court. It could not make sense of the evidence from ordinary Khoja members as to what Khojahood was and how it should be defined. The court therefore went through a lengthy process of arranging the evidence it collected from Khojas within the framework of an Islam deduced from 'experts' and objective Western knowledge. By this process the court defined the Islam that was being professed by the various parties in the case. The Khojas could not define themselves as Muslim and at the same time give their own definition of Islam in the law courts. In this process many of their current practices and beliefs were classified as either irrelevant, ignorant or superstitious or false.

The representation of Khojas as based on their religious beliefs meant that any individuals disputing elements of Khoja beliefs must adopt the path of the Sunni Khojas, that is, they must separate from the Khojas. The judgement in the Aga Khan Case that ruled that the Khojas were followers of the Aga Khan, established the relationship between the Khojas and the Aga Khan, and between the Aga Khan and Ismailism so firmly that neither could be questioned. Any group that broke away had to declare a change of faith.

Around 1879 a group of Khojas broke away from the Aga Khan and declared themselves to be Ithna ashariyya, just as other Khojas had claimed Sunni practices.[65] This group, like the Sunnis, built separate mosques, jamatkhanas and burial grounds. They did not ask for a share in the Khoja jamat's property. This demand did not come up very strongly because of the precedent set by the Aga Khan case in which the court made sectarian identification the basis for the Khoja's ability to use collective property. The court ensured that all members would have to demonstrate the same faith—that of the Aga Khan—if they were to continue in their property rights.

Cases of rights in property subsequent to the Aga Khan case did occur.[66] Most were decided on the grounds of the original religion of the group or the person in whose name the property was held. In an exceptional case in Mahuva, the court ruled that the Khojas of Mahuva were currently Ithna ashariyya and the property belonged to the jamat and therefore the Ithna ashariyya must also have a part of the property.[67] Here the court represented the Khojas as a contemporaneously determined 'polity' rather than 'original' sectarian faith. However, this practice seems to have been the exception rather than the rule.

NOTES

1. For a detailed description of numerous events of the dispute from the 1830s up to the Aga Khan Case see James C. Masselos, 'The Khojas of Bombay: The Defining of Formal Membership Criteria During the Nineteenth Century.' In *Caste and Social Stratification among Muslims*, edited by Imtiaz Ahmad (Delhi: Manohar, 1973).
2. Justice Arnould, 12 Nov 1866, in the judgement of The Advocate General *vs.* Muhammad Husen Huseni, 'The Aga Khan Case', reported in 12 BHR (Bombay High Court Reports), 1866.
3. A. Nanji, 'The Nizari Ismaili Tradition in Hind and Sindh.' PhD diss. McGill University (microfiche), 1972: 11.
4. H. H. The Aga Khan, *The Memoirs of the Aga Khan* (New York: Simon and Schuster, 1954).
5. Francoise Mallison, 'Les Chantes garabi de Pir Shams', *Litteratures medievales de L'Inde du nord*, contribution de Charlotte Vaudeville et de ses élèves (Paris: Ecole Française d'éxtrème orient, 1991); and her 'Hinduism as seen by the Nizari Ismaili Missionaries of Western India: The Evidence of the Ginans.' In *Hinduism Reconsidered* edited by G. D. Sontheimer and H. Kulke, South Asian Studies 24, Heidelberg, South Asian Institute (Delhi: Manohar, 1989); Faisal Devji, 'Conversion to Islam: The Khojas.' M.A. diss, University of Chicago, 1987.
6. 12 BHR: 323, while in the petition the Khojas are using the term 'community' to refer to their collective, since it is used in the context of their claims to be self-governing and their denial of governance by the Aga Khan, the term here has not been employed within the episteme of *Gemeinschaft* or pre-legal community.
7. In the formal texts such as the lettters to and from the government, in court affidavits, the first Aga Khan was known as Mohammed Hussein Hooseini (variously spelt: Hoosanee); see also Masselos, 'The Khojas of Bombay', for a description of events.
8. Hirbae and others *vs.* Sonbae in Perry, *Oriental Cases*, p. 111, discussed in this volume, Chapter 2.
9. Information filed on 21 Feb 1850, reported in the *Bombay Times and Journal of Commerce*, 21 July 1851.
10. Aga Jehangir Shah Ibn Aga Hasanali Shah, *Aga Jehangir Shahno Risalo, ie Ibrat e Afza,* tr. Adelji Dhunji Kaba (Amreli: Adelji Dhanji Kaba, 1912): 8-11. This text was being employed in a polemical battle to prove that the Khojas were originally Shia

Ithna ashariyya and not Ismaili. It claimed to be the memoirs of the first Aga Khan's son. I am assuming that the polemics in the text are confined to the nature of Shiism Aga Hasanali Shah was teaching, but am using the text to show that he was taking a serious interest in the religious behaviour of his Khoja devotees.

11. See Masselos, 'Change and Custom in the Bombay Mohurrum.' *South Asia* 5, 2, (1982): 52-53.
12. *Rast Goftar tatha Satya Prakasha* (RGSP) (22 April 1866): 252.
13. Quoted in RGSP 16 (1867): 164.
14. *'Khojaoni strioni halat ane rivaj,' Stri-Bodh* 6 (June 1868).
15. RGSP (13 Sep 1863): 465; (24 March 1867); (18 Nov 1866): 728.
16. Numerous articles in *Rast Goftar* critical of gurus, pamphlets like *Vishayi Guru Vishe*, articles by missionaries like Rev Wilson.
17. Aga Khan Case, 12 BHR: 348. This was criticized among the Vaishnav community, see also *Times of India,* 1 Feb 1862. It was described as an indirect tax and a burden on the ordinary consumer. The colonial state was extremely jealous of what it saw as its own sphere of relationship with the individual. Thus the collection of dues masquerades as an economic argument, actually constituting lines of power and authority.
18. Masselos, 'The Khojas of Bombay'; these were laid out in the notice sent to the plaintiffs on 23 Aug 1862 by A Soomar on behalf of the jamat convened by the Aga Khan's party; notice printed in the affidavit of A Soomar and others, 10 June 1864, Supreme Court 161/247 of 1864.
19. Masselos lists all these events very succinctly: 'The Khojas of Bombay': 8-15; affidavits of Abdul Rouzac and Ali Mohammed, 9 June 1864, Supreme Court 168/247 and 163/247 of 1864; at one point in 1863-1864, the Aga Khan party filed an action of trespass against Charles Forjett, then acting commissioner of police, for keeping sepoys at the jamatkhana: A. Soomar and others, affidavit filed on 10 June 1864, Supreme Court 161/247 of 1864.
20. Scoble, claiming precedence laid down by E. Perry in Gungbae *vs.* Thavur Moolla, reported in *The Bombay Gazette*, 25 June 1866: 3.
21. 12 BHR: 323.
22. Quoted in the 12 BHR: 327.
23. Listed in detail in the Bill of Complaint filed with the Supreme Court, Equity side, 2 June 1866, bundle no 248, doc no 18: 2 and 3; also in the Supreme Court doc no 163 of no 247, 1864,

para no 4; Bill of Complaint, 2 June 1862: 10, para 13, Supreme court, 18/248, 1866.

24. Plaint filed on 21 Feb 1850, reprinted in 21 July 1851 *Bombay Times and Journal of Commerce*.
25. Scoble replaced their earlier attorney, Anstey. Scoble's last major argument on 23 June 1866, quoted in *Bombay Gazette*, 27 June 1866: 3.
26. Bill of Complaint, 2 June 1862, p 1, para 14; if they had made a trust argument, they could have said that the property was dedicated to all Khojas and therefore it must be available for use by all. Kozlowski discusses how the British refused to recognise *waqf* in the name of family members and insisted that it be for 'charitable and religious purposes'. Justice Amir Ali's opinion was that the British claim for *aqaf* to be only for charitable purpose according to Muslim law is based on a footnote in Hamilton's English translation of the Persian translation of the Arabic *Hedaya:* Gregory C.Kozlowski, *Muslim Endowments and Society in British India* (Cambridge: Cambridge University Press, 1985).
27. *RGSP* (18 Nov 1866): 278.
28. Bill of Complaint filed 2 June 1862, para I, Supreme Court Records, 18/24, 1866.
29. *The Times of India*, Saturday, 28 April 1866: 3.
30. *The Bombay Gazette*, 13 June 1866: 3.
31. 12 BHR: 325; 360.
32. Evidence submitted by Howard on behalf of the defendants, *The Bombay Gazette*, 13 June 1866; Letter from the Aga Khan to the Khoja jamat of Thunda Mahomad Khan, a village in Sind, appointing the witness the Kamaria in the evidence of Ismail Saliani reproduced in *The Bombay Gazette*, 22 June 1866.
33. *The Bombay Gazette,* 27 June 1866.
34. *The Bombay Gazette*, 13 June 1866.
35. Borradaile's *Report of Civil Cases Adjudged by the Court of Sudder Dewanee Adawlut for the Presidency of Bombay from 1800-1824,* vols 1 and 2 (Bombay: Educational Society Press, 1863) is full of such instances. Also see the case of the Khoja property dispute which the judge referred to the attorneys authorizing them to collect the caste and settle the matter (see Chapter 2, this volume); 12 BHR 325.
36. Justice Erskine Perry's notebook, BHR (June 1847): 33-34.
37. 12 BHR: 228; 328.
38. Described in Chapter 2, this volume: 'usage, which being a matter of fact can only be determined by the examination of witnesses, or such evidence as the case may admit of.' Court of

Directors to Government of Bombay, letter of Dec 1827, India Office Records 0/6/20 Personal Records.

39. Examination of Gulam Rasool, *Times of India*, 26 April 1866: 3.
40. *The Times of India*, 28 April 1866.
41. Reported in the *Bombay Telegraph and Courier*, 24 June 1847.
42. *The Times of India*, 28 April 1866.
43. Sir Erskine Perry, *Cases Illustrative of Oriental Life:* 114.
44. *Bombay Times and Journal of Commerce*, 21 July 1851.
45. In Mallison, *Seventeenth garabi of Pir Shams*, Pir Shams is represented as the incarnation of God ('Morara', according to Mallison, 'Murari'). V. N. Hooda, 'Some Specimens of Satpanth Literature', *Collectanea*, vol 1, The Ismaili Society series A, no. 2 (Leiden: Ismaili Society, 1948): 74; Mallison, 'Les Chants garabi de Pir Shams': 126.
46. The judge described his arguments in the judgement reported in 12 BHR: 352-355.
47. Until the testimony of Allarukhia Soomar, halfway through the case, *Desatir*—the name of the Persian text—is used almost interchangeably with *Dashavatar*.
48. Marc Gaborieau, 'A Nineteenth-Century Indian "Wahhabi" Tract Against the Cult of Muslim Saints: *Al-Balagh al-Mubin.*' In *Muslim Shrines in India*, edited by Christian W. Troll (Delhi: Oxford University Press, 1992).
49. Examination of Karim Khan reported in *The Bombay Gazette*, 9 June 1866.
50. *The Bombay Gazette*, 13 June 1866.
51. Adelji Dhanji Kaba, *Khoja Komani Tawarikh* (Amreli: Adelji Dhanji Kaba, 1912); Ahmed argues that such conversion practices were undertaken by Sunnis; see also. Rafiuddin Ahmed, *The Bengal Muslims, 1871-1906: A Quest for Identity* (Delhi: Oxford University Press, 1981).
52. See Edward Said, *Orientalism* (New York: Pantheon, 1978) for a full description of De Sacy's activities and projects; Sylvestre De Sacy, *Exposé de la réligion des Druzes, Tire des livres religieux de cette secte, et précedé d'une introduction et de la vie du Khalife Hakem-Biamr-Allah*, vol 1 (Paris: L'imprimerie Royale, 1837).
53. A. Soomar and others, affidavit filed 10 June 1864, Supreme Court 161/247, 1864; para 8 mentions that the Sunni performance of the 'Moulood' ceremony during a marriage and also the Sunni celebration of Peeram Peer on the eleventh day after the rising moon of every month were not undertaken by the Khojas.
54. 12 BHR: 356.

55. These practices are not inherently Shia and constructed as such by one party. Later, similar constructions of 'smoothening the path to conversion' are used by Sunnis to explain other kinds of practices which cannot be explained by the classical image of Sunnism-as-Islam that is built up.
56. Farhad Daftary, *The Ismailis: Their History and Doctrines* (Cambridge: Cambridge University Press, 1990): 479.
57. 12 BHR: 353.
58. His questions were:
THIRDLY—Who and what is the first defendant, Aga Khan?
FOURTHLY—Who and what (independently of their distinctive religious belief) are the Khojas, and what are and have been their relations with the first defendant and his ancestors?
FIFTHLY—What have been the relations of the first defendant, Aga Khan, with the particular community to which the relators and plaintiffs belong, viz. the Khoja community of Bombay?
59. India Office Records (IOR), Bombay Secret Consultations, 4 April-27 June 1849, vol 2.
60. Justice Perry's notebook, gives the major arguments made in the case: 23-27; *Bombay Times and Journal of Commerce*, 21 July 1851; Perry, *Cases Illustrative of Oriental Life:* 113, n a.
61. This reference to Imamy as opposed to Ismaili probably reflects the ambivalence of the Aga Khan's practice between 'twelver' or Ithna ashari Shiism and 'sevener' or Ismaili Shiism.
62. Perry, *Cases Illustrative of Oriental Life:* 113, n a.
63. Wladimir Ivanow, *Satpanth (Indian Ismailism), Collectanea,* vol 1 (Leiden: Ismaili Society, 1948); J. N. Hollister, *The Shia of India*, 2nd ed (Delhi: Oriental Books Reprint Corp, 1979).
64. The various evidence as summed up by the judge in 12 BHR: 352; Kaba, *Khoja komani tawarikh;* 294.
65. Letter of Rahimtullah Sayani to J. Mcpherson, 2 Sept 1884, vol 27, 1884, Maharashtra State Archives, said that in 1879 only four Khojas followed Ithna ashariyya practices, but lately the number had increased to about twenty-five. In 1900 a much larger group broke off. They argued that the Khoja practices were actually Shia Ithna ashariyya and not Ismaili; Adelji Dhanji Kaba, *Khoja komani tawarikh*; Masselos, 'The Khojas of Bombay' describes these schisms in detail.
66. Kaba, *Khoja panth darpan:* 34, 41.
67. Mahuva Commission Case adjudged by Justice Mr. Mirza; quoted in ibid: 34.

CHAPTER 4

Caste, Religion and the Law: The Vallabhacharya Vaishnavas

A MOVEMENT FOR religious reform among the Vallabhacharya Vaishnavas (*Pushtimargis,* followers of the path of grace) culminated in the Maharaj Libel Case (MLC), as well as other events of conflict within the religious polity. The Maharaj Libel Case demonstrated that several castes of the Pushtimarga *sampradaya* (religious tradition) were intimately involved in the reform movement. These caste authorities exercised some control over practices which were religious, even as religious authority regulated the internal functioning of the caste. Together the caste and religious authorities governed what I call a 'polity'. When the reform controversy was brought to the colonial court, the nexus of caste and religious authorities was delegitimized in the legal process, which in turn did not permit the development of internal self-governance and the settlement of disputes. Instead the court privileged a classical textual definition of the religious group. The court's nonrecognition of the ability of the polity to determine disputes regarding its religious practices meant that the latter would be defined for it by an external body. Since the Pushtimarga claimed to be Hindu, its concurrence with Hinduism was seen in court as 'natural' and not as negotiated through its own interpreters. This treatment of the Pushtimarga in court may be characterized within the episteme of community.

It is generally accepted that caste persists despite conversion or change of religion,[1] and that religious authority can reorganize or maintain the relationships between castes through organizing local caste hierarchies. This power has been noticed by Arjun Appadurai in the South Indian context and by Maya Burger in the case of the Vallabhacharya Vaishnavas. In Burger's study of the temple town of Nathadwara, she remarks that the caste-rankings in Nathadwara were different from those in the surrounding area. She attributes this differential ranking tc the temple authorities who ranked certain 'low' castes higher in Nathadwara because the services performed by these castes were important in Pushtimarga ritual practices.[2]

The fact that religious heads governed disputes internal to member castes, as opposed to their governance of the caste system as a whole, has not been noticed by any extensive anthropclogical study. Nor has it been noticed that the heads of individual castes themselves exercised control over religious heads.[3] The links between the maharaj (priests or *gurus*) of the Vallabhacharya Vaishnavas and the Bhatias and Kapol castes of Bombay demonstrate that enormous cooperation and negotiation went on between caste authorities and religious authority.

The judicial courts restricted the jurisdiction of castes to fewer and fewer subjects (see Chapter 2). Earlier the courts were expected to consult castes on substantive law. Such consultations, however, became marginal after the accession of the crown and the employment of the Bengal Presidency model in Bombay, the drawing up of the Indian Penal Code, and codes of procedure. Though the courts generally treated religious groups as wholly self-governed, they retained the right to adjudicate religious disputes that affected matters of public interest. Thus the absence of consultation in the judicial sphere pushed caste out of the public domain, defined as a space in which individuals come together to debate, discuss and govern—be political.[4] As a non-participant in the public space then caste was prominent as community. Caste in itself was no longer recognized as a political space of debate, dispute, hierarchy but was seen instead as a self-governed and fixed community which was present in the public as an attachment to an individual. The public and not caste became an arena for the individual and the state. Caste became an area of sameness and cohesion, giving identity to an individual. This process saw the corollary to the rise of the individual (for which the nineteenth century in India is justly famous): the rise, and not the demise of, the community.

During the reform controversy the maharaj found that he could not employ caste authorities to enforce his will on devotees, and the castes too could not rely on the maharaj commanding the obedience of his devotees. When this dispute came to court in 1862, the court did not recognize either caste or the maharaj as reliable authorities regarding the interpretation of the 'true' religion of the Vallabhacharya Vaishnavas, that is, Hinduism. The court employed two main legal arguments to deny these powers to caste. One, that the court as an organ of Her Majesty the Queen had absolute sovereignty and it could not permit any other body to interfere in its pursuit of a settlement of a 'civil' dispute. Two, that matters of public interest must be dealt with by the public through its instrument, the state. The conjunction of these two arguments deprived caste men of the power to govern the religious polity and accorded it to the colonial judiciary. That Vallabha sectarians came from certain castes then became merely a descriptive sociological fact rather than a matter of active social control and governance. Yet, prior to the legal trial, caste authority was important to the reformers in controlling the social behaviour of caste members. Caste organizations were associated with the Pushtimarga maharajas. The reformers tried to mobilize caste authority for reform of the Pushtimarga religious tradition—to influence the behaviour of caste members and that of the religious authorities.

AS A RELIGIOUS POLITY

In mid-nineteenth century Bombay, young reformers criticized the maharajas of the Vallabhacharya tradition. Vallabhacharya was a sixteenth-century acharya (teacher and founder exponent of a school of philosophy). He was a Telegu brahmin whose uncle was a member of the Vijayanagar court. He lived at Adel near Benares and founded a temple and sect in Braj, a small forest settlement near Mathura. He taught the worship of the child-God Krishna and wrote a major commentary on the *Brahmasutras*. His descendants, through the male line, are called maharajas and they preside over the numerous temples of the sect, spread over Mathura, Rajasthan, Sindh and Gujarat.

In Gujarat the sect attracted the well-to-do among trading and farming castes: mainly the Bhatia, Lohana, bania, and Kanbi castes. In 1860 there were sixty or seventy maharajas in India. In Bombay, the first temple of this religious tradition was established in 1811 (Vikram Samvat 1867) by Gokulnathji Maharaj who had been living in Bombay for three years before the temple was established.[5] Other maharajas like Chimanlalji and Ghanshamlalji came to Bombay later and took up residence here. Jivanlalji Maharaj succeeded to Gokulnathji's seat in Bombay. In the 1860s there were four or five maharajas residing in Bombay.

Individuals from many castes were involved in the movement to reform the Vallabhacharya Vaishnava maharajas, of whom the banias and the Bhatias were the most prominent and important. While one talks of the banias as a caste, in actuality the caste is made up of numerous *jnatis* like the Kapol, Nagar and Dasha Shrimali. The most prominent of these jnatis in Bombay were the Kapols. The *sheth* or head of the Kapols also controlled the cloth market of Bombay and other trade organizations (*mahajanas*). The Bhatia were primarily two jnatis: the Kutchi Bhatias and the Halai Bhatias.

The brahmins amongst the reformers, such as Narmadshankar Lalshankar, were not themselves from the Vallabhacharya Vaishnava sampradaya. The Nagar and Dasha Shrimali banias in Bombay who were from the Vallabhacharya Vaishnava tradition and who participated in the reform did not enjoy much power in the Bombay mahajan or in the religious tradition. Thus, the Kapol Banias and the Bhatias were the main actors in the nexus between caste and the Vallabhacharya Vaishnavas of Bombay.

The reformers were criticizing the Vallabhacharya maharajas for licentious, tyrannical and immoral behaviour. Much of this discussion took place in 'public' societies and was published in public journals. The maharajas of Bombay, Jivanji being the chief of them, were worried about their personal reputations and that of their faith. Jadunath Maharaj of Surat, one of the most vocal and liberal-minded of all the maharajas came to Bombay in 1859 to combat the reformers. In Bombay he undertook all manner of activities to fight the reformers, which will be discussed later. An article published in the reformist newspaper *Satya Prakasha,* 21 October 1860, precipitated a crisis. It accused the maharajas of sleeping with the wives and daughters of devotees and of preaching heterodox doctrines. Jadunath Maharaj was named specifically as one who should put a stop to such practices.[6] In May 1861 he charged Karsandas Mulji, the author of this article and one of his most vocal critics and member of the Kapol bania jnati, and Rustomji Ranina, the publisher of *Satya Prakasha*, a Parsi, with libel, which became famous as the Maharaj Libel Case.

While only these two men were accused of libel by the maharaj, almost all the reform-minded men in Bombay, like Narmadshankar Lalshankar, Goculdas Tejpal, Mathuradas Lavji, Lakhmidas Khimji and Bhau Daji, were involved in fighting the case. This was a reformist event where the distinction between the 'intelligentsia' and merchant-princes, that Dobbin traces cannot be observed.[7] Prominent merchants like Goculdas Tejpal, Mangaldas Nathoobhoy, and Lakhmidas Khimji supported the reform effort of educated young men like Mulji, Narmad, Ranina, Bhau Daji and others. On the other side were the maharaj, caste leaders and rich merchants *(shethiyas)* like Varjivandas Madhavdas, along with clerks and government employees like the court translator Narayan Dinanathji. Jadunath Maharaj, the man who brought the libel charge, was considered the most 'forward-looking' of the Vaishnava establishment. He supported the opening of girls' schools in Bombay. He established the Vaishnava Dharma Prasaraka Sabha, society for the propagation of Vaishnava dharma.[8] He published two journals, the *Vaishnav Punch* and the *Svadharma Vardhak ane Samshaya Chhedaka,* and released handbills regularly, and so on. His father, Brajratanji Maharaj of Surat, was known for his love for education. Brajratanji and Durgaram Manchharam Mehtaji (Gujarati school teacher in Surat, reformer and founder of the Manav Dharma Sabha as well as the Pustak Prasarak Mandali) used to discuss questions of superstition, magic and the need to reform current practices with him.[9]

THE IMPORTANCE OF CASTE IN EARLY SOCIAL REFORM

Most studies of reform in nineteenth-century Bombay have concentrated on reform 'movements' or campaigns like the ones for widow remarriage, women's education, raising the age of consent and others against infanticide, sati and so on. They have not comprehensively studied the range of interests that the reformers exhibited. The early reformers of the 1850s urged numerous reforms upon local society in Bombay. A close scrutiny of the articles written on improvement in the fifties and sixties suggests that a significantly large proportion of the essays written about changing customs and manners were addressed to caste leaders and social/caste communities. Even where the concern was expressed for a religious group—Hindus—the focus of attention was on caste and caste authorities. For example, an article entitled 'The Need for Reform among the Hindus' talked of the power of castes to change the behaviour of the religious group.[10] In other words, the article assumed that the power to change lay with caste rather than with a religious head or philosophy. It even suggested that reduction of the power of castes to ostracize or make members outcastes would improve the chances of reform.

In Mulji's essays from 1855 to 1859 collected in *Nibandhamala*, the reformist appeal was addressed to caste leaders (*natanan shethiya*)[11] asking for arrangements to be made within the castes. Even on the question of building schools for girls he appealed to leaders of caste and trade organizations for funds. Since the local society was categorized by caste, the accusation of backwardness was directed according to caste: Mulji described the local refusal to educate girls as 'Bhatias do not send their girls to schools.' On the question of the marriage ceremony, complaining about the excessive expenditure and display of wealth during wedding celebrations, he said that the 'vaniya, Bhatia do this especially.'[12]

Other reformist essays also classified indigenous society by castes. In this classificatory system Parsis and Khojas were both treated as castes. Thus groups like Khojas or Parsis were not seen as parallel to Hindu or Muslim communities 'in general,' but as similar to castes like Bhatias and banias. Society was visualized as a caste society, especially upper caste society (see Chapter 5). The practices that Mulji targeted were described as social and caste evils and not as 'religious' evils of Hinduism. Thus the singing of obscene songs at marriages, festivals, beating on one's own chest at funerals to express grief, were seen as practices that could be stopped through caste *bandobasts* (arrangement) rather than by religious preaching.

The Holi festival, the subject of much reformist writing, was represented as a social event, not a religious one. Perhaps this representation of Holi was facilitated by the fact that different local 'religious' communities participated in the festival. At Holi, Parsi and Hindu women of various castes worshipped the Holi fire, fasted, and so on. None of the contemporary mythological explanations linked the Holi festival with the present routinely attested story of Vishnu, Prahlad and Holika. All the stories explaining Holi relate the death of a woman—either an evil daughter of a trader or the demise of demonnesses (*rakshasi*) (in two versions). These stories enjoin the worship of fire in her memory, to protect the people from her wrath.[13] The story had no sectarian references to specific Gods or other mythologically well-known figures.

Another example of the reformers taking the social group as basis for reform and religious change is Mulji's criticism of the worship at Mount Mary (an old shrine of the Madonna in a Bombay suburb). Mulji condemned Parsi women for offering wax figures at Mount Mary. He decried the persistence of this superstitious practice in spite of their education, and that of their husbands who had become doctors of medicine. None of his criticisms was on the grounds that this worship at Mount Mary was not 'true' Parsi worship, he merely called the worship superstitious.[14] These changes were urged not on religious or spiritual grounds but on the grounds of moral behaviour. On the ground of morality one could change one's behaviour without benefit of 'religious' instruction. Mulji and the reformers were not therefore looking for correct religious instruction. They were public-minded reformists who believed that their duty as social critics gave them the right and authority to criticize all groups. The reformist paper criticized the Khoja leaders for not pursuing the proper course in educational instruction and good behaviour along with their opposition to their religious head.[15]

In reformist articles the caste or social polity was seen as possessing social authority, which it was urged to employ in order to effect reform. In most instances of reform, caste barriers were respected. In nineteenth-century Bombay Presidency there were very few reformers working towards removing caste boundaries; a few of them, such as the Paramahamsa Sabha, remained small, secretive and found it difficult to survive. The more important mode for most reforms was that of recognizing the importance of caste and attempting to use caste authority for reform.

Durgaram Mehtaji (one of the oldest reformers in the Presidency) expressed this sentiment most clearly. He did argue for the destruction of pride born of caste, he maintained that it was wrong to consider Dhedhs (a caste of sweepers and cleaners) 'untouchable,' that the human race was one family and individuals should not object to eating and drinking with one another. However, he did not break caste rules regarding touch, purity and pollution. In reply to Krushnaram Dayaram's question as to why he did not break caste rules, he said that while he had thought of doing so, he was advised by friends that he could exercise a more beneficial influence from within the caste. He believed that he should convince more people to his point of view before getting out of the caste system.[16] Thus Durgaram regarded caste as an important tool for change and believed that influencing caste leaders would actually lead to greater reforms and change than breaking caste authority. Most reformers accepted the barriers between castes. For example, a *Rast Goftar tatha Satya Prakash* article urging the formation of a reformist 'club' said that the club would respect caste hesitations regarding inter-dining and there would be no dining at the club.[17]

From the 1870s onwards the caste organization itself became the subject of reforms. Reformers concentrated on ensuring that the shethiyas gave up their control on caste affairs and caste funds. They attempted to make the functioning of castes more transparent, and demanded a democratization by asking for the inclusion of more people in the management of caste affairs. This was to be achieved through the formation of caste councils, through regular elections, writing of constitutions of the councils and caste associations, and so on.[18] Thus, castes became the subjects of reform but were not eliminated by the improvement efforts. Caste governance was important to the reformers in organizing social change. Religious authorities also worked through the caste organizations of their followers. The employment of caste leaders by reformers and caste authorities suggests how important caste organizations and governance were in organizing society. The role of caste heads was of a 'public' nature in that they could be addressed not merely by their own members but also by men of other castes to govern better. As the domain of the public grew with the rise of newspapers, larger educational institutions with debating societies, public libraries and lectures, judicial courts, and so on, caste organizations were dragged into the public arena. They may be castigated for obstructing change but nevertheless they were criticized in public and were asked to use their power constructively. Castes were seen as active agents in this public space and not regarded as an anachronistic identity that survived in it. This challenges the common understanding of the growth of civil society as being characterized by atomized individuals. It was possible for castes to be considered a 'polity' in the early public sphere.

CASTE AUTHORITIES AND THE MAHARAJAS

One of the most crucial functions of governance of the religious polity was the collection of revenue for the upkeep of the maharajas' religious establishment. The maharajas levied a tax on almost every important article of trade, which was collected through the trade organizations of the city. In fact, non-Vaishnava merchants in the cloth market also paid trade levies to the Vallabhacharya maharajas and closed their shops on events like birth or death of a maharaj. This occurred because in Bombay the Kapol and Bhatia castes dominated the cloth market and its trade organization.

The maharaj also collected a levy on every marriage, pregnancy, birth, death and other events in the life of the devotee. The annual account and reports of the Halai Bhatia jnati of Bombay were published from 1863 onwards. These reports were published by the caste 'manager'—a leading member of the caste, Lakhmidas Khimji, who was also active in the reform movement. The reports primarily give details of the accounts of the caste organization and record any major controversy regarding its management.[19] These reports record that the caste collected a levy (called *laga*) at major life-events from caste members and sent a part of the collection to the various maharajas in Bombay, Kutch, Kathiawar and Gujarat. Letters from the maharaj mentioning receipt of this levy also mention receipts of goods like sugar, saffron and books.[20] Thus, the caste helped the maharajas procure important goods as well as money.

When Gokulnathji Maharaj first came to Bombay in 1811 the heads of the more important castes met him and signed an agreement promising support for building and maintaining a temple. Thus castes, through their own organizations, and through associated trade organizations, were important means of collecting revenue for the maharaj. The maharaj also employed caste authority to exercise his power. *RGSP* published an instructive list of such events when the maharaj exercised his authority over castes:[21]

(i) In 1855 the maharaj had quarrelled with the Bhuleshwar brahmins and asked his devotees to boycott them. The Bhatia caste mahajan, accordingly, resolved to ostracise those Bhatias who had helped the brahmins.

(ii) In 1858-1859 the Bhatia and Kapol caste leaders or seths agreed to punish any journalist who wrote against the maharaj.

(iii) In 1860 when Manekbai, a Bhatia widow, complained in court about harassment by the maharaj, the Bhatia caste leaders settled the question out of court.[22]

Gopaldas Madhavdas alleged in court that the maharajas decided caste disputes and themselves 'fell into' caste disputes. Around 1853 the Kapol caste headship was transferred from Gopaldas Madhavdas' hands to his brother Varjivandas Madhavdas with the help of Jivanji Maharaj. In 1858 the maharaj punished Mathuradas Lavji for not observing the proper mourning rules (*sutak*) and celebrating his daughter's marriage at a time of a death in the family. Mulji accused the maharaj of interfering in the social life of his devotees. In 1861 Jivanji Maharaj in Bombay arbitrated in a dispute in the Luvana caste. Karamsi Mulji advised the caste members not to allow the maharaj to interfere. Jivanji Maharaj called a caste panchayat in his temple and fined Karamsi Mulji for this interference and ostracized him for a month.[23]

Another report in 1867 mentions how the Narodawala Vrajratan Maharaj attempted to settle a dispute with some local Bhatia, Vallabhdas Lakhmidas, in Mandvi. In order to settle the dispute the maharaj collected the Bhatia caste members and organized a Bhatia *panchat* (panchayat) to solve the problem, but he dropped the prosecution when he felt he wouldn't succeed. A report from Ahmedabad in 1867 charged that when a Meshri baniya caste member was thrown out of the caste, he gave a donation to the Vallabhacharya maharaj of one hundred and fifty rupees. The maharaj then succeeded in getting the caste to take him back.[24]

If the instances just cited demonstrate that the maharajas manipulated the caste and settled its internal disputes, there are also instances which demonstrate the authority of the caste organizations over them. Caste leaders advised the maharajas on how they should behave and even punished them for incorrect behavior. Thus the Bhatia caste organization of Mandvi, a city in Kutch, complained about four different maharajas and their immorality to the Kutch Durbar (native court), who were then expelled from the city.[25] The caste organization also forced the maharaj to accept its decision of ostracizing a member. For example, the Bombay Bhatia caste forced the maharaj of Junagadh to accept their decision. Its secretary, Lakhmidas Khimji, wrote to the Junagadh maharaj, Gokaleshaji, on 17 April 1876, warning him of the consequences of not following the caste decision. Khimji accused the maharaj of acting out of monetary greed, and favouring an immoral and *vatlayela* (converted/ ostracized) Bhatia of Junagadh in *contravention* of the caste's disapproval. He ended the letter thus:

> 'We are advising you to maintain good counsel and warn you that the mahajan will not be scared of you and will act according to its wishes and do what is right. If you pressurize the Junagadh Bhatia caste men then we will have to complain to the Nawab saheb and the Kathiawar Political Agent and you will have to taste the bitter fruits . . . we hope you will not harass the caste organization.'[26]

These instances have been cited to demonstrate how caste organization was employed by the maharaj to establish his authority and how the caste accepted the responsibility to discipline the maharaj. Examples will be given of how the devotees and critics of the religion used the caste authorities to control the maharajas. This mutuality of authority and control did not mean that all members of the caste were compelled to follow one religion. Some families amongst the Kapols were Shaivas and some others Jain.[27] These differences of belief did not negate the maharaj's authority to govern individual behaviour and settle disputes within the caste. Maharaj Brajratanji of Surat agreed that this was a role played by the maharajas.[28] In disputes between the maharaj and the caste, the political authority, as we saw, was also employed. This is seen in the exchanges between the Bhatias and the maharaj in Kutch and Junagadh. In these incidents the political authority was called on to enforce a judgement or decision reached by the caste, which indicated that the caste and religious heads were governable by the political authorities, and were not considered to be some ungovernable or self-governing private sphere to be 'interfered with' only in the interest of some higher individual good. The authority of the religious preacher existed often in cooperation with caste but sometimes in subordination to it. The subordination was not in the name of individual right but of caste authority.

CASTE AUTHORITIES AND THE MAHARAJAS

The reformers recognized the association between the Vallabhacharya maharajas and the Bhatia, Kapol caste authorities. In their effort to reform Pushtimarga practice as in their other reform efforts they followed and accepted caste authority in trying to enforce their own point of view. They directed their criticism of the religious tradition to the religious authorities as well as to the caste authorities. Let us examine the movement to reform the Vallabhacharya maharajas' behaviour from the point of view of analysing the role of caste authority. The earliest criticism of the maharajas' behaviour in Bombay emerged in 1855 from the Bhatia caste. Lakhmidas Khimji, Mathuradas Lavji, among others, criticized Jivanji Maharaj of Bombay and had won over many caste members to their position. Their popularity was attested by the fact that those Bhatias who were convinced by their opinions were called *Mathurapanthi*.[29] The content of this critique is largely unknown, however, according to newspaper reports, the Bhatia caste had convened a meeting in 1855 in order to put an end to the sexual misbehaviour by the maharajas and to stop the women from visiting the maharajas.[30] Thus the reform of the religious practice was effected by caste authority.

Later in the same year, the maharajas became involved in a controversy with the Shaivite priests of Bhuleshwar, who celebrated *chhappan bhog* (festival of food offerings) at their Shiva temple. They ate and distributed the *prasad* (offerings) of this festival. The Vallabhacharya maharajas condemned this practice. They insisted that eating the offerings made to Shiva was condemned by the Shastras and was done only by shudras, and denounced those who ate these as polluted. They went on to say that until the Shaiva priests did *prayashchitya* (penance), their patrons, many of whom were Bhatias and Kapols, should not accept them. Several members of the Vallabhacharya polity and other brahmins in Bombay opposed the maharajas who were criticized as being merely jealous of the popularity of the Shaiva priests. However, the Bhatia caste organization agreed to support the maharajas if they in turn agreed to the reforms suggested earlier by the caste. The maharajas conceded on the condition that the reform agreement be kept secret for a year. Thus, the reformers worked with the maharajas to effect their changes.

The Bhatia support of the maharajas was not enough and the incident with the Bhuleshwar brahmins provided the reformists with much matter for criticism. One, that to maintain their image as powerful religious preceptors, the maharajas staged a false apology from the Shaivite priests. This was exposed in the newspapers and thus to the 'public'.[31] Mulji started publishing *Satya Prakasha* (later to be merged with another reformist paper, the *Rast Goftar*, in 1860, and to become the *Rast Goftar tatha Satya Prakasha* [*RGSP*]). He and other reformers started writing more critically about the Vaishnava maharajas. These reformers urged the caste organizations to influence the maharajas to change. They argued that the maharajas would improve and reform only if the caste organization and its leading men took a stand against them and forced them to change. The reformers strongly criticized the caste leaders when the latter submitted to the authority of the maharajas.[32]

Reformist articles treated the maharaj as identified with the castes; for example, a *Rast Goftar* article criticized the crowd at the maharajas' temple at the time of the annual feast. It was headlined '*Vania tatha bhatia maharajano ankota*' (the feast of the bania and Bhaṭia maharajas) emphasizing the fact that the maharajas were spiritual authorities of the bania and Bhatia castes.[33] This article also commended the Bhatia and bania caste leaders to make better arrangements to ensure that women attending the feast were not molested or hurt by the temple attendants. In other articles Mulji criticized the affront to female modesty inside the temple, how women's clothes got disarrayed in the rush and they were man-handled. In these articles while the maharajas are exhorted to make changes, the caste leaders, especially the Bhatia and bania castes were also exhorted to influence the maharajas and to think of building an alternative temple.[34] While most of the time the reformers exhorted the maharajas and their devotees through newspapers and such public forums to reform their practices, some did try to force the caste leadership to take reformist action. For example, on 24 July, 1866, a Bhatia youth, Mulji Thakarsi, forced a meeting of the Bhatia caste to consider a handbill published about the immorality of the maharajas. Subsequently, a group of the Bhatia leaders allegedly met Jivanji Maharaj of Bombay and received an assurance from him that he would admonish the other maharajas for their immorality. *RGSP*, the reformist mouthpiece, urged the Halai Bhatia caste organization to make their sub-caste rules and recommended that one of the subjects should be some arrangement regarding the maharajas. Another issue had an anonymous essay accusing the maharaj of unfair behaviour, and it once again emphasized that the exact caste of the devotee mattered in organizing the religious group. The accusation against the maharaj was that he favoured his Bhatia devotees because of their greater wealth over his bania ones.[35]

As in other issues, the maharaj employed the caste authorities to fight back against the reformist attack too or at least attempted to do so. One such response was in 1858-1859 in the event now famous as the 'slavery bond' episode. Towards the end of 1858, the editor, Navrojaji Dorabji, of the weekly journal *Chabuk*, allegedly at the instigation of the maharaj, published several articles abusing and criticizing Bhatia reformers Goculdas Tejpal and Lakhmidas Khimji, and the latter took the editor to court for libel in January 1859. The editor was advised to call the maharaj of Bombay as witness. The maharaj refused to come to court and instead enforced an agreement to prevent a recurrence of such summons on the caste organizations of his devotees. This agreement was called the 'slavery bond' by the reformist papers.[36]

The provisions of the bond required various kinds of action from caste authorities:

(i) collection of money from all caste fellows to fund the exemption of the maharaj from appearing in court;
(ii) an assurance that the caste would ostracize any Vaishnava who summons the maharaj to court;
(iii) ostracize any Vaishnava who writes against him in any newspaper or handbill:
(iv) an assurance that, if the maharaj were to receive a summons from members of other castes who do not believe in him, then the Vaishnavas must settle the problem out of court, however high the cost.

All the clauses of this agreement required that the caste ensure the maharaj's protection. It was signed reportedly by almost all the big shethiyas of the Bhatia, bania and other castes including Varjivandas Madhavdas, Mangaldas Nathoobhai, Goculdas Leeladhar, Goculdas Tejpal, Lakhmidas Khimji, many of whom were reformers.[37] The maharaj managed to get their signatures by closing the temples. This action placed immense pressure on the devotees because many could not eat without *darshan* (viewing the deity). Everyone cursed the reformers as they were held to have instigated the editor to summon the maharaj. Women apparently took to the streets beating their chests and 'mourning' the reformers' deaths (*chhajiya leva madi*).[38]

In spite of the strong links between the maharaj and the caste organizations, this agreement between them did not work and articles *(ii)* and *(iii)* regarding excommunication, aimed at Lakhmidas Khimji and Karsandas Mulji, could not be executed. Mahipatram describes vividly how strongly this agreement was condemned in *Satya Prakasha* and *Rast Goftar* and in the other newspapers. The articles and handbills published in *Rast Goftar* were highly condemnatory of the maharajas and the caste leaders, the latter were termed 'slaves' of the maharaj and their agreement their 'slavery bond'. The reformers published handbills condemning the agreement and soliciting essays on the topic of the authority of the gurus. As a result of such protest the agreement between the maharajas and the caste leaders did not come into effect. Mahipatram reports that the signatories were afraid that if they ostracized Karsandas Mulji they would have to face and lose a court battle. Therefore they did not do so. Karsandas is also said to have got secret support from within the Kapol caste.[39] Thus, the maharaj failed in his attempt to employ caste authority in his fight with the reformers. Since the bond signed to prevent the maharaj from being summoned to court failed, Jivanlalji Maharaj had to leave Bombay to avoid the court summons.[40]

Karsandas' attacks on the maharajas continued. Four years or so later Jadunath Maharaj came from Surat to help restore the fortunes of the maharajas in Bombay. Since the caste channels had not worked to contain the reformers, he decided to use the weapons of his enemies along with the traditional means. He published his own newspaper, distributed handbills and held public meetings. He also established the

Vaishnava Dharma Prasaraka Sabha, as mentioned earlier, and held regular discussions and reading of essays and debates on religious issues. At the first opportunity he got, he attacked the reformers legally exercising his rights as a 'citizen'. The threat that had earlier worked against him, of being dragged to a law court, was rendered ineffective by the maharaj as he himself employed the court against the reformers.

During the court case witnesses from both sides, reformers and supporters of the maharaj continued to recognize the association between *Pushtimarga* the religious tradition and the caste. Gopaldas Madhavdas, the head of the Kapol caste, testified that, 'the Maharajas are not the preceptors or spiritual guides of all the Hindus, but only of the Bhattias [*sic*] and Banians [*sic*] and Brahmins.' He referred to the events of reform as caste events. When referring to the arrangements made to prevent evidence from being presented in court he made a significant slip. He said, 'I have heard . . . that an engagement has been entered into by Banians, Bhattias [*sic*] and all the *sects* to do their utmost to prevent the Maharajas from being called as witnesses.' In an opposite instance, Varjivandas Madhavdas referred to the discussion amongst the Bhatias as amongst the members of the Vallabhacharya caste.[41]

The use of the terms 'caste' and 'sect' as interchangeable by the devotees is significant. It would seem that the caste was so involved in the organization of the religious tradition that the differences in the categories of sect and caste were hardly important. The caste organization had religious or sectarian functions and the sect or religious group functioned through the caste authority.

Regarding this particular reformist dispute, however, the caste was not entirely amenable to the maharaj's control. The maharaj therefore had to seek a higher authority to enforce his opinions. Conventionally the political authority settled disputes between castes and religious heads, as discussed earlier (see also Chapter 1). The maharaj also sought the local political authority, a colonial one, to arbitrate in this dispute. The only way in which the British would enforce the maharaj's ruling was if he could prove the justice of his side. The maharaj sought counsel before initiating proceedings against the reformers.[42] Libel—the accusation of publishing a false statement injurious to reputation was the most justiciable of the reformer's offences. Thus, the maharaj filed a libel suit against Karsandas Mulji.

The maharaj's reputation was indeed in danger, for while the reformers did accept the maharaj's relationship to caste authorities and their attempts were often within the nexus of caste and religion, they were also using 'public' means to criticize him. They invoked social pressure from the larger society by exposing the evils of the maharaj in newspapers, public meetings and so on. The caste authorities were mobilized by both sides, the reformists and the maharajas. The castes were involved in this new public sphere and felt challenged by it. However, in this case they could not effectively stop the reformers nor could they influence the maharajas. The latter therefore were forced to employ other authorities to put an end to the reformist movement.

THE DELINKING OF CASTE AND RELIGION: THE BHATIA CONSPIRACY CASE

The maharaj went to the Supreme Court of the Bombay Presidency in an attempt to control the reformers' attacks on religious tradition. The simultaneous employment of the colonial court and the caste by the maharaj to settle the same dispute dealt a severe blow to the caste controls over the religious community. Maharaj Jadunathji Brajratanji sued Karsandas Mulji and his publisher, Nanabhai Rustomji Ranina, for libel because of an article that was published in the *Satya Prakasha* of October 1860. Once the libel case was filed by the maharaj, Karsandas Mulji and Rustomji Ranina put in their pleas of defence. The maharaj prepared to fight the case. Several important men close to the maharaj, Prabhudas and Dayal Bhagwandas among others, met the maharaj at his temple and decided that the castes should collectively undertake to punish Mulji and pressurize him not to fight the libel prosecution.[43]

The Kapols were unable to organize a meeting. Gopaldas Madhavdas, one of their caste leaders, said in court, that he was asked tô hold the meeting by Prabhudas and Jaykishandas who were banias and managed the maharaj's case. However, he clearly refused to call a meeting to prosecute Karsandas, since a case had been entered in court.[44] The Bhatias went through with their meeting. Dayal Bhagwandas went to Gopaldas Tejpal, one of the Bhatia caste leaders, to ask for permission to call a meeting of the caste and even though it was tacitly refused, Dayal and his colleagues went ahead and called such a meeting with many sheths present and presiding. It was called in the way caste meetings were usually called by using the *thanai* (a messenger) to announce it. The Bhatia caste meeting was held on 6 September 1861. At the meeting the caste leaders sat on higher ground and other members on a lower level. About 200 to 300 Bhatias were present. Proceedings commenced at half-past six. According to one account an agreement was proposed at the meeting. Its main purport was that those who accepted the view that their religion was the true religion and that the present maharajas did not commit adultery, should sign the agreement in the book. Those who did not agree should not sign. This agreement was intended to begin proceedings against the printers and publishers by the caste. Khattao Luddha, a Bhatia, testified at the conspiracy case hearing that during the caste meeting it was agreed that,

> the printers and publishers, and their abettors and aiders will be called to account according to law. They did not say what law, but I understood it to mean the law of the caste.[45]

Evidently the libel was still being treated as a dispute within the caste to be solved by excercising caste authority.

Another agreement that the caste leaders wanted their followers to reach was that the caste would punish any member for giving evidence against the maharaj in the law courts. The caste also assented to and passed a resolution to send a letter to the caste organizations of Kutch, Abhrasa and Halar to this effect. These towns are the original 'home towns' of the various Bhatia castes of Bombay. A special memorandum was addressed to the leading Bhatia caste men of Mandvi. It warned that a Bhatia agent from the reformers was being sent to the

Vahuji of Chhotaji Maharaj at Mandvi to obtain some compromising documents from her and from Shri Ranchhodji Maharaj. The memorandum asked the local Bhatias to request the maharajas not to hand over any document 'by mistake or forgetfulness' to such an agent of the reformers. Here too note how the caste and its leadership were mobilized to speak to the Mandvi Maharaj on behalf of the Bombay maharajas.[46]

In the colonial court this meeting of the Bhatias was described as a conspiracy to prevent evidence being brought to the court and to hamper the functioning of Justice. The Bhatia leaders were tried and convicted for conspiracy in the Criminal Sessions of the Supreme Court by Justice Arnould in December 1861. Justice Arnould described the meeting as a conspiracy to obstruct the course of public justice, by preventing witnesses from coming forward to give their evidence in a case pending in court.

What did the caste meeting mean to the castes themselves? In organizing this meeting the maintenance of religion was treated primarily as a concern of the Bhatia caste. Even the attorney for the defence characterized the Vallabhacharya religion as the '*Bhattia religion*'. The defence for the Bhatias had argued that the caste meetings were in public and not in secret and therefore the members of the caste couldn't be charged with conspiracy. The judge, however, argued that any 'combination' whether secret or public to hamper justice could be called conspiracy.

According to the 'conspirators' the Bhatia caste meeting was an attempt by the maharaj to use the authority of the caste in the tradition of cooperation between caste and religious authorities. As the attorney for the Bhatia 'conspirators' argued, 'this matter was wholly a caste matter . . . the East India Company had always made it a point not to interfere with the natives in their religion and matters connected with it; and the same freedom was held out by our present good and wise government [i.e. after the accession of the crown].[47] The first resolution or agreement to be reached at the Bhatia caste meeting seems to have been an attempt to achieve consensus within the caste that Mulji was wrong in the charges he made in his article, and therefore should be punished by the caste. All those who agreed with the maharaj's interpretation of the religious text were to declare themselves.[48] In a less desperate situation, the caste could have organized a more thorough and extensive prosecution of Mulji. For example, it could have arranged a meeting of Shastris (brahmins educated in classical Sanskrit literature), since maharajas were not necessarily so qualified to determine the correct interpretation of the commentary criticized by Mulji. Lakhmidas Khimji even made this suggestion.[49] Similar meetings of Shastris were organized to resolve different interpretations of recognized texts. For example, the Nagar bania caste of Surat organized such a meeting on the correct Shastra regarding foreign travel.[50]

Jadunathji was, however, more impatient. He chose not to follow this method of dispute settlement. He chose to employ the law courts and on finding that he would have to prove himself innocent of the charge of 'immorality' he tried to mobilize his 'resources' as the maharaj of a religious tradition to see his cause successfully defended. This led to the direct confrontation of the different logics operating in the two systems of authority and power: of the state system on the one hand and that of caste and polity on the other. The state system worked within the logic of recognizing the equality of individuals, the citizen, as opposed to the caste system which differentially ranked the maharaj and caste men.

In the court's view the meeting had obstructed the crown and law by preventing evidence from being brought forward to prove guilt. As repeatedly stated by the judge in the prosecution of the Bhatia conspiracy case, the Bhatia meeting was 'an unlawful *combination* to defeat the administration of justice in this Court'. As such, the caste meeting was an offence against the crown's right and authority to try cases and deliver Justice. The law and the crown demanded absolute sovereignty over Truth and relevant information.

This particular Bhatia meeting was caught in the contradiction of caste and state. The Kapols saw this contradiction and submitted to the state. Gopaldas Madhavdas of the Kapol caste saw this meeting as a parallel adjudication attempt. As mentioned earlier, he testified in court that he had refused to hold the Kapol caste meeting because he felt that 'if what Karsandas had published is false, the Court will punish him. I refused to interfere, as the Maharaj had brought a legal action against him'.[51] In his statement caste decision-making and trial to punish the guilty are directly replaced by the colonial law courts.

The caste could have had the power to protect the maharaj through an independent prosecution, but in these circumstances, when it was ineffective in organizing a settlement between the maharaj and his devotee, its only option was to organize a defence in the court of law. The caste had no locus standii in a criminal prosecution. It was declared to be an unlawful 'combination'. The term 'combination' was particularly significant. It was used in the prosecution of labour meetings. The court held 'labour combinations' to be seditious: threatening the authority of the crown. In employing similar language to describe the caste meeting, the court took the view that the caste was usurping the crown's right to protect citizen's rights.

The verdict in the conspiracy case was guilty. At the end of the trial the judge passed severe strictures against the Bhatia caste leaders. He read out the law for conspiracy from Lord Campbell's act, which empowered the judges to sentence the conspirators to hard labour with imprisonment for the whole term of the sentence. He said he would not be so harsh and sentenced the two leading men with fines of Rs.1000 each and others with fines of Rs.500 each. The proceeding of the case as a criminal offence and the harshness of the judge's statement at the time of sentencing demolished any belief of the caste leaders that the caste could exercise its authority simultaneously with the authority of the court. With this verdict and strictures passed at the time of sentencing, the power of the caste to organize religion was made illegitimate. Thus, the court, given its ideas about sovereignty which enjoined upon it the duty and the right to be the sole authority protecting every citizen's reputation against slander and defamation, was obliged to dismiss any other attempt to provide such protection.

Was this idea of sovereignty inevitable within an imperial state? Could the state have itself forced the jnati to take notice of the dispute and settle it with due process? Certainly, the court could have directed the caste to look into the dispute between the reformer and the maharaj (see Chapter 2).

The court could have held that the matter under dispute was a caste matter and therefore should be dealt with by the castes. It could have entertained the question whether the caste meeting held to discuss the question was conducted in a proper or just manner. But since 1857 the notion of sovereignty was becoming more encompassing, and it disallowed earlier notions of recognizing sovereignty in bodies like castes other than the state.

PUBLIC INTEREST AND THE MAHARAJ LIBEL CASE

If state sovereignty was one ground for displacing caste authority by the state, the other was the ground of public interest. The libel case filed by the maharaj was tried after the Bhatia Conspiracy Case on the original side of the Supreme Court of Bombay in 1862. The importance of the ground of public interest was visible because the two judges trying the case gave opposing verdicts on its basis. This split between the judges allowed us a glimpse into the alternative domains of discussion current at the time.

The difference of opinion between the two judges arose over the defence plea of not guilty on the general issue of libel. Mulji pleaded that the article was not libellous because it was published under circumstances which formed 'a justifying occasion'. Justice Sausse, described as a stern man who was a stickler for the law, ruled that the defendants were indeed guilty of libel as according to him the selection of a public newspaper as the medium for matter defamatory of private character was one of the strongest proofs of malice and withdrew the protection of the clause of justifying occasion. He said,

> There was clearly no legal duty either public or private cast upon the defendants to do so [publish matter on religion]. Nor was there any moral duty, public or private, cast upon them to make that communication [regarding the alleged immorality of the maharajas] to the public beyond what might, press upon any other individual who had heard a bad character of the plaintiff . . . and believed that report to be true. It would be a novel and a dangerous doctrine to lay down that every editor of a

> newspaper, . . . should be held justified . . . in making specific charges of a most defamatory character against the private life of individuals, . . . and [which] from their character it would be conducive to public morality to publish them.[52]

He even went so far as to describe what kind of occasion might have qualified as a justifying one given Karsandas' 'private interest' as a member of the samprayada. He said had Mulji convened a meeting of the sect and so revealed the defamatory matter to members directly concerned by it and interested in it, he might have had some defence as to justifying occasion. Justice Sausse's judgement on this point was so unpopular that it was completely silenced in the reporting of the case. The press criticized it with a great deal of restraint as evidence of Sausse's excessive 'legalism'.[53] His view was in marked contrast to the view of Justice Arnould, the assisting judge. Arnould entirely vindicated Mulji of libel. He said, that Mulji, in addressing himself to the public through the newspaper, 'had appealed to the right and under the circumstances, to the only available tribunal'. He said,

> A public journalist is a public teacher; the true function of the press, that by virtue of which it has rightly grown to be one of the great powers of the modern world is the function of teaching, elevating and enlightening those who fall within the range of its influence.
>
> To expose and denounce evil and barbarous practices, to attack usages and customs inconsistent with moral purity and social progress, is one of its highest most imperative duties . . . As editor, defendant . . . was acting within the clear limits of his duty—in denouncing to a public principally composed of Bhattias and Banians, the moral delinquencies of the Maharajas.[54]

Justice Arnould was educated at Charterhouse and then at Oxford. He joined the Bar only on marriage, which meant the need to earn a better living. He was known for the scholarly interest with which he wrote his judgements. While at the Middle Temple he wrote extensively on social topics.[55] This judgement was imbued with the spirit of reform, for which it was widely praised. His opinion was carried on the front pages of all the newspapers. It has been repeated in books on reform in nineteenth-century India, and even in the law reports. His judgement has become the dominant mode of approaching the libel case, however, it was at the time, only the dissenting opinion of an assistant judge. It was on the grounds of the Chief Justice's opinion that the sentence in the Maharaj Libel Case was passed. It was probably this aspect of the judgements that enabled the maharaj to celebrate the case as a victory.[56]

The issue obviously revolved around the notion of what is Public Duty. Given Justice Arnould's background, he considered individual morality a fit subject for 'public' discussion and in fact considered such discussion a matter of public duty. The link between the caste and the religion was denied and broken when Arnould said that 'the public' was the only tribunal available to settle the dispute between a member of the religious group and the leaders of the same group. On the other hand, Justice Sausse considered the religious collective as the proper forum to discuss and settle differences, moral or otherwise, between the devotee and the religious preceptor. According to him the public had no 'interest' in the matter. Questions of morality of the religious leaders should rightly be a matter of concern only to the collective to which such leaders felt responsible. I would characterize this collective as a 'polity'. In this case the 'polity' was the religious group of Pushtimargis dominated by several jnatis to whom the maharajas felt responsible.

The question of religious morality being subject to public scrutiny was obviously something uncomfortable to Sausse. Public scrutiny of individual moral behaviour was being promoted and pursued in the mid-nineteenth century but was an unresolved issue, leading to such contradictory judgements. Later historians have, indeed, held this case to be the first vindication of the importance of journalists and the recognition of their role in society.[57] Justice Arnould and the elite reformers of Bombay, however, were attempting to exercise the domain of the public over the question of religious morality. The case sits at that juncture of transformation where caste—the non-state domain where this issue could have been discussed—is not open to the ideas of change and therefore the reformers choose the newspapers. The employment of newspapers as a locale to criticize caste issues was accepted as a matter of the ideology of Improvement. For the reformers the newspaper was as much a tool in questioning caste as a handbill distributed outside the temple or read out in caste meetings.

Justice Sausse made the distinction between the newspaper as public domain and other kinds of communication as the private domain. This partitioning of domains was necessary to enable the courts to exercise their jurisdiction. It was on this basis of the notion of publicity that the difference between guilty and not guilty on one count went. Justice Arnould recognized the distinction but suggested that the topic under consideration was one fit for public debate. His statement delegitimized the notion of employing caste in controlling religion or even creating an arena or institutional support outside the state-sphere of the judiciary for settling religion related disputes.

CONCLUSION

The decision in the Bhatia Conspiracy Case was an effective diminution of the power of the concerned castes over the Vallabhacharya Vaishnava polity. The case demonstrated that the caste authority could not be exercised in competition with the court. The split judgement on the issue of libel in the Maharaj Libel Case also demonstrated the uncertain recognition of the arena of the 'general public' as the locale to discuss religious beliefs. On the one hand the crucial notion of state sovereignty led to the delegitimation of caste; on the other hand, the notion of publicity meant that the idea that the newspaper and thus the 'general public' was an acceptable forum for a discussion of religious issues and that there was no other tribunal but such a generalized 'public opinion' for the resolution of such issues was a victorious one. The combination of arguments based on sovereignty and publicity enlarged the role of the state over that of caste. What could have been seen as a caste question under Regulation II, section 21 of the Bombay Regulations continued to diminish. The shrinking of the role of caste and religious authorities created a larger role for courts and a generalized public sphere.

The maharaj's authority for the purpose of this trial was delinked from caste authority. It was delinked practically because the court would not allow simultaneous exercise of two sets of power. It was also delinked ideologically by the fact that the caste was not recognized as a religious body and the religion was classified not as a polity made up of castes and the religious gurus but as a sect of Hinduism (see Chapter 5). The fact that the Pushtimarga Vaishnavas worked through castes and continued to recognize the nexus even after the case, though perhaps in a reduced way, does not invalidate this conclusion. The devotees seemed to work through caste and political authorities simultaneously and alternatively.

NOTES

1. Imtiaz Ahmad, ed., *Caste and Social Stratification among the Muslims* (Delhi: Manohar, 1973).
2. Arjun Appadurai, *Worship and Conflict under Colonial Rule: A South Indian Case*, Cambridge South Asian Studies, vol 27 (New York: Cambridge University Press, 1981); Maya Burger, 'The Hindu Model of Social Organization and the Bhakti Movement: The example of Vallabha's Sampradaya.' In *Devotional Literature in South Asia: Current Research 1985-1988*, edited by R. S. McGregor (Cambridge: Cambridge University Press, 1992); see ibid for a discussion on the case of the painters of *pichhwai* (cloth paintings used in ritual).
3. Bernard Cohn has studied the governance of caste by social and political bodies, but not by religious heads: 'Anthropological Notes on Law and Disputes in North India.' In *An Anthropologist Among the Historians and Other Essays* (Delhi: Oxford University Press, 1987); Some of the major socio-historical studies of the Vallabhcharya tradition are: N. A. Thoothi, *The Vaishnavas of Gujarat* (Calcutta: Longman, 1935); Rajendra Jindel, *Culture of a Sacred Town: A Sociological Study of Nathdwara* (Mumbai: Popular Prakashan, 1976); M. C. Parekh, *Shri Vallabhacharya: Life, Teachings and Movement (A Religion of Grace)* (Rajkot: Shri Bhagvat Dharma Mission, 1969); Edwin Allen Richardson, 'Mughal and Rajput Patronage of the Bhakti Sect of the Maha-

rajas, the Vallabha Sampradaya, 1640-1760 AD', PhD diss, University of Arizona, 1979.

4. On definition of 'public' see Hannah Arendt, *The Human Condition,* 8th ed (Chicago: University of Chicago Press, 1973).
5. Thoothi, *Vaishnavas of Gujarat*: 92-93. Also description in the defence statement, *Maharaj Libel Case including Bhatia Conspiracy Case, no 12047 of 1861, Supreme Court, Pleas Side* (from now on *MLC*) (Bombay: D. Lakshmidas and Co, 1911): 177-178; I am grateful to Marika Vicziany for generously giving me her copy of this book; evidence of Gopaldas Madhavdas, 25 Jan 1862, *MLC*: 125; Ratanji Framji Vachha, *Mumbaino bahar* (Bombay Union Press, 1874): 133.
6. *MLC*: 1-3.
7. See Introduction, this volume, where I discuss her extremely competent description of Bombay society in the mid-nineteenth century, Christine Dobbin, *Urban Leadership in Western India: Politics and Communities in Bombay City 1840-1885* (Delhi: Oxford University Press, 1972).
8. Leeladhar Hari Thakkar, *Pushti margano itihasa tatha vaidik dharmanan sidhanto sathe pushti marganan siddhantoni tulana* (Bombay: Sevaklal Karsandas, 1890): 2; *Vaishnav Punch* 3, 1 (8 Nov 1860): 10, presented as evidence by Karsandas Mulji, *MLC:* 233-234.
9. Mahipatram Rupram, *Uttam kapol karsandas mulajinun charitra* (Ahmedabad: Ranchhodlal Gangaram, 1877): 27.
10. *'Hinduoman sudharo karvani ghani jarur.' Rast Goftar tatha Satya Prakasha (RGSP)* (5 April 1863), *emphasis added.*
11. Mulji, *Nibandhamala samsar sambandhi vishayo,* vol 1 (Bombay: Union Press, 1870): 29.
12. *Rast Goftar* (8 April 1858): especially pp 79-80, *emphasis added;* also (2 Jan 1859): 30-31.
13. See the essay on Holi in *Astri ganean mala: parasi astrione vaste vancava layaka babadono samgraha* (Bombay: Daftar Askara Press, 1859); Karsandas Mulji, *'Holini utpatti,'* 13 March 1959, in *Nibandhamala.* These explanations are strikingly different from the current explanation. They also seem to fit the practices better than the current Prahlad-Hiranyakashyapu-Holika story.
14. I thank A Yajnik for this reference.
15. *RGSP* (18 Nov 1866): 728 and (9 Dec 1866) criticized the Khojas for not being reformist enough; articles dealing with Khoja reform are present in *RGSP* from early on. The volumes of 1861 and 1862 even had a separate index section for Khojas.
16. Mahipatram Rupram, *Durgaram manchharam charitra,* vol 1

(Ahmedabad: Ahmedabad United Printing and General Co, 1879), notes written on 27 Jan 1843, p. 13; see discussion of 26 Feb 1843 with Pratapray and Ochhavram: 41-42, and note of 8 Sept 1844: 107.

17. *RGSP* (21 May 1865): 325, anon. article says *'nat jatnan harkatne lidhe jaman na kare.'*
18. This is true of the various castes, *Shri mumbayina halai bhatia mahajanano 101 varshano itihas* (Bombay: Shatabdi Mahotsav Samiti, 1961); also recorded for the Kutchi Visa Oswal caste in the biography of their leading shethiya, Anupchand Shah, *Shri Velji Lakhamasi* (Bombay: Kutchi Visa Oswal Sthanakvasi Jain Mahajan, 1961): 61; for the Kapols in 1879 described in Tribhovandas Mangaldas Nathubhoy, *Lectures on Hindu Castes, Ceremonies, Customs and Inheritance* (Bombay: Education Society Steam Press, 1896); also a brief description in Dobbin, *Urban Leadership in Western India.*
19. *Times of India,* 1 Feb 1862, based on a brochure published by Jivanji Maharaj, approximately ten years earlier, said that the collection from such a tax amounted to Rs 50,000 a year for Jivanji alone; Thoothi, *Vaishnavas of Gujarat*: 195, n 2; *Shri mumbayinahalai bhatia mahajanan hisab sam 1817-1918 sudhi varan beno* (Bombay: Lakhmidas Khimjina Hukamathi Metaji Chaturbhuj Valaji, 1863), 52pp, annual reports examined up to 1883.
20. In all the reports published from 1863 till 1873, see, eg, vol 1863: 10-11; in most reports from 1864 to 1867, eg, vol 1864: 22-23; vol 1865: 41.
21. Vachha, *Mumbaino bahar:* 133; *RGSP* (22 Dec 1861): 608.
22. *RGSP* (21 April 1861): 186.
23. *MLC*: 128; *RGSP* (13 Oct 1861): 488; Karsandas Mulji, *'Maharajano julam.'* In *Rast Goftar* (23 May 1858), included in his collection *Nibandhamala:* 83-86; Mahipatram says that Karsandas had published numerous articles about the maharaj in 1855 and onwards but these have not been included in any of his later collections or at the time of the case. This is the first available critique of the maharaj that Karsandas published; *RGSP* (26 May 1861): 242 in *'Nat bahar mukavyo'.*
24. *RGSP* (24 March 1867): 184; (25 Aug 1867): 531-532
25. *RGSP* (12 Aug 1866): 502.
26. Letter, 17 April 1876 [Chaitra vad 9] published in *Shri mumbaiyina halai bhatia mahajanno V.S. 1932* [1876] *no varshika hisaba tatha mahajanana sambandhaman thaela kamakajano report,* vol 16, year 18 (Bombay: Halai Bhatia Mahajan, 1877): 109-111.
27. Manjula Kakatiya, *'Brhad mumbaini kapol vaishya jnati : ek sa-*

majashastriya anveshan.' PhD diss. SNDT, Women's University, 1978.

28. Interview with Vrajaratanlalji Maharaj, Mota Mandir, main temple, Surat 1990.
29. Evidence given by Mathuradas Lavji, 14 Feb 1862, *MLC:* 280; and description by Mahipatram Rupram, *'Karsandas mulji charitra'*: 15; Leeladhar Hari Thakkar, *'Pushtimarga athava maharajono panth'*, 1890: 3. This reform is not mentioned in any of the descriptions of reform in Gujarati society, and there is no information of the exact content of the reform.
30. Translations of extracts from editorials, *Bombay Samachar*, 21 Dec 1855; *Jam-e-Jamshed*, 25 Dec 1855; *Samachar Darpan,* 29 Nov 1855, presented as evidence in the MLC, *MLC:* 239-242 for evidence presented during the case; I shall discuss these accusations in Chapter 5 to demonstrate the gendered character of this controversy.
31. Mahipatram, *Karasanadas mulji charitra:* 14; 16.
32. For example, in *RGSP* (22 Dec 1861): 608.
33. *Rast Goftar* (2 Nov 1856): 355-356.
34. These attendants called *jhapatiyas* (whips) were assigned the task of keeping the crowd of worshipping devotees moving so that others could also get a chance to obtain *darshan* (view). They did this by waving a whip with which they sometimes injured devotees. The whip was then replaced by a large cloth. Mulji, *'Mandiraman thati amariyada'* (21 Nov 1858), reprinted in *Nibandhamala:* 123-124; *RGSP* (21 July 1861): 342.
35. *RGSP* (16 Sept 1866); (22 Dec 1867): 804; (16 Nov 1856): 369-370.
36. *Rast Goftar* (16 Jan 1859): 32-33; Mahipatram, *Karsandas mulji charitra*: 20. The 'slavery bond' article was republished in Mulji, *Nibandhamala:* 133-142.
37. Mulji, *Nibandhamala:* 133-135.
38. Mahipatram, *Karsandas mulji charitra:* 19-20.
39. *Rast Goftar* (23 Jan 1859): 45-48; (30 Jan 1859): 53-54; continued to comment till as late as 27 Nov. 1859; Mahipatram, *Karsandas mulji charitra:* 24; while Mahipatram mentions no names, this person may have been Mangaldas Nathoobhai; see his son's short biography, Tribhovandas Nathoobhai, *Caste Rules*.
40. The reformer eventually won the case of libel and was awarded damages plus costs: Mahipatram, *Karsandas mulji charitra:* 24-25. Perhaps the precedent helped the maharaj eventually to start a similar prosecution.
41. *MLC: emphasis added*; 126; 127; 140.
42. Evidence of Laxmidas Khimji, *MLC:* 297.

43. Reconstructed from the evidence presented by several witnesses at the trial of the Bhatia Conspiracy Case, 12 and 13 Dec 1861, Supreme Court—crown side, fourth criminal sessions of 1861, printed in *MLC:* 69-91.
44. *MLC*: 127. Also see his clarification to the judge: 131; Gopaldas Madhavdas, *MLC*: 127.
45. Evidence presented by Khattao Luddha on Friday, 13 Dec 1861, *MLC*: 79-81.
46. Handbill of the Bhatias, translated by the court, reproduced in *MLC:* 76-77. The communication didn't take place directly from the *haveli* (palace, referring to both temple and residence) of one maharaj to another. Local caste hierarchies were explicitly involved in making the arrangements for the sampradaya.
47. *MLC*, p. 94. *emphasis added;* 95; the proceedings of the Bhatia Conspiracy Case are printed on 48, 63-120. Evidence of Harjivan Jivraj, 12 Dec 1861, *MLC:* 73; of Khatau Ladha on 13 Dec 1861, *MLC:* 79-81.
48. Lakhmidas Khimji said this to Lakhmidas Damji when he first heard of the Bhatia meeting; deposition in court on 12 Dec. 1862, *MLC*: 69.
49. *RGSP*, 8 May 1870: 303.
50. Bhatia Conspiracy Case, *MLC*: 95; Gopaldas Madhavdas' testimony: 127.
51. *MLC:* 402; Judgement of Sir Matthew Sausse: 406.
52. *MLC:* 409; however his judgement was used to prove the fairness of the British system of justice, which allowed the judge to give a verdict in favour of such an unpopular man as the maharaj. *Times of India*, 2 May 1866.
53. *MLC*: 437; 423.
54. George Smith, *Dictionary of National Biography: Earliest Times to 1900*, edited by Leslie Stephen and Sidney Lee, vol 22, Supplement (London: Oxford University Press, 1921-1922): 78.
55. *MLC*: 419; defendants were awarded costs for four issues: the pleas 3rd, 5th, 7th and 8th where the judge found in their favour. The maharaj did not receive costs for the plea of not guilty found in the his favour since, as the judge explained, the maharaj and his party were disbelieved for their testimony given under oath.
56. Makrand Mehta, 'Maharaj Libel Case: A Study in Social Change in Western India in the Nineteenth Century.' *Indo-Asian Culture* 4, 19 (1970): 26-39.

CHAPTER 5

Representation of Pushti Sampradaya: Religious Community and Hindu Sect

THE REFORM OF the Vallabhacharya Vaishnavas and the consequent libel case entailed an essential transformation of the religious polity of the *Pushti sampradaya*. The law court ignored the controls exercised by caste authorities in settling disputes within the religious polity and took on a more authoritarian role to handle indigenous disputes. As a secular court, it assumed judicial ignorance of religion and as a consequence, it did not need to admit any religious arguments nor judge between several interpretations of religion. In the Khoja case (see Chapter 3) a dismissal of the discussion of religious meanings led to a determination of membership through demonstrating an adherence to symbols and property. During judicial proceedings of the Maharaj Libel Case (Chapter 4), the Pushtimarga sampradaya was distinctly de-linked from caste in court representation and in self-representation.

Before the Maharaj Libel Case took place, considerable reform of the maharaj's religious practices had taken place, pursued through social pressure that was exercised through caste authorities. Legal intervention led to the delegitimization of the religious interventions of the castes. One would assume that such a replacement of caste by state would lead to a decline in the importance of religion; however, as we shall see, instead its importance has grown in the hands of the state. Thus, the legal handling of the disputes emphasized the religious character of the debate, and identified the Vallabhacharya tradition with 'Hindu doctrine' in general.

The reformers and the maharaj were involved in a controversy over the interpretation of the religious texts of the Vallabhacharya Vaishnava tradition, as well as the behaviour of the maharajas vis-à-vis their devotees, especially the women devotees. As discussed earlier (Chapter 4) the particular article that was cited as libellous by the maharaj was written by Karsandas Mulji and published by Nanabhai Rustomji Ranina in the *Satya Prakasha* of 21 October 1860. This article criticized the religious teachings of the maharajas and called for reform. In addition to being held to be libellous, the article was seen by the maharaj as a spiritual offence—a heresy. Mulji's biographer and contemporary, Mahipatram, has described how the maharaj was more disturbed by Mulji's criticism of the religious tradition than by that of others like Narmadshankar and Bhau Daji because the former was a member of the Vallabhacharya Vaishnava tradition.[1] This controversy over religious interpretation was tried in the court, which took a considerable time to accept that the said article was a libel and not a heresy. Once the article was admitted to be libellous, it was examined in court. During the trial the secular humanist court ruled on religious questions and established and upheld a brahminic, Sanskritic definition of Hinduism.

HOW THE DISPUTE WAS ADMITTED FOR TRIAL

If the libel charge was to be considered applicable, the court would have to interpret Mulji's statements in the article *not* as a spiritual discussion within a self-governing religious polity but as an attack on the personal reputation of the maharaj. This interpretation would create a separation between the person and his position of religious authority. Another effect of trying the case as one of libel instead of heresy was that Mulji's accusations had to be examined for their truth rather than for their validity as religious opinion. Both strategies of interpreting the libellous article dissociated its arguments from *sampradayik* discussion. Thus in order to permit the reformers to be tried in court, the question of a self-governing religious polity had to be sidestepped and the question of libel and citizen's rights had to become all important.

This process of giving primary importance to citizen's rights and seeking redress from secular processes rather than religious ones was important in the creation of the upper class citizenry: a non-differentiated public. This process of class formation has been noted in many spheres; in law it is especially interesting, as the subjects are giving up significant religious and caste identities and also the authority that went with these. In this instance the maharaj had to give up the right to persecute Mulji for heresy and had to claim the right to redress for libel from the state. The abdication of religious authority was neither easy nor obvious; it had to be argued not only to convince the judge but also the religious devotees. The state could only take over the maharaj's role of punishing guilty members of the sect in the context of the explicit statement granting respect to all religions. Thus the making of the public had peculiar religious connotations.

FROM RELIGIOUS PRECEPTOR TO CITIZEN

Jadunath Maharaj sued Karsandas Mulji and Nanabhai Rustomji Ranina for libel because in the latter half of the article, Mulji called directly upon Jadunath Maharaj by name several times. The most direct sentence was, 'Jadunathjee Maharaj, should you wish to propagate or to spread religion abroad, then you must personally adopt a virtuous course of conduct and admonish your other maharajas'.[2] On the strength of this reference, and that of associated statements in the article, Jadunath Maharaj sued for libel.

Before the trial could begin, the defendants, Mulji and Ranina, filed a special demurrer petition, which could be filed by the defence, suggesting that the court should not or could not hear the case. In a special demurrer, the defence specified the grounds on which the case should not be tried. In their demurrer the reformers pleaded that the alleged libellous piece was discussing general matters that concerned religious opinions and therefore the accusations were 'not a libel concerning his [Jadunath Maharaj's] private character, but against his religious office as maharaj'.[3] In this petition the reformers averred that the status of the maharaj was not the same as that of any ordinary citizen, that he did have spiritual authority, and that this status of spiritual authority did not change by coming into the law court.

Later in the trial, Anstey, the defence attorney, argued for a non-suit. He said that the plaintiffs had merely shown how the maharaj's character was a religious one; that the maharaj was charged as a religious personality by the libellous article. He pointed to the fact that the reformers, in fact, held Jadunath in very high esteem and did not mean to malign him personally. He referred to the survey of Jadunath's career carried in the *Satya Prakasha* of 18 November 1861, which had applauded the maharaj's activities.[4] According to the defence, Jadunath Maharaj was mentioned in the libellous article because the reformers had expected great reforms from him. He had helped them with the cause of women's education and discussed religious doctrine publicly. Thus, he was mentioned only because he was the most accessible representative of the class of maharajas. The defence therefore argued that since the statements were intended for the maharajas generally, Jadunath Maharaj had no cause to believe he had been personally accused.

The maharaj argued contrarily that he was accused not in his capacity as religious preceptor but in his personal capacity and the case was therefore valid for prosecution. His attorney said,

> This was the libel against the plaintiff, not in his spiritual capacity, but in his private character, and the mere fact of his being a Brahmin, a Maharaj, or a member of the sect of Vallabhcharya [*sic*], did not disentitle him to seek protection at law.[5]

The exigencies of the secular law forced the maharaj to portray himself as a common citizen. It forced him to dissociate himself from his religious authority. That the law required this transformation was clear from the arguments of the demurrer. It was established that if it was held that the maharaj was *not* personally implicated, he could not sue for libel. The interpretation of several sentences in the alleged libel which referred to the maharaj in the vocative became the pivot on which the decision was made as to whether there was a prima facie case for trial or not. The sentences could be construed as personal accusations or as general exhortations to the whole class of maharajas. The court tried to establish from several respectable citizens whether the particular vocative used for the maharaj was intended to refer to the general class of maharajas or the particular maharaj mentioned. Bhau Daji and others were questioned as to this point. They testified that the words referred to the individual as well as to all the maharajas generally. Indeed Bhau Daji said that the article in the original did not accuse Jadunath Maharaj personally but the English translation 'tends that way'.[6] This acceptance that the words could be interpreted generally meant that the article could not be accused of libel.

The Chief Justice, Sir Matthew Sausse, however, ruled that the article was applicable to Jadunath Maharaj personally, adding 'this was a libel against the plaintiff in his individual capacity, segregated from his character of priest'. This opinion was based on the principle enunciated in the case of May *vs.* Brown 3B and C138, according to which 'when a libel is of and concerning the plaintiff in various characters, it is a libel against him individually'. The Chief Justice pointed out that the several characters by which Jadunath was referred were 'Maharaj, Brahmin and member of the Vallabhacharya sect'.[7] The fact that the maharaj was addressed in several capacities meant that none other could be in the same position and therefore he was individually singled out. This does not recognize the fact all the maharajas would have these several capacities too.

Thus, in order for the case to be tried, the court reduced the multiple identities of individuals to several particular roles that only one individual could fulfil. The general reference of the original vernacular article was also ignored. In both instances, in the legality of the Chief Justice and the disregard of the vernacular, the colonial law and its particular requirements transformed the character of the maharaj from being a representative religious authority to a particular person, with rights which the court must recognize, a citizen.

Once the logic of citizen's rights operated, the maharaj had to argue as a citizen and give up his spiritual authority and status. This person whose reputation had been besmirched must then be protected or avenged by law. Until the case, the maharaj had tried to fight Mulji through the exercise of his religious and caste authority. Mulji had successfully evaded these authorities and continued to criticize the religion in the newly emerging upper class public sphere, which the maharaj was thus forced to occupy through the highest authority of the state. In this case he was unable to force the state to recognize his traditional authority as religious preceptor. Thus he had to come to the state on its terms, claiming rights as a 'citizen' of a 'private character', not as a brahmin or a priest. This demonstrates how necessary the state and the traditional authorities were in the governance of religious polities. This nexus of authorities to regulate polities and their disputes was unavoidable. The maharaj's defeat lay in the fact that while using the state authority for settling his complaint he subjected his own religious authority to it. The court clearly did not recognize religious authority and the maharaj's power to organize caste meetings, nor did it recognize his statements on religion as those of an authority. He was seen as a citizen, equal to all others. Once the logic of citizen's rights operated, the maharaj had to give up his spiritual authority and status. We shall see the implications for the interpretation of religious acts and texts later. Within the reformist trajectory and its entanglement with the law, the mechanisms for discussing and debating religion in public, which may have been developing, were delegitimized and the high ground of morality was occupied by the state and the citizen. This was one of the first instances when a religious authority willingly subjected itself to a court of law. Until 1858 the maharajas in Bombay were trying to collect money to send a barrister to England who would obtain a permanent exemption for them from being summoned to a law court.[8]

FROM HERESY TO LIBEL

The defence pleaded for dismissal of the suit on a general ground besides the special grounds mentioned in the demurrer petition. In the general ground of demurrer, the reformers suggested that the case should not be heard for reasons of public policy. In other words, as a spiritual head Jadunath Maharaj should not be allowed to use the secular law courts to enforce his religious opinion. As Anstey phrased it,

> not an instance could be discovered of an attempt like this, wherein a Maharaj or Hindu High Priest, sought, by the machinery of Her Majesty's Courts, . . . to enforce the discipline of his sect. It behoved the Court to decline to lend its jurisdiction to such uses.[9]

In this petition the maharaj was clearly seen as a religious authority. The defendants argued that Mulji's article expressed religious opinions with which the maharaj disagreed and the case was one way of punishing Mulji for challenging the maharaj. The article was, according to the reformers, continuing a debate over interpretation of the particular religious tradition between the reformers and the maharaj. Anstey said, 'On the face of the plaint, it [the libellous article] was clearly a spiritual offence, for which the plaintiff sued, for the Plaint sets forth his spiritual ascendancy.' Anstey said that since the Plaint described the maharaj as a high priest, Mulji's offence was against the maharaj as priest. Mulji's only offence, in this situation, was not according the maharaj the kind of respect he deserved as a high priest. As such the offence for which the maharaj was suing was a spiritual offence.

Anstey quoted several precedents and statements by previous judges to indicate that the courts were not to enforce religious discipline. He suggested that if such a dispute as that between Mulji and the maharaj arose in the Anglican church, it would be tried by the ecclesiastical courts. However since there were no such courts in India for the Hindus, this Plaint could not be tried.

The argument went that the rule of non-interference in religion has been laid down in the Acts of Parliament and applied by Charter to India. Indian courts and common law courts in general did not interfere in religious matters. Anstey said, 'How could His Lordship, prevented by Common Law from enquiring into heresy as respects the Scotch, the Irish, the Protestant, etc, determine the imputation of heterodoxy in this case.' As the demurrer insisted the article was 'a legitimate denunciation of faith imputing heresy; this is a legitimate difference of opinion and not a question of libel.'[10]

The general demurrer on the ground of public policy, that this was a case outside the jurisdiction of the court, was not allowed. Justice Sausse's reasons were purely technical. He said, he would disallow the demurrer because *(i)* no precedent was cited; and *(ii)* because by the court's Rules of Pleading (Rule no. 90), the defendant must plead only on such special grounds as were stated in the special demurrer. This ground of public policy was not included in the special demurrer filed by the defendants earlier and thus the later addition of a demurrer on a general ground was not admitted, and could not be argued.[11]

The question that the maharaj with his spiritual authority was actually charging Mulji and Ranina with heresy was set aside on technical grounds. The court took three significant steps: first, it did not recognize the authority of the caste in the *sampradaya*, second, it categorized the maharaj as a citizen; and third, it dismissed a petition which described this dispute as lying within an organized religious tradition. Thus the court came to establish the religious dispute as a dispute over 'public' reputation which could be avenged by the highest public authority: the state. The whole process of bringing the dispute to court required that religious and caste authorities be sidelined. As can be seen, this process was uneven and multi-faceted. It occurred out of the court jealously guarding its own jurisdiction and out of the legal anomalies of transposing British law to India with the mismatch in languages and connotations, sometimes at the insistence of the religious authorities themselves rather than the champions of the public sphere. The process was neither natural nor simple. If the spiritual authority had been recognized the court would have treated the Vallabha sampradaya as a polity. Not treating it as such was not obvious even given the judges' understanding about Indian religions (see Chapter 1). The court proceeded to examine the article which criticized the religion of the Vallabhacharya Vaishnavas.

FROM RELIGIOUS ACCUSATIONS TO SECULAR FACTS: GROUNDS FOR THE TRIAL

How did the court deal with religious criticism described in Mulji's article? The religious accusations made in the libellous article were discussed, not from a religious point of view, but as statements of facts, which had to be verified, not through religious discussion, but by evidence presented in court.

Once the court agreed to enter the Plaint under libel laws, the defence entered their Plea that Mulji's accusations were true, therefore, he was not guilty of libel. Mulji's article accused the maharajas of preaching as well as practising heterodoxy, heresy and immorality.

He stated that the Vallabhacharya sect came into being in the Kaliyuga, where according to the Shastra, all Kaliyuga sects would preach false religion. Thus, the Vallabhacharya doctrines were heterodox and heretical. He demonstrated the immorality of the teachings of the sampradaya by pointing to one of its mainstays, the *Brahmasambandha* mantra, as interpreted by Goḳulnathji Maharaj (the grandson of Vallabhacharya 1552-1641). This interpretation enjoined adultery by requiring that every devotee offer his wife or daughter for the sexual 'service' of the maharaj. Mulji further alleged that such religious beliefs were considered unacceptable and heterodox by Hindu religion, and that they were immoral and therefore he was not guilty of libel. The maharajas who were acting according to these doctrines were also heterodox, heretical and immoral.

The court was called upon to decide whether this accusation by Mulji was accurate or not. After the first few discussions the court gave up trying to decide the question of heterodoxy:

> Sir Joseph Arnould [the assisting judge]: We don't know what heterodoxy is, and we don't know what heresy is; for we don't know what the Shastras themselves are.

Sir Matthew Sausse [the chief justice] concluded,

> As at present advised, we should read the clause leaving out the words, 'Shastras' and 'Kali yuga' for there is no evidence to show what they are.[12]

Hence the truth of the allegation that the Vallabhacharya Vaishnavas did not follow the Shastra could not be ascertained. The court would confine itself to judge the accuracy of the charge of immorality; examining the immorality of the doctrines as preached by the Vallabhacharya Vaishnava maharajas as well as the practice of immorality by Jadunath Maharaj in particular. Even the maharaj's counsel agreed that the libel did not criticize the doctrines on doctrinal grounds alone but on moral grounds.

Once morality was held to be the grounds on which to judge the accuracy of the reformist accusations, the religion of the maharaj had to prove itself consistent with a universal morality; not with its own religious orthodoxy.

This examination of the doctrines of the Vallabha religion on the charge of immorality came about in the complex circumstances within which the reform debate was being carried out, and much of the reform of social practice was not considered to be a question of religion (see Chapter 4). However, religious change was also being urged and undertaken.[13]

Many of the same people were involved in both social and religious reform efforts. The grounds of reform were shifting. On the one hand, the reformers spoke on the grounds of morality and natural religion. For example, in their defence plea the reformers argued that their sole purpose of criticizing the maharaj was 'to promote the truths of natural religion'.[14] On the other hand, they urged reform on the grounds of true Hindu religion.

No studies of the employment of Dharmashastra tradition by the reformers are available. My reading of reform writing suggests that the reformers employed parts of the Dharmashastra for iconic purposes. Durgaram of Surat clearly stated that the Shastra was to be used in argumentation to convince others. When discussing caste and its necessary prohibitions on touch he said 'the Shastra has been written by men like you and me and therefore we must trust it only after giving it some thought'. He also implied that orthodox texts were only interesting and worth reading as much as they agreed with one's opinion.[15]

Narmadshankar Lalshankar's articles especially the ones on gurus and women have a similar instrumental relationship to the Shastra. One of the more vociferous protectors of the Shastra at the time was Vishnubuva Shastri.[16] Karsandas, commenting on him, said that it was not enough to talk about religious texts, our preacher and others should also preach morality and good qualities. He said that the most attractive aspect of Christianity was the regular moral advice given by the *padris*.[17] Mulji was not defensive about the Smritis or the injunctions of religion.

If this was the case why did the reformers quote or refer to the Shastra at all? Durgaram said that Shastra should be used to convince others. Some of the reformist essays quoting the Shastra were written in response to solicitations. Journals often advertised prizes for essays written on specific subjects. Often the specific condition was that the essay must quote from the Shastra, as was the case in the advertisement soliciting essays on gurus and women, on the authority of gurus, or on widow remarriage.[18]

Another place where the reformers were forced to consult the Shastra was in their debate with the maharaj. The most telling incident was when Narmad met Jadunathji Maharaj in a public debate for a discussion on the subject of widow remarriage, attended by almost a thousand people. It was arranged in 1859 after the widow remarriage bill had been passed and considerable debate had already taken place in Bengal where Ishvarchandra Vidyasagar and others had employed the Shastra to prove that widow-remarriage was permitted by orthodoxy. The maharaj began the debate by asking Narmadshankar whether he believed that the Shastra were God-created (*ishvarkrta*) or not. Narmad replied that he did not believe they were so created, at which the maharaj refused to debate any further by saying that those who did not believe in the Shastra could not interpret them faithfully.[19] This attempt to debate a 'moral' issue within *sampradayik* terms was an attempt to assert the authority of the religious polity of the maharajas. Narmad himself was not disappointed as he felt that he had addressed the need to discuss the issue and question the religious tradition from within and establish the grounds for the debate (see Chapter 1). The issue of widow remarriage did not find a place in the debate. The reformist newspapers were very upset, commenting that the debate led to a loss of face for reformists and a loss of public sympathy for the cause of reform.[20]

In his journal *Svadharma Vardhak ane Sanshay Chhedak* (henceforth *Svadharma Vardhak),* the maharaj challenged the reformers to write upon the *guru-shishya* relationship by quoting the Shastra. He also warned that 'he who would not do so should be unworthy of belief by his own people'.[21] Mulji taking to heart this repeated accusation of not following the Shastra then proceeded to employ Shastra-based arguments and produced the article which was accused of being libellous.[22] The debate over correct behaviour of the maharaj and other issues though deriving inspiration from moral teachings and published in newspapers was being conducted from within the sampradaya—through *shastrartha* and caste meetings and caste-based reform. Mulji's use of the Shastra was directed at the caste-religion nexus to induce it to carry out changes.

In his article Mulji used the Shastra in a simplistic manner, quoting that in the Kaliyuga numerous heretical and immoral religious opinions *(mat)* would arise. He then said that the maharaj's religion which was only four hundred years old had arisen in the Kaliyuga and therefore must be heretical. A major portion of the article described the immorality of the sect in preaching adultery and impurity. Thus, in reformist articles the Shastra was mostly employed to prove a moral point. Even in Mulji's allegedly libellous article while the Shastra was employed in criticizing the maharaj, the sense of morality and natural religion was always coupled with it. In the Plea for their defence too, the reformers described their view of orthodox religion in moral terms. They said that *religious* and *moral laws* prescribed the observance of piety, chastity, sobriety, that it was a wicked and impious thing for a mere man to pretend to be a God or to be capable of begetting a God and for maidens to have carnal intercourse before marriage.[23]

This coupling of orthodoxy with morality later allowed the court to dismiss all notions of orthodoxy and the Shastra and still judge the accuracy of an article which accused the maharaj of contravening religious orthodoxy. The dismissal of notions of orthodoxy, however, clearly removed the debate from being an 'internal' matter of a self-governing religious group to being a 'public' matter. The self-governing religious polity was delegitimized and disempowered by this move.

MORALITY AS A UNIVERSAL STANDARD

The court thus was enabled to employ morality as a substantive standard to examine the religious content of the maharaj's doctrines. If on the examination of facts the religion was found to be immoral and if the conduct of Jadunath Maharaj was found to be immoral then the article would be held to be true and therefore not libellous. The court collected facts from the testimony of witnesses. It had strict rules of admissible evidence and argument. The witnesses were not allowed to present their interpretations or opinions, nor were they allowed to voice their faith. As a witness, the person concerned could present only the truth. In this situation much of the testimony of the witnesses was not evidence. The testimony could not be accepted in court for it codified different meanings and values from those of the judges. This will become clear in the following examples of the questioning of witnesses in the court.

The problem over determining 'facts', given the court's inability to entertain different religious interpretations and meanings is particularly striking in the questioning of Jumnadass Sevaklal. He was a witness for the plaintiff and in cross-examination Anstey asked him if some banias believed the maharaj to be a God. He replied that they considered him to be their guru.

> Sir Matthew Sausse intervenes: 'Tell witness if he does not answer the question, he will be sent to jail.'
>
> Witness: 'What is the precise question?' [interpreter explains]. 'Some consider the maharaj a God in the shape of gooroo.'

> Mr. Anstey: 'Is Gooroo a God?'
>
> Witness: 'Gooroo is gooroo.'
>
> Sir Matthew Sausse: 'Tell him if he does not answer the question, most indubitably will he go to jail.'
>
> Witness: 'I don't know if others believe him as God; I consider him as simply a gooroo. I don't know under what name others worship him.'

The witness could not interpret his action and the belief regarding guru or religious preceptors. The term 'God in the shape of Gooroo' was a meaningless statement as far as the court was concerned. The witness merely had to give evidence as to action and belief. This evidence was evaluated as moral or immoral according to the value system recognized by the court. Believing a mere mortal to be God was clearly immoral in the court's judgement. In another exchange with Jumnadass Sevaklal this became more striking. Anstey asked about Holi, a festival where all participants threw *gulal,* a coloured powder, at each other, and the maharajas showered their devotees with it in the temples. It had been charged that this festival encouraged licentiousness and unacceptable sexual contact between female devotees and the maharaj. In response to questions about gulal and licentiousness, Jumnadass Sevaklal said,

> I don't think that throwing golal [*sic*] makes women pregnant. It is not the fact that young men throw golal and not the old. Throwing the golal has no relation to sexual intercourse. I would consider it a great insult for any other person, but the maharaj, to throw golal upon my wife. Throwing golal from a distance I don't consider as an outrage upon chastity.

At this point the witness was fined fifty rupees for not giving a direct answer. The judge maintained that the witness was fined for 'evasion, prevarication, and delay'. So the witness restated thus, 'if the maharaj, handled the breast or neck of a female, it would be considered adultery—not so his throwing golal on females.'[24]

The witness' earlier statement that the maharaj throwing gulal did not have the same meaning as another person doing the same was considered prevarication and evasion, for all men in the court's value system were equal. The maharaj could not be considered as a religiously significant person and the same act by him could not be admitted to have a different meaning. Thus the witness gave up trying to distinguish the different meanings of the same actions by different people and instead talked about different actions having different meanings. His scheme of evaluation was thus effectively replaced by that of the court's and by extension the defendant's.

This difference between the conceptions of the maharaj and his followers, and that of the court's was shown up again and again in the statements of the witnesses. Many of them drew similar distinctions. The story of Krishnadas who offered his wife instead of money to a shopkeeper to feed his guru was read out in court. It was used to prove that the religion preached and approved of adultery.[25] Similarly numerous translations from the Vallabhacharya scripture were presented and found to describe and preach immorality. These were studied on the principle that if such literature were found to be immoral then the accusations in the libellous article would be found to be true.

The method of collecting and sorting evidence did not permit the admission of the meaning of actions and literature of the believers. The hegemonic character of 'morality' and its universalism did not allow for any other kinds of interpretations and meanings. This is clearly captured in the concluding statement of Anstey when he said,

> The maharaj denies the singing of obscene songs, but perhaps to his perverted sense, or rather want of the sense of decency or shame, being provoked to unlawful love and those passages containing licentious sentiments appeared to be lessons of piety and morality![26]

The songs of the devotion of Radha and Krishna indeed appeared to be moral tales to the maharaj and his followers. In his journal *Svadharma Vardhak* the maharaj described how the accusation of adultery and indecency could never be applicable to the love of Krishna and the Gopis; God was made up of both man and woman and thus the story of his 'love-making' was really the story of how the Self enjoyed itself (*potani sathe raman kare*).[27]

This alternative interpretation as to meaning of God and the relationship with him was not admissible in court. The maharaj himself was examined from the nineteenth to the twenty-second day of the trial. He was the last witness to be examined. By this time he had been advised that he couldn't debate meanings of actions/stories in the court. Thus when the maharaj himself gave evidence regarding doctrines which were considered immoral, he did not attempt to challenge this characterization or debate the interpretations of texts in the court. He was left with the alternative of denying the existence of the allegedly immoral actions and beliefs. For example, he said, 'I never threw golal on the persons of the devotees at the temple of Luxmijee. . . . I do not know what is the meaning of *ras mandlee* (lit. love society). Other witnesses for the maharaj were also left with denial as the only defence, for example, Varjivandas Madhavdas said I am not able to state whether it is a part of our sect that Krishna had intercourse with 16,000 women, and that they had salvation thereby.[28] The maharaj and his witnesses did not provide alternative interpretations of the same actions: throwing gulal, singing songs or reading stories about adulterous women and their devotion to their lovers. Anstey, the defendant's lawyer, pointed out how the maharaj did not attempt to question the evidence put in by Mulji nor his interpretation or description of religious tenets and religious practices.[29] Alternative interpretations of the religious tenets are silenced. The tool of this silencing was the hegemonic notion of 'morality'. It came to be employed as the tool for evaluating evidence as the judges tried to come to some decision regarding the first accusation of the alleged libel: that the maharaj's religion preached immorality. By the employment of 'morality' as a sole criterion to judge the religion, the maharaj's role as interpreter of Hinduism was denied. The interpretive activity of all the devotees was also denied, and they were seen as practicing a faith without any consciousness. Faith was represented as demonstrated through actions or texts, which were not seen to be accompanied by any rational interpretive activity. Thus individual members were said to belong to a religion by being born into it and believing it involuntarily rather than voluntarily. I characterize this representation of believers as 'communal' rather than 'social'. The episteme within which the court viewed the religious group was that of 'community'.

REFORMIST MORALITY: ADULTERY AND GENDER CONSCIOUSNESS

The reformers based their claim to morality and reform on their efforts to remove the tyranny of the priests over all of their devotees but they were especially concerned to improve the condition of women. They believed that the application of morality as a standard to judge the behaviour of the Vallabhacharya priests would lead to a beneficial change for all devotees. Anstey concluded his speech for the defence by saying, 'The maharaj preyed upon the blind ignorance and credulity of his followers, and in the prosecution of his unholy ends brought his peculiar Shastras to his aid'. Any consciousness of action by any of the devotees was considered to be 'ignorant', 'blind', 'credulous'. It would seem that the maharaj was the one who was in control. But if one considers Anstey's words very carefully, it seems that the maharaj was employing his 'peculiar Shastra'. Thus it would seem that the maharaj's doctrine was to be blamed. Everyone was said to believe in it without any reasoning and without any difference, debate or dispute within themselves.

This image of the religious group persisted despite considerable evidence presented in the trial that every member of the sect did not believe the same thing. For example, Jumnadass Sevaklal said in his cross-examination, 'It is true that about half the bania caste does not believe in the maharaj. There are two sects of banias—believers and unbelievers.' Mathuradass Lavji, another witness, said, 'A few Vaishnavas do not consider the maharaj as a God. I do not, but my brother does consider them as such.'[30] This difference between the devotees of the maharaj was ignored in the court's examination. Differences within the devotees of religious groups were not seen as a sign of the need for organization and governance. Instead another argument was used to explain why such an adulterous religion was practiced. As described in the Plaint by the maharaj,

> [It is alleged] that abstinence from women was the profession of the maharaj; but the learned counsel [for the plaintiff] deemed it unnecessary to notice such a monstrous argument which bore absurdity on the face of it, for abstinence from women is no man's profession, and much less in a climate like this, where the passions are warm, where children arrive at puberty at a much earlier age than in the cold countries . . .[31]

This notion of natural sexuality is present in Mulji's biographer later,

> The Gujarati Hindu women were placed in an unfavourable situation in as much as they were illiterate, . . . that they lived in a climate which early developed their passions and that they resided in a moral atmosphere unfavourable to purity and delicacy, and to crown it all, that their gurus or spiritual guides took undue advantage of their superstitious beliefs.[32]

and in the judgement of Justice Arnould,

> The hymns sung by the women of the Vallabhacharya sect in honour of the maharajas . . . are passionate with all the passion of the East.[33]

Thus it would seem that none of the religious actors—maharaj or women—had the freedom to decide to commit adultery. They were controlled by their natures, climate and geography. Further, it would also seem that they were all objects in the grip of 'degradation', 'sensuousness', and 'passion'. Reform was necessary to control the natural tendency of the East to immorality. Thus, individuals were marked by their nature; in this sense they were members of a natural community or *Gemeinschaft*. They only existed doing 'natural' tasks, and, as just mentioned, climate and geography were the ruling elements. One of the implications of understanding sexuality and women's behaviour as being natural was that the only way to stop it was through some amount of control and regulation, which was precisely the action advocated by numerous reformers.

On the one hand, women were constructed as in the grip of their natural geographical situation, on the other they were seen as subordinate to the men in the sect, the maharaj or the family. For example, in Mulji's articles on the subject of the maharaj's degradation he said,

> Maharajas write in their books about enjoying the tender maidens, the people's wives and daughters, and they enjoy them accordingly. . . . Maharajas, acting up to that commentary, [you] defile the wives and daughters of your devotees. . . . The maharajas are offered the wives and daughters before they [the women] are put to their [the sectarian men's] own use.[34]

In this description, the males—the maharajas and the husbands—were the main actors in the sect. It was assumed that women had no agency at all—they were sent by their husbands to the maharajas who used them sexually. Thus the women were completely silent, though their actions were ever present. This image in reformist writing was consistent with the image of the women of the sect that emerged in the law court as well. In the entire case, though the main accusations against the maharaj, which had to be proven to be true, were concerning women, adultery and immoral practices, no woman was examined to present direct evidence as to her exploitation. As in the literature, in the court case too women were absent.

The construction of women as passive continued to persist despite several witnesses testifying to the women's willing participation in religious practices that the reformers considered immoral. The reformers cited the existence of ras mandalis at Bet Dwarka in Gujarat, among other places where married couples participated in licentious sex. Many other instances were cited of women swinging the maharaj on the swing, sitting with him in their gardens, visiting him in the afternoon, playing Holi, singing songs to him, giving him offerings and so on. Many witnesses corroborated that the women often took the initiative in making the contact with the maharaj, participated in the activities, went on their own and came out smiling. In his judgement too the judge mentions the women's participant role

> The wives and daughters of these sectaries (with their connivance in many cases if not with their approval), went willingly—went with offerings in their hands.[35]

Another report of women's dramatic action was in 1858 when the maharajas and reformers were involved in the dispute over whether the former would be summoned to court in another case. The maharaj had closed his temple for days and disallowed darshan. The women took to the streets and undertook a symbolic mourning of the death of the reformers.[36]

In contrast to this evidence, in the reformers' testimony and their articles, women were infantalized 'tender maidens', and so on. They were made possessions of people: 'wives' and, 'daughters'. They were always the objects of an act: (they were) 'defiled', 'enjoyed', 'used', and so on. And women reduced to this position of being objects were described as 'degraded and abused'.

Given the reformers' view of women as infantile and degraded, governed by their environment or their superstitious faith, the change in their behaviour had to be brought about by others. The maharaj reportedly refused to stop the women from visiting him and claimed that women were his main support and source of financial gain. Thus the responsibility of stopping women rested on control by the husbands and the families. Mulji made the statement very clearly in the *Satya Prakasha* of 18 November1861. He said,

> Divest your females of the notion that the intercourse with the Maharajas is an honour, and that amorous connection with them is bliss . . . Claim them as your own only, and bind them to yourselves and your families by the strong and hallowed ties of conjugal, parental, and

> filial affection. Let not your homes have the scent of the impurities of the temple, whose odour should be disgust ing to your nostrils.[37]

Thus reform actually seemed to mean regulation. It allowed for the imposition of a different power over women: 'conjugal,. parental, filial'. This could be seen in other articles by the reformers as well. A letter written to the *Times of India* described the Vallabhacharya practices as 'luring' women from the family and suggested that such preaching was subversive of male authority. It described the maharaj as 'surreptitiously administering . . . spiritual advice to females . . . when [the licentiousness became] known [it] has been put down by the male members of the family.' *Rast Goftar* suggested that the libel case should shame the men who sent their women to the maharaj's temple. It asked Vaishnavas to find ways to protect family honour and reputation (*abaru*). The discussion in the reform literature concentrated on the question of the morality of the temple and its effect on women, family and the home.

Many of the actions suggested as solutions to the maharaj's adultery also reflected this attitude towards women. One complaint of the reformers was that the maharaj entertained women in his women's quarters (*zenana*) in the afternoon. The author of the article suggested that such darshan must be stopped. As prevention, he suggested several rules:

(i) women should have darshan only from 7 a.m. to 9 a.m.;
(ii) women should enter the zenana only to meet the maharaj's wife and daughters when the maharaj was busy with other work;
(iii) women should not be allowed to visit in the afternoon;
(iv) women should not be allowed to visit the maharaj to offer him fruit in privacy.

Rast Goftar reported that four or five large families had determined that the women of their homes would not be allowed to visit the maharajas. The paper also reported that these families tried to stop the women's attendance at the temple, some of them even used force and violence.[38] None of the articles advocated such general restrictions on male activity.

The 1855 resolution of the Bhatias, widely claimed to have attempted to rectify the maharaj's adultery, had the following provisions:

> Bhattia women should not go about in their Garries without 'purdas' or screens . . . women should not sit on the roads on the occasion of any death in the caste; . . . they should attend early at the general caste dinner, etc.[39]

A particular kind of woman and her exploitation by the maharaj was of greater concern than the general absence of sexual abstinence on his part. Even though there was considerable evidence of the maharajas being patrons of prostitutes, these events did not bear the brunt of the criticism. It was the maharajas' sexual liaisons with women within the households that was discussed most often, and evidence was presented for these rather than for those with courtesans. Thus the strongest complaint against the maharajas was that they were teaching illicit sexual behaviour to their disciples and their wives and daughters. For example, there was a specific accusation that the maharaj was fondling women's breasts during the celebration of the Holi festival. This was described as taking place with a woman who was 'neither wife nor lawful concubine' or again throwing gulal on the breasts of women who were 'neither wife nor lawful concubine.'[40] The employment of these categories to describe the victimized woman indicates that the reformist complaint was not about the maharajas forcing unwanted sexual attention on women, but about his promiscuity with other men's wives or daughters.

The most vitriolic accusations in reformist writing were made against the older woman—widow and 'crone' who 'spoilt' the young bride, took her to the temple, and so on. It would seem that the young girl and the child bride had to be protected and in her defence action would have to be taken. Perhaps it was this concern with the 'rights' of the younger and dependent woman that led the media and the reformers to ignore the case of an older widow who prosecuted a maharaj in a law court. A Bombay maharaj—Gokuleshdhishaji (variously spelt as Gokildasaji) sent a legal notice to a Bhatia widow named Manekbai in February of 1861 to sell her house and give him the money since she had allegedly gifted that house to him. He threatened to sue her about the house. Instead of bowing down to the maharaj's threats she employed Anstey (the same lawyer who was later employed by the reformers), to pursue the matter legally. She accused the maharaj of having pressurized her to sign over her home to him by harassing her. The maharaj pleaded in court that she had no right to complain. The Supreme Court gave a verdict in her favour that she had every right to sue the maharaj, thus Gokuleshdhishaji had to pay Rs.700 as costs and was given time to enter his plea. Anstey served an attachment order on the maharaj to force him to remain present in court. On 28 February he tried to serve a notice on the maharaj to remain present in court but the person delivering the notice was thrown out. The case was settled out of court by the leaders of the Bhatia caste who forced Manekbai to withdraw the case and to pay the maharaj a sum of Rs. 1,600 to release her building, which was valued at Rs.14,000. The maharaj was compensated to give up the claim to the house, which he had forced out of her. Her brother allegedly helped her through the dispute and its settlement.

During this period when the two sides served summons and pleas against one another, the reformist beacon *RGSP* only mentioned these proceedings, once in the comments page but mostly as small news items. None of the reformers took this as an opportune moment to criticize the maharaj. Nor did they hold felicitation ceremonies for the widow Manekbai who dared to challenge and summon the maharaj to court. The reform magazines and societies did not recognize her pursuit of the maharaj in court as a modern or contemporary challenge to the maharaj, and did not celebrate it as such. They did not criticize the maharaj for having forced the widow to donate the house to him. This action was listed merely as the sign of the maharaj's foolishness: the heading of the *RGSP* comment was '*maharajoni murkhai*' (maharaj 's foolishness).[41]

Contrast this disregard towards an independent older woman's struggle against a maharaj with the events following two other complaints against the maharaj. A young Bhatia girl complained that a servant of the maharaj had made away with her jewels. When some leading Bhatias heard of the this, they complained to the maharaj and requested him not to allow women to see him at untimely hours. He however refused. The report goes on to say that Bhatias convened a general meeting of the caste the same afternoon, and resolved that no Bhatia female should stir out at night and that the violation of this order should be attended by a fine and that in virtue of this resolution several fines were collected.[42] Thus when a younger woman complained about the maharaj's behaviour they invited control over their own behaviour rather than that of the maharaj.

The newspapers reported another instance of the maharajas' exploitation of women. They reported that an unnamed maharaj was accused of raping and causing the death of a twelve-year-old girl in Bombay. The reformist newspapers severely criticized the parents of the girl and the caste leadership for not taking this maharaj to court, and urged the parents to do so. The maharaj who was afraid that this might happen was trying to prevent such an eventuality by making bandobasts.[43]

Manekbai's courage in taking the maharaj to court for harassment was not celebrated, while the parents' cowardice in not pursuing the maharaj was bemoaned. The reformers' could not appreciate the older woman's independence. Their championship of the cause of women seems to have been limited to the need of protecting young marriageable women. There is considerable literature which argues that the nuclear patriarchal family was the basis for much of the call for the emancipation of women by the nineteenth century male reformers.[44] While concerned elite women have expressed themselves on the questions of education and the age of consent and claimed these as emancipatory gestures, no woman seems to have participated, or claimed any benefits at all from the reform addressed to remove the sexual exploitation of women by religious gurus.[45]

I do not wish to suggest that the religious polity was necessarily less exploitative of women than the family. As we saw, the caste authorities did attempt to control women's actions within the religious sphere. According to several scholars of religion, women did see religion as an alternative to the family.

Also as we see in various accounts women seem to have largely supported the maharajas' temples against the recommendations of the reformers. The importance and necessity for temples and religious spaces were recognized even in the *RGSP* which suggested therefore that the reformers should build different kinds of temples.[46] I have, however, also quoted several instances of exploitation and harassment of women by the maharajas. The value or lack thereof of the Vallabhacharya sampradaya to women would form a different kind of investigation and analysis. Here, I merely wish to point out in brief the nature of the reformist alternative for women and caution that my critique of the reformers should not be seen as a valorization of the relationship between women and their gurus. As members of the sampradaya women were undertaking different actions and could play one authority of the polity (family or caste) against the other (the maharaj). One may reflect that the reformers' image of women's actions conceived them as belonging unquestioningly within the family.

REFORM AND ITS RELIGIOUS CONSEQUENCES

During the case, in the allegedly libellous article and in the defence plea no 7, discussed later, the reformers were associating orthodoxy with morality in their critique of the maharajas. We have so far merely discussed the aspect of morality and the Shastra in the reformers' writings. The Maharaja Libel Case was seen as a major defeat of superstition and religious tyranny and celebrated as the beginning of 'modernity' and as a victory for 'Hindu reformers'. The success of the reformers in the case was welcomed as a sign that a newer and better Hinduism would be established. As the Gujarati newspaper *RGSP* said, 'even after exposing the degradedness of the community [*kom*; Arabic *qaum*] [referring to the exposure of the evils within the Pushtimarga sampradaya in the case] Mulji still follows the Hindu religion'. Later, Karsandas Mulji, the defendant, was described as

> the leading and directing spirit [of Hindu reform], just as the great personality of Martin Luther stood at the head of the Reformation of the Papal despotism.

Thus Karsandas was described as reforming Hinduism, clearing out impurities and heresies that had cropped up within it. The *Times of India* said that this reform was an indication of 'the progress of the times and *the progress of Hindoo society*.'[47]

The religion of the maharajas was seen as deviating from Hindu orthodoxy. The defence plea no 7 asserted that the Vallabhacharya sect was holding practices and professing opinions as to religions and morals quite opposed to the ancient religion and moral laws of Hindus.[48] This plea was framed to support the argument in Mulji's allegedly libellous article, where he accused the maharaj of heterodoxy and immorality. Even though the law court refused to examine what Hinduism meant and whether the Vallabha sampradaya was truly heretical, the position of Hinduism was strengthened during the course of the trial, as seen in the public comments subsequent to the case.

The two charges in the libel, as discussed earlier, were: *(i)* holding heterodox opinions; and *(ii)* improper conduct. In the judgement the question of whether it was heterodox or not was dropped, for the judges were unable or unwilling to determine what was the true religion, and the court judged the Vallabhacharya religion on the grounds of morality. It also classified the Vallabhacharya sampradaya as a Hindu sect, whereas Vallabhacharya's teachings *described* as sampradaya would have had some independence from Hinduism and could be seen as self-governing and self-determined. When described as a sect, the teachings were seen as established in some original moment without any contemporary means to determine them and debate them.

One consequence of the court's ignoring the self-governing aspect of the religious polity and examining the reformist dispute from the point of view of morality alone was that certain practices of the Vallabhacharya tradition were silenced and women were firmly placed within the sphere of the family. Another important consequence was that the reformers had to prove in court the truth of their statement that the maharajas were not good Hindus. The second statement had the effect of constructing the maharajas as belonging to the Hindu religion without any negotiation, or authority, which may be characterized as 'communal'.

Just as the Pushtimarga doctrine could not be debated and interpreted in court, 'Hindu' doctrines could also not be discussed in court. Thus the nature of the maharaj's Hinduism had to be based on the outward signs of concurrence with Hinduism—a Hinduism that the court understood from its own recognized authorities. For the most part, as shown earlier, the maharajas were judged to be Hindus by the evidence of their use of Sanskrit texts, the Veda and the Dharmashastra, their being brahmins, their acceptance of caste barriers, the origins of their religion being ancient, and so on. Bhau Daji, a witness for the defence, and a renowned reformer and indologist, quoted from *Mitakshara*, a Hindu law book, and from *Manusmriti* to describe the various actions which Hindu orthodoxy classified as adultery to prove that Hindu orthodoxy considered adultery an offence. This argument would then be employed to judge the maharajas and if they seemed to approve of adultery then they were considered not to be true Hindus. In several articles on the subject of widow remarriage and others, Mulji also quoted explicitly from Manu.[49] These texts quoted by Bhau Daji and Mulji were admitted in court as evidence because they were recognized as authoritative texts of Hinduism. For example, Bhau Daji quoted from a Government of Bombay translation of the *Mitakshara* published in 1844.

If one source of understanding Hindu doctrine in court was quotation from the Orientalist translations of texts, another was the testimony of learned Sanskrit scholars and indologists. One of the crucial testimonies regarding the maharaj and his place in Hinduism was the testimony of Rev. John Wilson, a respected Scottish Presbyterian missionary in Bombay. He was a member of several learned societies in England and in Europe, he had been President of the Bombay Branch of the Royal Asiatic Society for seven years and had published several works on Indian religions.[50] He testified on various aspects of the maharaj's divergence from Hinduism. Other sources of criticism of the maharaj were known. Sectarian criticism of the maharajas was older than the reformist criticism, which was read by some of the reformers. However, these aspects of the criticism of the sampradaya were not allowed into the court and were not examined by the court. For example, Wilson himself wanted to quote a sectarian Sanskrit play of 1637 which criticized the Vallabha sampradaya, but it was disallowed on the grounds that it was not a professional treatise and could not be recognised as a historical authority'.[51] It was the court that determined what constituted as authoritative and acceptable Sanskrit texts and authorities. The court drew such knowledge from Orientalists like Wilson himself, who had reduced the status of the play by saying that it was probably never performed but that was probably written for circulation among friends.[52] This was a masterly reduction of sectarian disputation within Hinduism.

The debate in court emphasized certain ideas about the characteristics of Hindu orthodoxy. One characteristic was that Hinduism must be based on the Vedas alone. This nature of Hinduism was also established in Orientalist knowledge. Haberman has argued at great length how the Hinduism described in court by the reformers and the court matched the Orientalist knowledge of Hinduism.[53] In response to the reformist argument that Hinduism must be Vedic the maharaj stated that the Vedic and Puranic ideas differed but they had the *same* roots. The maharaj said, 'The original courses of the Vedas and the Puranas having gone forward, have diverged into different ways.'[54] The maharaj's argument of different paths arising from the same Veda was countered by the reformers thus:

> What a deceitful proposition this is. Out of one religious system ten or fifteen by-ways must not branch off. The course of religion and *of morals must be one only*. What necessity is there to quit the straight road?[55]

They emphasized that Hindu orthodoxy must be single. This claim to singularity cannot be viewed as a polemic claim between competing interpretations of Hinduism. In court, as mentioned earlier, there was no room for admitting interpretations. Thus the claim for singularity (which in another arena could have allowed for debate) in court only permitted demonstration of a singular Hinduism. The maharaj's religion would have to demonstrate that it followed the single

Vedic path by showing its identity with pre-defined forms rather than prove its orthodoxy through arguments in court.

Vedic religion was described as an ancient religion. The reformers said that they were attempting to 'promote the *truths of natural religion* and to get rid of all superstitions and religious abuses which are but *of very modern growth*, and not to be traced to the *mysterious past.*' Thus the ancient is the original, is the true religion, and once again this ancient religion is coupled with natural religion and morality. The Hindu truth is pushed to a distant past which is mysterious and the modern is discounted by these 'modernists'. The term 'ancient' is used here as an ideological term, referring not just to time but to practices of purity and morality. Haberman argues that this interpretation of Hinduism is the 'most important dimension of the trial, where the effects of the Orientalists can be seen most clearly'. He goes on to demonstrate how the idea of a true Hinduism being ancient was crucial in Orientalist knowledge.[56] This knowledge was the only kind of knowledge that the court would admit. History and ideology were associated in the term 'ancient' to create a dubious history for the merely 400-year-old religious teachings of Vallabhacharya. Since the religion of the maharajas was not ancient, they were by definition impure and therefore false Hindus.

In court it was also argued that Hinduism was brahminic. The plaintiff's attorney said, 'none but Brahmins study it [the Hindu religion], and some thirty years are required for that purpose'. In the defendants' attempt to prove that the maharaj was not an acceptable preacher of the orthodox religion, they spent a considerable time showing how the maharaj was not a good brahmin. The statement of the defence at the outset said that,

> Maharajas . . . were not, nor are, the chiefs or heads of the class of Hindus . . . called Brahmins.[57]

Mulji deposed that the maharajas were excommunicated by their brahmin caste, they were not preceptors of ancient Hindu religion to anybody. Other witnesses were called to prove that they were not good brahmins with whom others would inter-marry, that they had been ostracized by their caste—the Tailanga Brahmins—and in order to marry into their caste they had to pay a considerable amount to the bride as presents. Again Rev. John Wilson's evidence was the most significant. He provided the professional opinion and 'the history' of the outcasting:

> They are not chiefs or heads of any single sect of Brahmins. The descendants of Vallabha are considered as outcasted Telinga Brahmins . . . it is not possible for Brahmins to hold such intercourse with the Maharajas as members of one caste hold with each other.

As such they had no right to preach the religion of the Hindus. Thus the reformers were privileging a particular caste as teachers of Hinduism and the Pushtimarga was again proven to be false by this sign of non-belonging.[58]

The knowledge of Sanskrit was regarded as another sign for belonging to true Hinduism. The Vallabhacharya religion was described as particularly false because most of its texts were written in Braj—not a classical language, but a spoken language of Mathura, Vrindavan and surrounding regions. Sanskrit was employed in the reformist writings in popular journals and essays often in response to advertisements soliciting such articles. The reformers employing Sanskrit also followed a fixed pattern of 'dharmic' discourse: an argument was begun by choosing the *praman* (first statement as general principle from which to derive an argument) from an authoritative Sanskrit text and then extracting one's point from it. By thus employing Sanskrit the reformers were constructing an audience that understood Sanskrit and condemning the religious tradition of the vernacular languages. After the case, the maharaj too denounced all the texts of the sampradaya written in Braj.[59] Since Sanskrit was known only to the brahmins, this emphasis once again privileged the upper caste in defining religion.

During the trial an image of Hinduism was created as possessing a single Shastra and a single tradition. An orthodoxy was constructed which placed its faith in a unitary, original, primitive Hinduism as laid down in the Vedas, Puranas, and the *Manusmriti* and as expounded by the brahmins. At the same time, the reformers argued for Western education and morality and rationality—the death of superstition and abuse. This latter claim gave them the right to be considered modern. In representations of the reformers, by themselves and by others, westernization was emphasized more strongly while their invocation of Hinduism was underplayed.

The maharaj failed to counter this discursive combination of orthodoxy and morality, though he brought witness after witness who testified that he was a respected guru and a teacher of the sect, and that the doctrines were 'proper', that is, orthodox. But the court had refused to participate in a theological discussion to understand orthodoxy, therefore what was 'proper' had to be identified as morality. His case was entirely based on establishing the good character and importance of the maharajas. This was done by testimonies on his behalf from caste leaders of the bania Kapol caste, Justices of the Peace and other men of standing. They testified that they had great faith in the maharaj and that he was a true representative of their religion. This policy was strictly followed so that witnesses even denied all knowledge of the libellous article and denied that it had affected their devotion to the maharaj. At one stage the defence even argued that the libel was not proven, since the plaintiff's reputation was not affected by Mulji's article and therefore the case should be declared a non-suit.

Mulji brought several witnesses who testified as having heard of the maharaj's adulterous behaviour. However, no woman was produced who could give direct evidence as to the maharaj's extramarital affairs. Thus the hearsay evidence of one side was set off by the hearsay evidence of the other. As the judge said, much of the evidence was a question of oath against oath, and 'the truth must be tested by other means'.[60] Evidence of the maharaj's immorality and adultery was provided by two doctors Dr. Dhirajram and Dr. Bhau Daji. They testified that the maharaj had consulted them because of a syphilitic infection, which they diagnosed and treated.[61] The detection of syphilis—the disease of the dreaded 'lal bazaar' (the neighbourhood where prostitutes were segregated, monitored and permitted to pursue their work), proved that the maharaj was immoral and adulterous. The disease provided the incontrovertible evidence required by law. Victorian prejudice about venereal disease proved the truth of the reformers' accusation as to immorality. Mulji's accusations were judged to have been true and he was exonerated of any charge of libel.

In the collection of evidence to prove Mulji's accusation of the maharaj's preaching of adultery, no discussion of meanings of actions was admitted from the believers Long passages were translated from the Vallabhacharya scripture: the *varta*, and from commentaries, as well as from Jadunath Maharaj's discussions in Gujarati. Whatever might be the interpretations of the passages, the court only took the literal meaning of the words of the text and interpreted it according to its notions of morality. The maharaj's interpretations of the sectarian texts differed from that of the court's; nevertheless, he was identified with the religion defined by the court and his personal behaviour and physical health provided the justification for judging the religion. Thus according to the court it was proved that the maharaj preached an immoral doctrine (whether heterodox or orthodox Hindu) and he undertook immoral practices. The reformers were vindicated as to the truth of their accusation. Such a vindication led to an implicit conviction of the maharaj and an establishment of the authority of the reformist opinion. The trial and its impact was tremendously powerful and caused those who believed in the maharaj and the maharaj himself to change their way of looking at their religious tradition.

THE IMPACT ON THE VALLABHACHARYA VAISHNAVAS

The reformers celebrated the case with lectures, congratulatory meetings, public meetings, notices in newspapers, handbills and subscriptions to pay for costs of the case. It was celebrated as a vindication of the truth of the reformer's claims. It demonstrated to those who opposed the reform that their opposition could not be sustained. The proceedings of the Maharaj Libel Case were published immediately after the case in Gujarati and English. They were popularly read for entertainment. Two histories of the Vallabhacharya Vaishnava tradition were also written based on the case. One was by

Karsandas Mulji and the other by Leeladhar Hari Thakkar. The last also went through three editions.[62] In these representations, the Vallabhacharya Vaishnavas were held to be degraded and degrading and not orthodox Hindu. The Maharaj Libel Case was cited as the most effective source that put the label of degradation on the Vallabhacharya Vaishnavas. As noted by a committee appointed to examine the cause of the downfall of the Bhatia caste in 1924, forty-four years after the case, 'even though all the accusations (during the case) were false, the taint [*kalanka*] has not been washed out'.[63]

On the other hand, the case triggered the movement within the sampradaya to change its reputation. The prevailing establishment allowed the Vaishnavas to redeploy and reinterpret their literature and assert themselves as Hindu. Thus, subsequent to the case, several leading Pushtimargi maharajas emphasized their 'Hindu' characteristics. Immediately after the case Jadunath Maharaj himself denounced those texts of the sect that were written in Braj bhasha and declared that they were composed by people who did not understand the true religion taught by Vallabhacharya. He insisted that devotees read and follow only the Sanskrit texts.[64] Leading thinkers of the sect, particularly Pandit Gattulalji, nephew of the Bombay Maharaj, from the 1870s and Devakinandanacharya who came to Bombay in 1878, actively worked at preaching and propagating a self-consciously reformed Vaishnava sampradaya. They gave public lectures on the 'principles of Vaishnava dharma', *'guru-shishya'* (preceptor-pupil/devotee) relationship, and these were reported in newspapers, and highly praised. They published polemical handbills and relied on the Sanskrit text of the *Subodhini* (Vallabhacharya's commentary on the *Brahmasutras*), though it was hardly mentioned in the case.[65]

Tanika Sarkar suggests that because the Maharaj Libel Case was the first public criticism about religious authorities, it became a sign for Hindu corruption and set the terms for a self-reflexive debate within Hinduism even in Bengal. She adds that this kind of reflection was being undertaken by all kinds of groups in Bengal and that these groups could not be characterized as either modernist or revivalist.[66] Her analysis of the impact of the case bears out with the developments in

Bombay as well, where the differences between the maharajas' supporters and the reformers considerably narrowed and the maharajas became involved in critical self-reflection. However, in some of this self-reflection, the characterization of Hinduism became entangled with Orientalist notions of Hinduism—establishing that brahminism and Sanskrit-speaking were the characteristics of good Hindu religious groups. The authority of the maharajas was nominally re-established after the case but the ties between the maharaj and the devotee were manifestly different. The changed ties were most obvious in the temples that were built after the case. These temples followed many of the Pushtimarga practices but they were removed from caste and religious authorities. They were built by individual patronage and were known by the names of these patrons.

New temples in the city in the 1870s and 1880s were built by Gokuldas Tejpal, a Bhatia leader and reformer before the case; by Mulji Jetha, a Bhatia leader, not closely associated with the reformers during the case, as well as by Varjivandas Madhavdas, a Kapol bania leader and supporter of the maharaj during the case. The newspapers had been urging this reform in order to ensure that the maharajas not be patronized. These articles suggested that in such temples there was no need of either a maharaj or an idol; with these absent it would establish the original Hindu religion based on Vedic truth. While the temples did not follow the newspaper prescriptions regarding idols or Vedic truth, they did do away with the maharaj in day-to-day worship. Subsequently numerous major temples were built by the Vaishnavas that followed the rituals of the sampradaya but which did not have a 'haveli' of the maharaj; for example, the Murlidhar temple built by the Thackerseys in Santa Cruz in 1960; or the Vallabhasadan temple in Ahmedabad, the trust for which was set up in 1954.[67]

The printing and publishing of Vaishnava texts increased, the *Vaishnava Dharmapataka* advertised to collect old texts and requested donations to print copies of the old texts and maintain Vaishnava libraries.[68] The availability of religious-sampradayik literature increased, so did the use of the Gita and other non-sampradayik literature. These developments undermined the caste and maharaj's authority to organize the faith and beliefs of the members of the sampradaya. We may celebrate the decline of absolute authority, with the reformers. But the court's manner of achieving this delegitimization of religious authorities did not create or support a means of dispute settlement within the sampradaya. They marked the judgement of religious practices of a Hindu sampradaya by an externally defined Hinduism not an internally debated Hinduism.

CONCLUSION

The history of Pushtimarga in the latter half of the nineteenth century was assuredly more complicated and complex. The story of the Hindu revival and the popularization of philosophical and spiritual literature in the late nineteenth century were a part of it. After the case, some of the supporters of the reformers invited Dayanand Sarasvati to Bombay and they founded the Arya Samaj in Bombay in 1874.[69] This history is still to be written and is much more complex than what can be attributed to the effects of the case.

The Vallabhacharya Vaishnava religious polity was represented as a community during the legal controversy between the reformers and the maharajas. Outside the legal arena the religious polity was governed by religious and caste authorities (maharajas and *shethiyas*), who in court were represented as citizens—the same as other citizens. In court the religious authorities were submitted to a legal scrutiny which examined their testimony not for its interpretive truth but its truth as concurring with the court's notion of morality and Hinduism. When found wanting on those counts, some of the faith and practices of the religious tradition were silenced. The establishment prevailing after the court case permitted Pushtimargis to reinterpret their religion in the image of the 'true' Hinduism, which was also being discovered by reformers, other Orientalists like H. H. Wilson and missionaries like John Wilson. Jadunath Maharaj said in his journal that the '*shuddha vedamarg*' advocated by the reformers was the Brahmo Samaj of Rammohan Roy.[70] While the court case was not the sole source of a definition of true Hinduism, it was the arena in which this meaning of Hinduism was applied to categorize religious polities like the Pushtimarga.

NOTES

1. Mahipatram Rupram, *Uttam kapol karsandas mulji charitra* (Ahmedabad: Ranchhodlal Gangaram, 1877): 12-13.
2. Official translation from *Satya Prakasha*, 21 Oct 1860, in *MLC*: 4.
3. *MLC*: 13.
4. Speech for the defence, 1 Feb 1862, *MLC*: 183.
5. Ibid: 31.
6. Bhau Daji's testimony, *MLC*: 289, 290-91.
7. Chief Justice's ruling on the demurrer petition, delivered 18 July 1861, *MLC*: 37.
8. Karsondas Mulji, 'slavery bond', in *Nibandhamala: samsar sambandhi vishayo,* vol 1 (Bombay Union Press, 1870): 133-142. Such exemptions were common in the nineteenth century. One government list exempted two maharajas of Ahmedabad from such appearance in 1859. The Aga Khan was exempted between Oct 1865 and Aug. 1866. *Historical Note on the Privilege of Exemption from Personal Appearance in Civil Courts in the Bombay Presidency* (Bombay: Government Oriental Press, 1896).
9. *MLC*: 13.
10. Ibid; Anstey's argument on demurrer, ibid: 14-15; 18, 19.
11. *MLC*, Judgement of Justice Matthew Sausse, 18 July 1861: 36. These points were more clearly argued by Bayley (attorney for the maharaj): 23; and Judge Sausse: 27.
12. *MLC*: 60, the eighth plea on behalf of the defendants; 'The said supposed libel . . . is . . . true in substance and effect'; Seventh plea of defence: 43-59; 150.
13. R. L. Raval, *Socio-Religious Reform Movements in Gujarat during the Nineteenth Century* (Delhi: Ess Ess Publications, 1987); Charles Heimsath, *Indian Nationalism and Hindu Social Reform* (Princeton, NJ: Princeton University Press, 1964); Kenneth W. Jones, *Socio-Religious Reform Movements in British India, Cambridge History of India,* vol 3, pt 1 (Cambridge: Cambridge University Press, 1989).
14. *MLC*: 14
15. Durgaram's diary entry describes this conversation: '*mein kahyun ke dharmashastra tumara amara jeva manasanun banavelun chhe, mate tena par vichar karine bharoso rakhavo a*

joyiye.' Mahipatram Rupram, *Durgaram charitra:* 30-31, 42 and 43; *my translation;* Durgaram said, *'mara vichar pramane juo to gitaman shun kahyun chhe te apana vichar sathe male chhe tethi te vancava jog chhe.'*

16. Narmadshankar Lalshankar, *Junu narmagadya* (Bombay: Gujarati Press, 1912), most striking in essays like *'Guru ane stri'*: 99-127; Frank Conlon, 'The Polemic Process in Ninteenth-Century Maharashtra.' In *Religious Controversy in British India: Dialogues in South Asian Languages*, edited by Kenneth W. Jones, SUNY Series in Religious Studies (Albany: State University of New York Press, 1992).
17. Mulji, *nibandhamala:* 55; first published in *Rast Goftar*, Aug 1857.
18. Narmadshankar, *Junu narmagadya*: 99, 143; advertisement, *Satya Prakasha,* 23 Jan 1859, quoted in *Guruni satta vishe* (Ahmedabad: Dalpatram Ambaram, 1859); advertisement, *Rast Goftar*, 3 April 1853.
19. Narmadshankar Lalshankar, *Mari hakikat ane anya atmakathaniya lakhano*, edited by Dhirubhai Thakar (Ahmedabad: Gurjar Grantharatna Karyalaya, 1983): 73.
20. Mahipatram Rupram, *Karsanadas mulji charitra:* 29-30.
21. Yadunath Maharaj Suratvala, *Svadharma vardhak ane sanshay chhedak*, 2nd ed, vol 1 (Ahmedabad: Haridas Zaverdas, 1911): 20. Also quoted by Anstey in speech for defence, *MLC*: 182. Throughout the period concerned, the maharaj was referred to as 'Jadunath'; hence this spelling has been kept in the book, though in later publications 'Yadunath' has been used in keeping with the greater use of Sanskrit in the later period.
22. Justice Arnould quoting the defendant while giving his judgement, *MLC*: 432-433; the maharaj's articles in the *Chabuk* and *Svadharma Vardhak,* 16 and 29 Sept 1860. Sumit Sarkar notes that Ishvarchandra Vidyasagar's early article against child-marriage (1850) was marked by a total absence of textual exegesis unlike his later articles on widow remarriage. 'Vidyasagar and Brahmanical Society', in *Writing Social History* (Delhi: Oxford University Press, 1998): 261.
23. *MLC*: 44-45.
24. During cross-examination on Monday, 27 Jan 186, *MLC*: 134-135; 136-137.
25. *MLC*: 145; later I shall examine the gender consciousness of the reformers who did not interpret this action as exploitation of women.
26. *MLC*: 367.

27. Yadunath Maharaj Suratvala, *Svadharma vardhak:* 24.
28. *Ras* has been translated in numerous ways depending on the context. It means essence or flavour, emotion or mood. In the context of the discussion, however, the emotion or mood was definitely of love, whether of *gopi* (cowherdess) or *sakhi* (friend); *MLC*: 342-343; examined Monday, 27 Jan 1862: 139.
29. *MLC*: 367.
30. Ibid: 134, 281, 365.
31. Ibid: 31.
32. B. N. Motiwala, *Karsondas Mulji, A Biographical Study* (Bombay: Karsondas Mulji Centenary Clebration Committee, 1935): 157.
33. *MLC*: 441.
34. *MLC*: 4.
35. Evidence of Lakhmidas Khimji, 20 Feb 1862, *MLC*: 298, Evidence of Kalabhai Lalloobhai on the same day: 302, others: 309; 430-431.
36. Mahipatram Rupram, *Karasanadas mulji charitra:* 19-20. This discussion does not delve into the meanings of this kind of protest by women and its reporting in the narrative of the reformers; I intend to pursue this question separately.
37. Motiwala, *Karsondas Mulji:* 142.
38. *Times of India*, 16 Feb 1862; *RGSP* (12 May 1861): 219; these efforts were described as failures, (9 June 1861): 226; (7 Sept 1862): 431.
39. Evidence of Bhimjee Purushottam, 25 Feb 1862, *MLC*: 333.
40. In several newspaper accounts accusations against maharajas in Udaipur and elsewhere, *RGSP* (19 May 1861); (26 May 1861); *MLC*: 53.
41. *RGSP* (17 Feb 1861): 78; (3 and 24 March 1861); (21 April 1861).
42. *Times of India*, 2 May 1862; newsletter from Kutch Mandvi, April 1862: 3; *RGSP* (4 May 1862): 218-219 quotes the same report.
43. *RGSP* (24 Sept 1865): 613.
44. Padma Anagol, 'The Age of Consent Act (1891) Reconsidered: Women's Perspectives and Participation in the Child Marriage Controversy in India.' *South Asia Research* 12, 2 (Nov 1992); Himani Bannerjee, 'Mothers and Teachers : Gender and Class in Educational Proposals for and by Women in Colonial Bengal.' *Journal of Historical Sociology* 5, 1 (March 1992): 1-30; Amrita Shodhan, 'Rakhmabai: A Woman's Voice in the Age of Consent Controversy,' in *Strijivanvishayaka sthityantar: Mumbai Parisar (A.D. 1876-1950)* (Bombay: SNDT University, 1992); Mrinalini

Sinha, 'The Age of Consent Act : The Ideal of Masculinity and Colonial Ideology in Late Nineteenth Century Bengal.' *Proceedings of the Eighth International Symposium on Asian Studies*, 1986: 1197-1214.

46. Kinsley Davis, 'Devotion as an Alternative to Marriage in the Lives of Some Hindu Women Devotees.' In *Tradition and Modernity in Bhakti Movements*, edited by Jayant Lele *International Studies in Society and Social Anthropology,* vol 31 (Leiden: E. J. Brill, 1981); *RGSP*, 9 June 1861, 21 July 1861, 26 Oct. 1862.
47. *RGSP* (26 July 1863): 373, *'komani badi ughadi padi chhatan acaranna Hindu dharmanoj chhe'; my translation;*. Motiwala, *Karsondas Mulji:* 65; *Times of India*, 3 March 1862: 2. *emphasis added.*
48. *MLC*: 44.
49. Bhau Daji's testimony, *MLC*: 288. Most reformers quoted Sanskrit texts that had become more accessible recently through English and vernacular translations. He quoted from the Marathi translation by the Government of Bombay in 1844; Mulji, *'lagnasambandhi manusmriti'; 'vidhawa vivah vishe Manuna vichar.' Nibandhamala:* 238, 240.
50. *MLC*: 253; George Smith, *The Life of John Wilson: For Fifty Years Philanthropist and Scholar in the East* (London: John Murray, 1878).
51. Selections from the play were published by Karsandas Mulji in 1869, *Pakhand dharma khandan nataka,* 2nd ed (Bombay: Induprakash Steam Press, 1910).
52. Sir Matthew Sausse, *MLC*: 254-255.
53. David Haberman, 'On Trial: The Love of the Sixteen Thousand Gopis.' *History of Religions* 33, 1 (1993): 44-70.
54. Maharaj's letter in *Chabuk,* quoted and translated in *MLC*: 229. In his newspaper he published a detailed discussion of how and why the religion of the Vedas and Puranas was different. Some of the reasons he cited as leading to differences within religious texts were human failings and differences in religious goals. *Svadharma Vardhak:* 63-68.
55. *MLC*: 2, *emphasis mine.*
56. *MLC*: 14; Haberman, 'On Trial': 54-55.
57. *MLC*: 29; 42.
58. Mulji's testimony, 4 Feb 1862, *MLC*: 190-191, 258; any attempt to debate brahmininhood would have to be thrown out of court as being a 'technical' matter of which the court had no knowledge. Expert opinion as to the truth of the maharajas' brahminhood was sufficient for the court.

59. After the case, *Svadharma Vardhak,* 20 July 1862 (dated Chaitra Samvat 1917) contained a notice for all Vaishnavas declaring that the vernacular language commentaries on Vallabhacharya's texts did not match the meanings of the Sanskrit works and their meanings were quite different. Thus these Braj bhasha books were unacceptable. *RGSP* (27 July 1862): 352, quotes *Svadharma Vardhak:* 147-148.
60. *MLC*:151, 456.
61. Evidence of Bhau Daji, 14 Feb 1862, *MLC*: 285, evidence of Dhirajram Dalpatram, same day: 292.
62. *Times of India* printed the verdict in full for a week and Arnould's concluding remarks every day for a month from 29 April-29 May 1862; The transcript of the case was published first by Daftar Askara Press in 1862 in two versions: Gujarati, 1500 copies; English, 1000 copies, *Granth ane Granthakara*, vol 5 (Ahmedabad: Gujarat Vernacular Society, 1934); the English version was reprinted several times (Bombay: 2nd ed, Union Press, 1879; 3rd ed D. Lukhmidass and Co, 1911). Also see Karsandas Mulji, *History of the Sect of the Maharajas, or Vallabhacharyas, in Western India* (London: Trubner, 1865); Leeladhar Hari Thakkar, *Pushtimargano itihasa tatha vaidak dharmana siddhanto sathe pushti margana siddhantoni tulana* (Bombay: Vallabhdas Ranchhodadas, 1st ed. 1890, 2nd ed. 1919, 3rd ed. Damodar Sundardas, 1926).
63. Before the case the Vallabhacharya sect was regarded as the quintessential example of moral degradedness by Christian missionaries, Orientalists and Shaivites. Captain James McMurdo, 'An Account of the Province of Cutch and of the Countries Lying between Guzerat and the River Indus: with Cursory Remarks on the Inhabitants, Their History, Manners and the State of Society.' *Transactions of the Literary Society of Bombay* 2 (1820) (Bombay: Bombay Education Society Press, 1876): 217-255; H. H. Wilson, 'A Sketch of the Religious Sects of the Hindus.' *Transactions of the Asiatic Society of Bengal,* vol 16. A Shaivite critique quoted during the case was Damodar Pandit's '*Pakhanda dharma khandan nataka*' [637] published later by Mulji in 1869, see n51. For other Shaivite accounts see quotations from Kaurma Purana by Leeladhar Thakkar, *Pushtimarga athava maharaj ono pantha* (Bombay: Sevakal Karsandas, 1890): 446-447. See also *Bhatia komani avanati ane tenan karanoni udati tapasa*, Bombay: n.p (1924): 56-58. That the taint remained was the conclusion reached by a committee appointed by the Bhatia caste to examine the reasons for the

downfall of the caste. For other such characterizations of the Maharaj Libel Case see Leeladhar Hari Thakkar, *Pushtimargano itihasa;* B. M. Malabari, *Gujarat and the Gujaratis: Pictures of Men and Manners Taken from the Life,* 3rd ed (Bombay: Fort Printing Press, 1889), Patwari, Ranchhodadas Vrindavandas, *Pushtimargiya siddhanta: atmanivedana ane laibel kesa samiksha* (Ahmedabad: Patwari Ranchhodadas Vrindavandas, 1926); N. A. Thoothi, *The Vaishnavas of Gujarat* (Calcutta: Longman Green, 1935): 96.

64. See n59.
65. Article on *'Sridevakinandanacharyaja maharaj,'* in *Vaishnava dharmapataka,* vol 1, part 1 (Bombay: Pushtimargiya Sahitya Prachara Karyalaya, Gordhandasa Goculdas, 1916); Devakinandanacharya, *Pushtisampradaya vaidik hai,* 1909, in Hindi, quoted in Keshavlal Maganlal Trivedi, *Pushtimarga kalpit chhe: etle vedabahya nirdhar chhe* (Ahmedabad: The Ahmedabad United Printing Press, 1910).
66. Tanika Sarkar, personal communication, 3 May 1995.
67. It is also interesting to note that Tejpal's and Varjivandas' temples were dedicated to the Laksmi-Narayan icon of Vishnu and Lakshmi as opposed to either the child Krishna as in the Vallabha temples or to Radhakrishna in the Bengal Vaishnava temples. The idea of Lakshmi Narayan is more in line with a Vedantic idea of paired deities; *RGSP* (9 June 1861); (21 July 1861); (26 Oct. 1862); see inscription in Gujarati in the Murlidhar temple premises: 'ground breaking' or beginning the construction, date 1956, establishment of the idol, 1960; interview with Navnital Sakarlal, trustee of Vallabhasadan Trust, 5 Sept 1990.
68. Vaishnave Dharmapataka, vol 1, part 2.
69. Damodar Sundardas, *Mumbai aryasamajano itihas athava maro aryasamaj* (Bombay: Damodar Sundardas, 1933); J.T.F. Jordens, *Dayananda Saraswati: His Life and Ideas* (Delhi: Oxford University Press, 1978): 127-128.
70. Yadunath Maharaj Suratvala, *Svadharma vardhak,* vol 5: 41.

Conclusion

> If the state recognises the presence of local collective structures it thinks of them as 'nations'—groups with a 'prepolitical subjective will'. As such groups then they should have laws but not decision-making mechanisms, they should have language but not language-making mechanisms. Thus frozen and stuck in time they surrender all decision-making to the imperial power, who then will administer their laws and languages. As such an administrator, the state is bound to make changes. . . . Such changes . . . will follow the logic of the state and the international or collective mode that has logics that are quite different from the ones that may operate at the level of the local collective.[1]

SPECIFIC AND LOCAL investigations of small communities and their individual histories are normally found 'interesting' only as they illustrate some general theory or proposition. However, often the creation of the generalized picture obscures the particular ways in which such developments work. This study by focusing on two particular communities, the Khojas and the Pushtimarga Vaishnavas, hoped to highlight those points of view that were silenced and ignored, even as larger processes were illustrated. I will not claim any general propositions applicable to all of Indian society; but there are several perceptions and understandings that have developed during this study that I would like to share. Local polities existed through processes of self-governance recognized and supported by external polities. When in the nineteenth century, colonial government attempted to organize the governance of local disputes they did not recognize the power of religious and caste groups to govern themselves and therefore did not provide such polities with a space outside the state to settle disputes regarding their faith and practice.

In the mid-nineteenth century, groups like *jnati* (caste), *jamat* (association) and *sampradaya* (religious tradition) may be better understood in the episteme of 'polity'. There was a disjuncture between the colonial judicial treatment of religious and caste groups and their local governance in the early nineteenth century. The social and religious authorities that controlled the Khojas and the Vaishnavas created a dynamic though elitist and patriarchal polity. The colonial legal system was unable to accept the active, constitutive, changing nature of caste and religious polities. These polities were, therefore, relegated to the private sphere and treated as vestiges of an ancient, natural community.

M. N. Dwivedi, a contemporary philosopher and litterateur, was a perceptive observer of the changes that were taking place. While describing the socio-political effect of British rule in India, he commented that the ideal of Indian political morality (*niti*) was one which gave primacy to the collective (*samshtipradhan*): where the principal ruler of the country was the king, but his subjects—whether in a wider region outside his court, or the village—managed their administration through the assembly, the panchayat (judicial collective), the *mahajan* (the leading men of the caste). He suggests that this had been entirely set aside and the king's authority was established as the overwhelming dominant one, thus creating an individual-centred polity (*vyashtipradhan*).[2] This understanding has been repeated in a 'commonsensical' and unexamined way in numerous Indian histories.

To understand this larger process of replacing local and overlapping polities, I chose to study two of the most 'celebrated' cases of the nineteenth century which were held responsible for re-organizing the particular religious collectives involved. A trial is a good location to examine disputes because, it forces the participants including the state to express their ideas and ideologies most clearly whether they are in agreement or in disagreement with each other. It highlights the voices that don't fit the narrative and provides the clues to the places where new and different categories are becoming dominant. If we examine these court trials as arenas of dispute resolution, then our attention will be focused on how colonial courts, not supposed to investigate religions, actually did so. Thus, in the Aga Khan Case the religion of the Khojas was determined on the basis of colonial scholarship on Islam and in the Vallabhacharya Vaishnava case, the religion of the sampradaya was examined in terms of the true Hinduism as understood by Western and westernized scholarship. An analysis of the nature of these religious identities would substantiate the claims made by many regarding the creation of the colonial 'orientalized' image of the religious traditions of Hinduism and Islam in India.[3] The definitions of religious communities in court—given the studies of colonial knowledge in general—were Orientalist and patriarchal, privileging a family which retained exclusive rights to control female sexuality.

To focus merely on the issue of the Orientalism of the definitions accepted in the court, however, would obscure the question of how such an inquiry into religion came about. It was the attempt to understand this latter question which led me to observe the trial as a space for the actual working out of the colonial legal jurisdictions and to query the judgement as a form of social knowledge about Indians.[4] This led me to an examination of the categories of knowledge of the Indian 'person' encoded in the court's jurisdiction. In both cases the court worked with a notion of group membership as *religious community* which could be identified in 'fact', whether belonging to a sect or a church of a particular religion. This group was represented as existing without any need to dispute its religion. The absence of need was presumed, for as a community, the group was assumed to exist in a pre-political, primordial form. Any actual dispute as to religion was settled in court by reference to the original religion of the community in fact, not by the testimony of religious belief in court. This *factual* inquiry discovered the 'true' beliefs by evidence of experts—either Western or westernized scholars or such texts. The disputes over religious beliefs could alternatively have been settled not in the colonial court but within the nexus of the jamat or caste and religious authorities. The nexus of caste and religious authorities, the polity of the *Pushti sampradaya* was replaced by the court's notions of its own jurisdiction.

In order to give some depth to this history of collective rights in the court's jurisdictions I examined in brief how the legal system in Bombay Presidency represented 'caste' as the collective which would organize group life of the local populace in the early nineteenth century (see Chapter 2). The term 'caste' was applied in judicial practice to cover tribes and sects also.[5] The 1827 Bombay Regulation restricted the jurisdiction of castes to 'private' spheres of life, reserving for the state the settlement of group disputes which affected 'public' matters. But even as it described caste and small religious polities' internal jurisdiction over private matters as independent from the state, certain residual means provided for the court's consultation with these polities for resolving disputes. Individuals retained the right to appeal to the court against actions by these polities. As discussed in Chapter 2, the early practice of the courts was to discover collective opinion regarding practice, during the trial, from the local polities. The court also facilitated settlement of disputes within the polities but through court appointed arbitrators. To the extent that the court consulted castes or retained for them the right to resolve caste questions, it was treating the caste and religious group not as a community but as an active polity.

Subsequent to 1857 there was an expanded understanding of the role of the state and the public, laws regarding numerous matters were formulated and codified. The judicial model of the Bengal Presidency was applied in Bombay and judicial systems of the three Presidencies were regularized and unified. While the clauses of 1827 Regulation that admitted the jurisdiction of 'polities' over their own questions continued, they became less important. These developments led to the marginalization of the judicial model of the Bombay Presidency that had developed around customary law. Simultaneously the conviction that it was politically important not to interfere with religious beliefs was gaining ground. It was at this conjuncture of the growing power of the state and its increasing fear of religious beliefs that the Aga Khan Case and the Maharaj Libel Case were examined by the Bombay courts.

The court had earlier treated the Khoja dispute as a 'caste' matter and therefore to be determined outside the court, however, with its help. Later it treated the same dispute as a question of use of sectarian or charitable property and therefore lying fully within the court's own jurisdiction not requiring reference to the Khoja polity. In the Pushtimarga case while one judge treated the discussion of religious matter as a private affair of caste or religious group and thus its public discussion as libellous, the other felt that this discussion was entirely a question of public interest and therefore appropriate for public discussion. Because the ideas of what was public and what was private differed, different verdicts were reached in the same case. Religious disputes had to be presented as disputes over public issues before they could be entertained in court. Such a transformation required the surrender of adjudication of disputes undertaken through a caste or religious or political organization or some combination of the three. The surrender of rights of the local polities meant a further concentration of power in the hands of the state.

I would like to draw attention to two different implications of the general process to which the polities of the Khojas and the Pushti sampradayis were subjected. The judicial proceedings in the two cases determined the true religious beliefs of the group because an inquiry into origins of the religions was conducted, which represented the Khojas and the Pushtimargis as sects of the larger religious communities of Hinduism and Islam. Firstly, the construction of the Khojas and the Pushtimargis was out of the nexus of the social and religious authorities governing their particular religious traditions. Secondly, this construction of pre-determined Islam and Hinduism had no space for historically grounded definitions of their polities. The court definitions were constructed by reference to origins.

Thus, in this process, when groups or individuals within the Khoja or Pushtimarga polities had differences regarding their practices or beliefs, there were no mechanisms for them to be heard except in 'public' newspapers. If the dispute went to the state—the only alternative to traditional group leaders—the differences were not discussed. Those who argued for a change of the status quo had to prove that what they believed was the original religion of the community, which was independently determinable. With the distancing of religious beliefs from collective social and religious governance (by the maharaj and the caste or by the Aga Khan and the jamat) and making the religious belief independently determinable, the individual believer was joined in community with a larger group of Hindus or Muslims.

For the Pushtimargi reformers the denial of sampradayik governance meant becoming part of an integrated Hindu community. This sampradayik identity was only asserted on the question of temple entry, otherwise even the maharajas hastened to be included within the fold of 'orthodox Hinduism' as defined in court.[6] Thus, we may suggest that with the denial of the maharaj and separate caste jurisdictions over religion, a *savarna* (those with a higher caste-ranking) identity of Hindus was constructed.[7]

For the Khojas the denial of jamat governance still retained the special rights of the Aga Khan. However, it also joined them with the larger Muslim community. Whereas in the 1850s Khoja differences of social practices like inheritance were not seen as threatening to the Islamic identity of the collective, in 1937 they were so, and in the Shariat Act of 1937 the Khojas were denied customary rights of inheritance.[8] The history of these integrated communities of Islam and Hinduism is larger than the scope of this study, but surely any such history must take these events into account. The construction of the universal integrated religious community is contingent on the destruction of the governance of collectives based on such smaller *panths*, jamats and sampradayas. For the Muslims of India the construction of a homogeneous Muslim identity occurred in a more dangerous and threatened environment.

The documentation of the actual eroding of the governance of the Khojas and the Pushtimargis would be a different investigation. The Khoja Law Commission failed to come to a decision about specific laws applicable to the community, Khoja *justis* (village judicial councils) were replaced by the Shia Imami Ismaili Council in 1906.[9] Various acts of government, reduced the effect of caste excommunications and even enabled the challenging of such caste actions, while the economic and political developments made local networks and associations less important. The social organization of the Bhatias and Kapols also changed with the organization of caste associations and councils. Here let me only suggest that court proceedings like these undermined the local polities of social and religious authorities—caste, jamat, pir, guru, maharaj—and created a discourse and a knowledge of the polity as being part of the religious communities of Hindus and Muslims.

These religious communities of Hindus and Muslims were unmarked or undifferentiated. While the Khojas and the Pushtimargis still retained their sectarian identifications, legal governance gave more importance to the larger religious communities and understood these smaller groups by reference to the larger one. The story of the integration of different groups into a larger universal Hindu and Muslim community is much larger and includes many more developments and historical circumstances. Khojas and Pushtimargis had to change, and so did the larger society.

The study indicates that representation of the Khojas and the Pushtimargis as homogeneous communities of Hindus and Muslims was not a simple miscarriage of justice nor was the court going beyond its powers and jurisdictions. Within the law these prosecutions were 'legal' or correct. Scholars have suggested that the judiciary of modern India also gets involved in such active definitions of Hinduism.[10] The legal treatment of religious groups and communities was not a suppression of the narrative of community, but rather a consistent deployment of this narrative to strengthen the supreme authority of the colonial state.

The discussions during the trial suggested that there were no simple battle lines between the external colonial and indigenous Indians. Elite Indians of the nineteenth century and their project of Improvement were implicated in opening up debates within religious polities and also in demanding changes of traditional authorities. These changes were often gut wrenching and involved not merely 'civil' debates but street violence. The colonial exercise of legal power transformed the religious/political struggles into statements regarding religious membership. The state and the court did not permit examination of the grounds on which the religious debate should occur, and on which the religious polity should come together.

A colonial study always begs the hypothetical question: What if there had been no colonization? Sometimes it is assumed that the pre-colonial situation would have continued. Sometimes it is suggested that whatever the indigenous people were doing in 'their own' spheres, outside the purview of the colonial realm, would have continued. To provide a contrast to the developments of the 1860s, I have examined not a pre-colonial period but the earlier period of colonial rule 1819-1861. Contrasting one strand in colonial strategy with another reveals that the very presence of alien rule does not mean that it was pre-determined or fixed. By the same token, the indigenous modes of governance were changing and they too were multi-pronged or multi-valent. Thus, one should not imagine a fixed trajectory of historical development either for the pre-colonial or the colonial.

By taking a 'Hindu' and 'a Muslim' case it may seem that I am discounting the fact of the difference between these two religious groups and their collective functioning. One reason in examining these two polities was because they were *not* described as a 'Hindu' and a 'Muslim' community to start with. Subsequent to the two cases, however, it became possible to categorize them as such. This is not to suggest that the terms 'Hindu' and 'Muslim' were not applied to the Pushtimargis and the Khojas before the cases, but to recognize that after the cases, they were determined in their beliefs and practices by reference to these larger religious definitions. These two particular groups, the Khojas and the Pushtimargis, were similar in their social histories and collective structures, and also their inter-linkages at the time (see Introduction). Both collectives were governed by assemblies of men in combination with the religious authorities: the maharaj or the imam. These similarities aided the simultaneous discussion of otherwise different groups.

The analysis of the two cases attempted to show how or whether the construction of the Hindu and Muslim religious communities out of existing locally differing polities was affected differently by the colonial exercise of power. While to a large extent the Khojas had to submit to an unvarying and Orientalist definition of Islam as the Pushti sampradaya had to do so to a definition of Hinduism, later developments are interestingly different. Pushtimargi practice was extensively re-examined subsequent to the case, and external definitions of the sect continued to draw on the case (see Chapter 5). But members of the sampradaya were able to define their religious practice as *also* Hindu practice. A similar reformulation of Islam as also inclusive of Khoja practices has not occurred; the Khojas have, instead, been integrated into the larger Muslim community. The differences between the Orientalist version of Islam and the Orientalist version of Hinduism may have contributed to this difference. The circumstances of majority tradition and minority tradition may also have played some role in the restraint and diffidence with which the Khojas defined their religion. The construction of an integrated Muslim identity occurred in a more dangerous and threatened environment: of being subsumed and marginalized within the dominant representation of Indians as Hindus.

In 1909 the Morley-Minto reforms represented these undifferentiated communities of Hindus and Muslims in the political sphere as important in forming representative government. This recognition may have been for all kinds of political reasons, and did not involve or support governance of the collective body of Hindus and Muslims or even the creation of a consensus within it.[11] Thus the collectives were treated as communities: organic, pre-political.

If one were to take a lesson from this story of the treatment of polities in India as communities, one would realize that the assumption by the state of the existence of independent communities would suppress or make insignificant the hierarchies within these polities. The treatment of aggregates of individuals as if they have no relevant disputes over what they should collectively believe and practice, does not necessarily make that aggregate equal and democratic. It seemed, at least, in the nineteenth century, to make the aggregate objectified. It stifled a free discussion of group beliefs and made voices of individuals meaningless and gave greater credence to adherence to symbols of membership.

One could suggest that the Khoja and Pushtimarga polities

came into being or were re-constituted in the acts of governance at times of disputes between members. If at such times of dispute, the adjudicatory authority was unwilling or unprepared to listen to the beliefs of the members but determined 'true' beliefs by external referents then the polity was bound to be objectified with a predetermined teleology. This kind of predetermination was projected as providing a total prescription of what the polity was, leaving no room for internal differences. The assumption of the ungovernability of collectives was therefore counter-productive and submitted the collective to a totalizing state authority. It removed the possibility of recognizing the historicity of actual practices and dissent from within. The rhetoric of the face-to-face, ungoverned community which was supposedly nurturing and 'safe' fell apart.[12]

On the other hand, recognizing governance of and by groups constituted by birth but maintained through disputation and dispersed authorities could open up the possibility of discussing contemporary faiths and meanings held by their members. Such recognition would obviously not be without problems. However, the possibility of such recognition allows us to frame more important questions. Questions regarding the nature of governance, and the character of the state. We can focus on the distinction between governance of collectives, which is participatory—including different perspectives—and one which is imposed from outside. We question the concentration of all power and authority within the state. While these issues are much bigger than this study, reflecting on the processes that we observe in the nineteenth century enables us to ask these larger questions.

Recently the moral imperative of the community has been given increasingly greater prominence as questions of the plurality of groups and cultures continue to become crucial in the Western metropoles. In an attempt to establish diverse and plural societies, communitarians, writing at this time in the USA and Canada, for example, Taylor and Etzioni, amongst others, also suggest recognizing communities and giving them representation. Their examples of communities include religious groups, ethnic groups like the Quebecois in Canada. In their view, community is seen to exist in some natural manner, either due to traditional bonding through language or kin. They insist that the functions of shared culture and cohesiveness are essential to the maintenance of a sense of self. In order to assert this integrity they seem to deny the very notion of governability and negotiated changes. They assume that communities need only recognition by the state to ensure their 'survivance'.[13]

To a large extent the assertion of the importance of community rests on a historical argument regarding its prevalence in the pre-modern period, which is associated with an integrated life, in contrast to the degradation of modern life, associated with the loss or attrition of ancient communal integration. This historical argument cannot be sustained. As we have seen in this book, in the early colonial period with the acceptance of 'caste' as an integral part of public life, the changes and tensions that the Khojas and the Pushtimargi Vaishnavas experienced were very much a part of public life. The press and the judicial system were mediating these changes. This mediation was simultaneous with other discourses on the universal public and the individual subject/citizen. The universal public is defined as par excellence a realm of associations of individuals *(Gesellschaften)*. This episteme of the modern public—in the way it organized legal and judicial order—enabled the formation of the object community: *gemeinschaften*, inward looking, ungoverned, affinal and 'safe' from the outside.

In the 1860s when the idea of closed community was incorporated in law and governance, the judicial courts accepted the responsibility of resolving the disputes of the Khojas and the Pushtimargis. These disputes and disputants were dealt with as if encroaching on public jurisdiction. Resolutions were sought by confining the disputes within the space of the respective communities, defined as fixed at the time of origin and knoweable in their essentials by expert outsiders rather than determined by discussion. The community was thus defined due to the organization of judicial knowledge and jurisdiction rather than by the self-understanding of the Khojas and the Pushtimargis. Indeed, they were defined in opposition to their self-understanding and contemporary practices.

This historical discussion which describes the transformation of the polity to community should remove the historical argument at the base of the society-community divide and destroy the notion of the ancient, integrated self-contained community. The idea of the contractual individual was created in contradistinction with the affinal community. This construction of contradictions has to be recognized just as the contradiction between the rational public man as opposed to the hysterical private woman has been recognized. With such recognition we can percieve the possibility of bringing the community into the public sphere—more amenable to coexistence with society and social change.

The idea of community, as we have seen, has many closures in it. Paul Hirst, also interested in the same goal of plural societies, uses the term 'group' or 'association' to refer to collectives rather than the term 'community'. He discusses how the groups must be organized according to rules and be governed from the outside.[14] This challenges most ideas of community and politics being proposed as alternatives between the two extremes of civil libertarianism and multicultural states. To question the colonial production of communities is hopefully to retain possibilities of self-constituting polities.

NOTES

1. Jonathan Ree, 'Internationality.' *Radical Philosophy* (Spring 1992): 60.
2. Manilal Nabhubhai Dwivedi, *'Purva ane pashchin: deshio upar angreji kelavanini asaro.'* In *Manilalana tran lekho* (first published in serial form in *Sudarshan*, 1890-1896), edited by Dhirubhai Thakkar, 2nd ed (Ahmedabad: Gujarat Vidyasabha, 1954), *author's translation and paraphrase.*
3. David Haberman, 'On Trial: The Love of Sixteen Thousand Gopis.' *History of Religions* 33, 1 (1993): 44-70, limits his examination of the Maharaj Libel Case precisely to uncover this Orientalized image of Hinduism established in court.
4. That the court cases were creating a body of knowledge about indigenous society which was widely disseminated can be attested by the extensve reporting of the cases in newspapers, the publication of the judgement and the entire proceedings of the Maharaj Libel Case in Gujarati and in English. The book on the case proceedings ran through three editions by 1911. Both cases, as seen in the earlier chapters, were quoted in histories of the

sects, scholarly as well as popular.

5. I have suggested that the recognition of caste was a reduction of multiple authorities involved in constituting collective life earlier. In the Khoja case, the recognition of caste was probably also a transformation of the category of the local religious collectives accepted in Islam.
6. Personal communication, Vrajratanji Maharaj, main temple, Surat, 1993.
7. Personal communication, Dr. Sujata Patel, then head, dept of sociology, SNDT Women's University, Bombay, August 1994.
8. Asaf Ali Asghar Fyzee, *Outlines of Muhammadan Law,* 3rd ed (Oxford: Oxford University Press, 1964): 68.
9. The Khoja Law Commission was established to frame the Khoja Intestate Succession Act and functioned from 1879-1884. The act which it proposed generated a gret deal of organized opposition and the plan to frame such a law was shelved. Maharashtra State Archives, Judicial Dept, vol 36, 1878; vol 31, 1880, vol 27, 1884; Chunara Vazirmohammad Janmahommad, *Nurammobin* (1st ed, 1936) 4th ed (Bombay: Ismailia Association for India, 1961), in Gujarati.
10. Partha Chatterjee, 'Secularism and Tolerance', *Economic and Political Weekly* (9 July 1994): 1768-1777; Marc Galanter, 'Hinduism, Secularism and the Indian Judiciary.' In *Law and Society in Modern India,* edited by Rajeev Dhavan (Delhi: Oxford University Press, 1989).
11. Some leading explanations are listed by A. R. Desai, *Social Background of Indian Nationalism,* 3rd ed (Bombay: Popular Prakashan, 1998): 369-371.
12. Others have criticized how this image of the community falls apart from other points of view and very powerfully from the feminist point of view: eg, Ray Pahl, 'Friendly Society', *New Statesman and New Society* (10 March 1995): 20-22; Iris Marion Young, 'Polity and Group Difference: A Critique of the Ideal of Universal Citizenship.' In *Theorizing Citizenship,* edited by Ronald Beiner (Albany: State University Of New York Press, 1995).
13. Charles Taylor, *Multiculturalism and the Politics of Recognition* (Princeton: Princeton University Press, 1992): 58; Amitai Etzioni, described by Martin Walker, 'Community Spirit', *Guardian,* 13 March 1995.
14. Paul Hirst, *Associative Democracy: New Forms of Economic and Social Governance* (Amherst, Ma: University of Massachusetts Press, 1994).

A Select Bibliography

GOVERNMENT RECORDS

India Office Records, Board of Control's Collection, 25950-26035, vol. 926, 1827-1828.

India Office Records, Bombay Secret Consultations, 4 April-27 June 1849.

India Office Records, Personal Records, vol. O/6/20.

Judicial Department (JD) volumes, Maharashtra State Archives, vol. 36, 1878; vol. 31, 1880; vol. 27, 1884.

Justice Erskine Perry's Notebook, June 1847, Bombay High Court Records.

Supreme Court Records, 168/247; 161 and 3/247, 1864, Maharashtra State Archives.

Supreme Court Records, 18/248, 1866, Maharashtra State Archives.

NEWSPAPERS

Bombay Times and Journal of Commerce, 1847-1851.

Bombay Telegraph and Courier, 1847-1848.

Bombay Gazette, 1851.

Khoja Dost, 4 May 1861.

Rast Goftar, 1853-1854, 1856, 1859.

Rast Goftar tatha Satya Prakasha (*RGSP*), 1861-1873.

Stri-Bodh, 1859-1863, 1868.

Times of India, 18 May 1861-30 June 1868.

PRINTED BOOKS AND PAMPHLETS

Aga Khan, H.H., *The Memoirs of the Aga Khan*, New York: Simon and Schuster, 1954.

Aga Jehangir Shah Ibn Aga Hasanali Shah, *Aga Jehangir Shahno Risalo, i.e., Ibrat e Afza*, trans Adelji Dhunji Kaba, Amreli: Adelji Dhunji Kaba, 1912.

Ahmad, Imtiaz, ed., *Caste and Social Stratification among the Muslims*, Delhi: Manohar, 1973.

Ahmed, Rafiuddin, *The Bengal Muslims, 1871-1906: A Quest for Identity*, Delhi: Oxford University Press, 1981.

Altekar, A. S., *A History of Village Communities in Western India*, Bombay: Oxford University Press, 1929.

Anagol-Mcginn, Padma, 'The Age of Consent Act (1891) Reconsidered: Women's Perspectives and Participation in the Child-Marriage Controversy in India.' *South Asia Research* 12, 2(1992): 100-118.

Anderson, Benedict, *Imagined Communities: Reflections on the Origin and Spread of Nationalism*, London: Verso, 1983.

Anon, *Astri ganean mala: Parasi astrione vaste vancava layaka babadono samgraha*, Bombay, Daftar Askara Press, 1859.

Anon, *Bhatia komani avanati ane tenan karanoni udati tapasa*, Bombay: n.p., V.S. 1980 (1923/1924).

Anon, *Guruni satta vishe*, Ahmedabad: Dalpatram Ambaram, 1859.

Anon, *Porva: Surati dasha porvad hitechhu sabhani jubilee mahotsavanun smarak pustak*, Bombay: Sabhani Pustak Samiti, 1922.

Anon, *Sir Thomas Erskine Perry*, London: E. W. Allen (repr. from the *Biograph*, Feb 1880), n.d.

Appadurai, Arjun, *Worship and Conflict under Colonial Rule: A South Indian Case*, Cambridge South Asian Studies vol. 27, Cambridge: Cambridge University Press, 1981.

Baker, J. H., *An Introduction to English Legal History*, 3rd. ed, London: Butterworths, 1990.

Ballhatchet, Kenneth, *Social Policy and Social Change in Western India 1817-1830*, London: Oxford University Press, 1957.

Bannerjee, Himani, 'Mothers and Teachers: Gender and Class in Educational Proposals for and by Women in Colonial Bengal.' *Journal of Historical Sociology* 5, 1 (March 1992): 1-30.

Barrier N. G., ed., *The Census in British India: New Perspectives*, Delhi: Manohar, 1981.

Barz, Richard, *The Bhakti Sect of Vallabhacarya*, Faridabad: Thomson Press, 1976.

Bengalee, Navrojajee Sorabjee, *Life of Sorabjee Shapurjee Bengalee*, Bombay: Navrojajee Sorabjee Bengalee, n.d.

Bhagavatsinhiji, *Bhagavadagomandal*, 8 vols., 2nd ed. Rajkot: Pravin Prakashan, 1986.

Bhattacharya, Neeladri, 'Remaking Custom: The Discourse and

Practice of Colonial Codification.' *Tradition, Dissent and Ideology: Essays in Honour of Romila Thapar*, edited by R. Champakalakshmi and S. Gopal (Delhi: Oxford University Press, 1996).

Bombay High Court Reports, vol. 12, 1866.

Borradaile, Arthur Frederick, *A Sketch of the Borradailes of Cumberland*, London: Maclure and Macdonald, 1881.

Borradaile, Harry, *Gujarat Caste Rules Published from the Original Answers of the Castes*, 2 vols., Bombay: Mangaldass Nathoobhoy, 1887.

——, *Reports of Civil Causes Adjudged by the Court of Sudder Dewanee Adawlut for the Presidency of Bombay from 1800-1824,* vol. 1, 1800-1821, cases decided in Bombay; vol. 2, 1821-1824, cases decided in Surat, Bombay: Educational Society Press, 1863.

Burger, Maya, 'The Hindu Model of Social Organization and the Bhakti Movement: The Example of Vallabha's Sampradaya.' *Devotional Literature in South Asia: Current Research 1985-1988*, Papers of the fourth conference on Devotional Literature in New Indo-Aryan Languages, Wolfson College, Cambridge, 1988, edited by R. S. McGregor, Cambridge: Cambridge University Press, 1992.

Carroll, Lucy, 'Law, Custom, and Statutory Social Reforms: The Hindu Widows' Remarriage Act of 1856.' In *Women in Colonial India: Essays on Survival, Work and State,* edited by J. Krishnamurthy, Delhi: Oxford University Press, 1989.

Chatterjee, Partha, 'Secularism and Tolerance.' *Economic and Political Weekly* 28, 29 (July 1994): 1768-77.

——, 'Response to Taylor's Invocation of Civil Society.' In *Working Papers and Proceedings of the Centre for Psychosocial Studies*, no. 39, Chicago: Centre for Psychosocial Studies, 1990.

Choksey, R. D., *Mountstuart Elphinstone, The Indian Years 1796-1827*, Bombay: Popular Prakashan, 1971.

Chunara Vazirmahommad Janmahommad, *Nurammobin* (1st ed. 1936), 4th ed., Bombay: Ismailia Association for India, 1961, in Gujarati.

Cohn, Bernard S., *An Anthropologist among Historians and Other Essays*, Delhi: Oxford University Press, 1987.

——, 'Law and the Colonial State in India.' Paper presented at the international symposium, Ethnohistorical Models for the Evolution of Law in Specific Societies, Bellagio, Italy, 1985.

——, 'Notes on the History of the Study of Indian Society and Culture.' In *Structure and Change in Indian Society*, edited by Milton Singer and Bernard S. Cohn, Chicago: Aldine, 1968.

Colebrooke, T. E., *Life of the Honorable Mountstuart Elphinstone*, 2 vols., London: John Murray, 1884.

Collingwood, R. G., *The New Leviathan, or Man, Society, Civilisation, Barbarism*, Oxford: Clarendon, 1944.

Conlon, Frank, 'The Polemic Process in Nineteenth Century Maharashtra: Vishnubawa Brahmachari and Hindu Revival.' In *Religious Controversy in British India: Dialogues in South Asian Languages*, edited by Kenneth W. Jones, State University of New York series in religious studies, Albany: State University of New York Press, 1992.

Daftary, Farhad, *The Ismailis: Their History and Doctrines*, Cambridge: Cambridge University Press, 1990.

Dahyabhai, Dalpatram, *Jnatinibandh*, 4th ed, Ahmedabad: Gujarat Vidya Sabha, 1885.

Davis, Natalie Z., and John Bohstedt, *Riots and Community Politics in England and Wales, 1790-1810*, Cambridge, Ma: Harvard University Press, 1983.

De Certeau, Michel, *The Writing of History*, tr. by Tom Conley, New York: Columbia University Press, 1988.

De Sacy, Sylvestre, *Exposé de la réligion des druzes, Tirc des livres réligieux de cette secte, et précedé d'une introduction et de la vie du Khalife Hakem-Biamr-Allah*, vol. 1, Paris: L'Imprimerie Royale, 1837.

Derrett, J. D. M., *Religion, Law and the State in India*, London: Faber, 1968.

Desai A. R., *Social Background of Indian Nationalism*, 5th ed. Bombay: Popular Prakashan, 1998.

Devji, Faisal, 'Conversion to Islam: The Khojas'. M.A. diss, Department of History, University of Chicago, 1987.

Dhareshwar, Vivek, '"Our Time": History, Sovereignty and Politics.' *Economic and Political Weekly* 30, 6 (Feb 1995): 317-324.

Dirks, Nick, 'Castes of Mind.' *Representations* 37 (Winter 1992): 56-80.

Divetia, Krishnarao Bholanath, *Bholanath Sarabhainun jivancharitra*, Bombay: Nirnayasagar Press, 1888.

Dobbin, Christine, *Urban Leadership in Western India: Politics and Communities in Bombay City 1840-1885*, Delhi: Oxford University Press, 1972.

—, *Basic Documents in the Development of Modern India and Pakistan 1835-1947*, London: Van Nostrand, 1970.

Dumasia, N., *The Aga Khan and His Ancestors: A Biographical and Historical Sketch*, Bombay: Times of India Press, 1939.

Dwivedi, Manilal Nabhubhai, *'Purva ane paschim: deshio upar angreji kelavanini asar.'* In *Manilalna tran lekho*, edited by Dhirubhai Thakar, Ahmedabad: Gujarat Vidyasabha, 1954. (1st pub. in serial form in *Sudarshan* from November 1890 to 1896.)

Elphinstone, Mountstuart, *Report on the Territories Conquered from the Peshwa*, Calcutta: Government of India Press, 1821.

Forbes, Alexander Kinloch, *Rasmala: The Hindu Annals of the Province of Gujarat*, tr. by Ranchhodbhai Udayram, Bombay: Pharbus Gujarati Sabha, 3rd ed. 1927.

Forrest, George, *Selections from the Minutes and Other Official Writings of Mountstuart Elphinstone*, London: Richard Bentley and Son, 1884.

Foucault, Michel, *The History of Sexuality,* vol. 1., trans. Robert Hurley, New York: Vintage, 1980.

Freitag, Sandria, *Collective Action and Community: Public Arenas and the Emergence of Communalism in North India*, Delhi: Oxford University Press, 1990.

Fukazawa, Hiroshi, 'The State and the Caste System *(jati)*.' In *The Medieval Deccan: Peasants, Social Systems and States Sixteenth to Eighteenth Centuries*, Delhi: Oxford University Press, 1991.

Fyzee, Asaf Ali Asghar, *Outlines of Muhammadan Law*, 3rd ed, London: Oxford University Press, 1964.

Gaborieau, Marc, 'A Nineteenth-Century Indian "Wahhabi" Tract against the Cult of Muslim Saints: *Al-Balagh al-Mubin'* In *Muslim Shrines in India*, edited by Christian W. Troll, Delhi: Oxford University Press, 1992.

Gait, E. A., *Census of India 1911*: *Reports*, vol. 1 part 1, Calcutta: Government of India Press, 1912.

Galanter, Marc, 'Hinduism, Secularism and the Indian Judiciary.' In *Law and Society in Modern India*, edited by Rajeev Dhavan, Delhi: Oxford University Press, 1989.

——, 'Group Membership and Group Preferences in India.' In *Law and Society in Modern India*, edited by Rajeev Dhavan, Delhi: Oxford University Press, 1989.

——, 'Changing Legal Conceptions of Castes.' In *Structure and Change in Indian Society,* edited by Milton Singer and Bernard S. Cohn, Chicago: Aldine, 1968.

Gazetteer of Bombay City and Island, vol. 1 (1909), Pune: Government Press, 1977.

Geertz, Clifford, 'The Integrating Revolution: Primordial Sentiments and Civil Politics in the New States.' In *Interpretation of Cultures*, London: Hutchinson and Co. 1975.

Ghose, Benoy, *Ishwarchandra Vidyasagar*, New Delhi: Government of India, 1965.

Gnan Prasharak: Etalej elam tatha honarano felavo karnar copaniyun, Bombay: Gnan Prasharak Mandali, *The Journal of the Stu-*

dents' Scientific and Literary Society, vols. 1-3, 1849-1851.

Government of Bombay, *Historical Note on the Privilege of Exemption from Personal Appearance in Civil Courts in the Bombay Presidency*, Bombay: Government Oriental Press, 1896.

Government of Bombay, *Report of the Board of Education for the Year 1842*, Bombay: 1843.

Government of India, Legislative Department, *The Bombay Code*, vol. 1, 4th ed., Calcutta: Superintendent Government Printing, 1924.

——, *Chronological Tables of Indian Statutes*, Calcutta: Government Printing Press, 1909.

Granth ane Granthakara, vols. 5, 8, Ahmedabad: Gujarat Vernacular Society, 1934.

Growse, F. S., *Mathura: A District Memoir*, s.l. rev. and abridged 3rd ed. Allahabad: North West Provinces and Oudh Government Press, 1883.

Gune, V. T., 'The Judicial System of the Marathas.' Deccan College Dissertation Series: 12, Pune: Deccan College Post-Graduate and Research Institute, 1953.

Haberman, David, 'On Trial: The Love of the Sixteen Thousand Gopees.' *History of Religions* 33, 1 (1993): 44-70.

Halévy, Elie, *A History of the English People in 1815*, trans E. I. Watkin and D. A. Barker, New York: Harcourt, Brace, 1924.

Harirayaji, *Chaurasi vaishnavan ki varta (tin janma ki lila bhavana vali),* edited by Dwarkadas Parikh, 3rd ed., Mathura: Dwarkadas Parikh, 1960.

Hawley, John Stratton, *Surdas : Poet, Singer, Saint*, Seattle: Publications on Asia of the Henry M. Jackson School of International Studies, University of Washington, vol. 40, 1984.

Heimsath, Charles, *Indian Nationalism and Hindu Social Reform*, Princeton: Princeton University Press, 1964.

Hill, Michael, 'Sects.' In *Encyclopaedia of Religion and Ethics*, edited by Mircea Eliade, vol. 13, New York: Macmillan, 1987: 154-159.

Hirst, Paul, *Associative Democracy: New Forms of Economic and Social Governance*, Amherst: University of Massachusetts Press, 1994.

Hobsbawm, Eric, and Terence Ranger, eds, *The Invention of Tradition*, Cambridge: Cambridge University Press, 1983.

Hollister, J. N., *The Shia of India*, 2nd ed, Delhi: Oriental Books Reprint Corp., 1979.

Hooda, V. N., 'Some Specimens of Satpanth Literature.' *Collectanea* 1, The Ismaili Society Series A no. 2, 1948.

Hutton, John H., *Caste in India: Its Nature, Function and Origins*,

Cambridge: Cambridge University Press, 1946.
Inden, Ronald, *Imagining India*. London: Blackwell, 1990.
Ivanow, Wladimir, 'Satpanth (Indian Ismailism).' *Collectanea* 1, The Ismaili Society Series A, no. 2, 1948.
Jindel, Rajendra, *Culture of a Sacred Town : A Sociological Study of Nathdwara*, Bombay: Popular Prakashan, 1976.
Jois, Rama, *Legal and Constitutional History of India,* 2 vols., Bombay: N.M. Tripathi, vol.1 1984; vol. 2, 1990.
Jones, Kenneth W., *Socio-Religious Reform Movements in British India*, Cambridge History of India, vol. 3, pt. 1, Cambridge: Cambridge University Press, 1989.
Jordens, J. T. F., *Dayananda Sarasvati: His Life and Ideas*, Delhi: Oxford University Press, 1978.
Kaba, Adelji Dhanji, *Khoja panth darpan*, vols. 1-4, Amreli: Adelji Dhanji Kaba, 1913-1915.
——, *Khoja komani tawarikh*, Amreli: Adelji Dhanji Kaba, 1912.
Kakatiya, Manjula, *'Brhad mumbayina kapol vaishya jnati: ek samajashastriya anveshan.'* PhD diss, SNDT Women's University, 1978.
Kaul, Minoti, 'Commons, Community and Courts in Colonial Punjab.' *Indian Economic and Social History Review* 29, 4 (Dec. 1992): 393-436.
Kaviraj, Sudipta, 'The Imaginary Institution of India.' In *Subaltern Studies,* vol. 7, edited by Partha Chatterjee and Gyan Pandey, Delhi: Oxford University Press, 1992.
Kikani, L. T., *Caste in Courts or Rights and Powers of Castes in Social and Religious Matters as Recognized by Indian Courts*, Rajkot: the author, Ganatra Printing Works, 1912.
Kinsley, Davis, 'Devotion as an Alternative to Marriage in the Lives of Some Hindu Women Devotees.' In *Tradition and Modernity in Bhakti Movements,* edited by Jayant Lele. International Studies in Society and Social Anthropolgy vol. 31, Leiden: Brill, 1981.
Kozlowski, Gregory C., *Muslim Endowments and Society in British India*, Cambridge: Cambridge University Press, 1985.
Llewellyn, Woodward, *The Age of Reform: England 1815-1870*, 2nd ed., Oxford: Oxford University Press, 1992.
Maclean, A. J., 'Law (Christian, Anglican).' In *Encyclopaedia of Religion and Ethics*, edited by James Hastings, New York: Scribner's, 1915.
Macnaghten, William Hay, *Principles of Hindu and Mohammadan Law*, edited by H. H. Wilson, 9th ed. London: Norgate, 1885.
Maharaj Libel Case including Bhatia Conspiracy Case, 12047, 1861 Supreme Court, Plea Side, Bombay: D. Lukhmidass and Co, 1911

(1st published in two versions English and Gujarati, Bombay: Daftar Askara Press, 1862; 2nd ed. Bombay: Union Press, 1879).

Mahipatram, Rupram, *Durgaram manchharam charitra*, vol. 1, Ahmedabad: Ahmedabad United Printing and General Co., 1879.

——, *Uttam kapol karsandas mulji charitra*, Ahmedabad: Ranchhodlal Gangaram, 1877.

Maine, Henry Sumner, *Village Communities in the East and West*, London: John Murray, 1907.

Malabari, Behramji Merwanji, *Gujarat and the Gujaratis: Pictures of Men and Manners Taken from the Life*, 3rd ed. Bombay: Fort Printing Press, 1889.

Mallison, Françoise, *'Les chants garabi de pir Shams.'* In *Litteratures medievales de L'Inde du nord*, Contributions de Charlotte Vaudeville et ses élèves, Paris: École Française d'extreme orient, 1991.

——, 'Hinduism as seen by the Nizari Ismaili Missionaries of Western India: The Evidence of the Ginans.' In *Hinduism Reconsidered*, edited by G. D. Sontheimer and H. Kulke, Delhi: Manohar, 1989.

Mani, Lata, 'Contentious Traditions: The Debate on Sati in Colonial India.' In *Recasting Women : Essays in Colonial History*, edited by K. Sangari and S. Vaid, Delhi: Kali for Women, 1989.

Marriott, Mckim, 'Little Communities in an Indigenous Civilisation.' In *Village India*, edited by McKim Marriott, Chicago: Chicago University Press, 1955.

Marshall, P. J., *The British Discovery of Hinduism in the Eighteenth Century*, Cambridge: Cambridge University Press, 1970.

Masselos, James C., 'Change and Custom in the Bombay Mohurrum.' *South Asia* 5, 2 (1982).

——, 'The Khojas of Bombay: The Defining of Formal Membership Criteria during the Nineteenth Century.' In *Caste and Social Stratification among the Muslims*, edited by Imtiaz Ahmad, Delhi: Manohar, 1973.

McMurdo, Captain James, 'An Account of the Province of Cutch and of the Countries Lying between Guzerat and the River Indus: With Cursory Remarks on the Inhabitants, Their History, Manners and the State of Society.' *Transactions of the Literary Society of Bombay*, vol. 2 (1820), repr. Bombay: Bombay Education Society Press, 1876.

Mehta, Makrand, and Achyut Yajnik, *Karsandas mulji: jivan nondh*, Ahmedabad: Gujarat Vishamata Nirmulan Parishad, Karsandas Sardha Shatabdi Prakashan, vol.1, 1983.

Mehta, Makrand, 'Maharaj Libel Case: A Study in Social Change in Western India in the Nineteenth Century.' *Indo-Asian Culture* 19,

4 (1970): 26-39.

Meschievitz, Catherine S., 'Panchayat Justice: State Sponsored Informal Courts in Nineteenth Century India.' Disputes Processing Research Program Working Papers series 8, Madison: University of Wisconsin–Madison Law School, 1987.

Motiwala, B. N., *Karsondas Mulji, A Biographical Study*, Bombay, Karsondas Mulji Centenary Celebration Committee, 1935.

Mulji, Karsandas, *Nibandhamala: samsar sambandhi vishayo*, vol.1, Bombay: Union Press, 1870.

—, *Pakhand dharma khandan nataka*, 2nd ed. Bombay: Induprakash Steam Press, 1910 (1st published 1869).

—, *History of the Sect of the Maharajas, or Vallabhacharyas in Western India*, London: Trubner, 1865.

Mulla, D. F., *Jurisdiction of Courts in Matters Relating to the Rights and Powers of Castes*, Bombay: Caxton Printing Works, 1901.

N.A. [Editor of the *Imperial and Asiatic Quarterly Review*], *The Biographies (with portraits) of their Highnesses the Present and the Two Preceding Aga Sahibs of Bombay, the Chiefs of the Khojas and other Ismailians: The History of the Dynasty and the Organization of the Khojas*, Woking, England: Oriental University Institute, 1894.

Nanji, A., 'The Nizari Ismaili Tradition in Hind and Sind.' Ph.D diss., McGill University, 1972 (microfiche).

Narmadshankar Lalshankar, *Mari hakikat ane anya atmakathaniya lakhano*, edited by Dhirubhai Thakar, Ahmedabad : Gurjar Grantharatna Karyalaya, 1983 (written in 1869, 1st published Mumbai: Gujarati Press, 1933).

—, *Junu Narmagadya*, Bombay: Gujarati Press, 1912.

Nash, Manning, *The Cauldron of Ethnicity in the Modern World*, Chicago: University of Chicago Press, 1989.

O'Dea, Thomas, Sects. *International Encyclopaedia of the Social Sciences*, vol. 14, edited by David Sills, New York: Macmillan, 1968: 130-136.

Olsen, Gerald Wayne, ed., *Religion and Revolution in Early-Industrial England: The Halévy Thesis and Its Critics*, Lanham Va: University Press of America, 1990.

Pahl, Ray, 'Friendly Society.' *New Statesman and Society* 10 March 1995.

Pandey, Gyanendra, *The Construction of Communalism in Colonial North India*, Delhi: Oxford University Press, 1990.

Pandita Ramabai, *The High Caste Hindu Woman*, Bombay: Maharashtra State Board of Literature and Culture, 1981 (1st published 1887).

Pant, R., 'The Cognitive Status of Caste in Colonial Ethnography: A Review of Some Literature on the North-West Provinces and Oudh.' *Indian Economic and Social History Review* 24, 2 (1987): 145-162.

Parekh, M. C., *Shri Vallabhacharya : Life, Teachings and Movement*, Rajkot: Shri Bhagvat Dharma Mission, 1969.

Patwari, Ranchhodadas Vrindavandas, *Pushtimargiya siddhanta: atmanivedana ane laibel kesa samiksha*, Ahmedabad : Patwari Ranchhodadas Vrindavandas, 1926.

Perry, Sir Thomas Erskine, *Cases Illustrative of Oriental Life and That Application of English Law to India Decided in Her Majesty's Supreme Court at Bombay*, London: S. Sweet, 1853.

Pollock, Sheldon, 'The Idea of Shastra in Traditional India.' In *Shastric Traditions in the Indian Arts*, edited by Anna Libera Dallapiccola et. al. Contribution to South Asian Studies no. 125 (Stuttgart: Steiner, 1989).

Radcliffe, C.J.R., *Mountstuart Elphinstone*, The Romanes Lectures delivered in the Examination Schools, 25 May 1962, Oxford: Clarendon, 1962.

Rahimtoola, Jaffer, *Khoja Komano Itihas*, Bombay: Sanj Vartman Press, 1905.

Rankin, George Claus, *Background to Indian Law*, Cambridge: Cambridge University Press, 1946.

Raval, R. L., *Socio-Religious Reform Movements in Gujarat during the Nineteenth Century*, New Delhi: Ess Ess Publications, 1987.

Redington, James, *Vallabhacharya on the Love Games of Krishna*, Delhi: Motilal Banarsidas, 1983.

Rée, Jonathan, 'Internationality', *Radical Philosophy* (Spring 1992).

Richardson, Edwin Allen, 'Mughal and Rajput Patronage of the Bhakti Sect of the Maharajas, the Vallabha Sampradaya, A.D.1640-1760.' Ph.D diss, University of Arizona, 1979.

Rocher, Ludo, 'Schools of Hindu Law'. In *India Major*, edited by J. Ensink and P. Gaffke (Leiden: Brill, 1972): 167-176.

Roy, Sripati, *Customs and Customary Law in British India*, Calcutta: Hare's Press, 1912.

Said, Edward, *Orientalism*, New York: Pantheon, 1978.

Sangari, Kumkum, 'Politics of Diversity: Religious Communities and Multiple Patriarchies.' *Economic and Political Weekly* (Dec. 1995): 3287-3309.

Sarkar, Sumit, *Writing Social History*, Delhi: Oxford University Press, 1998.

—, 'Popular Culture, Community, Power: Three Studies of Modern Indian Social History.' *Studies in History* 8, 2 ns (1992): 309-323.

Sastri, D. K., 'Agiyaramathi solama shatakana vaishnavabhaktinun pruthakkarana.' In *Aitihaśika Samshodhana*, 2nd ed., Ahmedabad: Gujarati Sahitya Parishad, 1977.

Savailal, Harilal, *Samaldas Parmanandas*, Bombay: Tata Vivechaka press, 1912.

Shah, Anupchand, *Shri velji lakhamasi*, Bombay: Kutchi Visa Oswal Sthanakvasi Jain Mahajan, 1961.

Shodhan, Amrita, 'Rakhmabai : A Woman's Voice in the Age of Consent Controversy.' In *Strijivanvishayaka sthityantar: mumbai parisar (A.D. 1876-1950)*, edited by S. Shirgaonkar, Bombay: SNDT Women's University, 1992.

Sinha, Mrinalini, 'Colonial Politics and the Ideal of Masculinity: The Example of the Age of Consent Act of 1891 in Bengal.' *Proceedings of the Third National Conference on Women's Studies*, vol. 2, Chandigarh: Indian Association of Women's Studies, 1986.

Smith, George, *Dictionary of National Biography: Earliest Times to 1900*, edited by Leslie Stephen and Sir Sidney Lee, vol. 22, supplement, London: Oxford University Press, 1921-1922.

—, *The Life of John Wilson: For Fifty Years Philanthropist and Scholar in the East*, London: John Murray, 1878.

Spivak, Gayatri, 'Can the Subaltern Speak? In *Marxism and the Interpretation of Culture*, edited by Cary Nelson and Lawrence Grossberg, Urbana: University of Illinois Press, 1988.

Shri mumbayina halai bhatia mahajanano 101 varshano itihas V.S. 1915-2015, Bombay: Shatabdi Mahotsava Samiti, 1961.

Sri mumbayina halai bhatia mahajanana hisab : sam 1917-1918 (1860-61) to sam 1940 (1883) Bombay: Lakhmidas Khimjina Hukamathi Metaji Chaturbhuj Valaji, annual reports 1863 to 1883.

Steele, Arthur, *The Hindu Castes, Their Law, Religion and Customs*, Delhi: K.M. Mittal, 1986 (1st published Bombay: Courier Press, 1827).

Suarez-Smith, R., 'Rule-by-Records and Rule-by-Reports: Complementary Aspects of the British Imperial Rule of Law.' *Contributions to Indian Sociology*,. 19, ns1 (1985):153-196.

Sukhalalji, Pandit, *Darshana ane cintana : pandit sukhalalajina gujarati lekhono samgraha*, Ahmedabad: Gujarata Vidya Sabha, 1957.

Sundardas, Damodar, *Mumbai aryasamajano itihas*, Bombay: Damodar Sunderdas, 1933.

Taylor, Charles, *Multiculturalism and the Politics of Recognition*, Princeton: Princeton University Press, 1992.

Thakkar, Leeladhar Hari, *Pushtimargano itihasa tatha vaidak dharmana siddhanto sathe pushti margana siddhantoni tulana*, 3rd ed, Bombay: Damodar Sundardas, 1926 (1st ed, variously titled, *Pushtimarga athava maharajono panth*, Mumbai: Sevaklal Karsandas, 1890; 2nd ed, Bombay: Vallabhadas Ranchhodadas, 1919).

Thakkar, Usha, 'Puppets on the Periphery: Women and Social Reform in Nineteenth Century Gujarat.' Paper presented at the Second International Seminar on Gujarat Development and Deprivation. Surat: Centre for Social Studies, 6-8 Dec. 1994.

Thibaut, Anton Friedrich (1772-1840), *An Introduction to the Study of Jurisprudence: Being a Translation of the General Part of Thibaut's Systém des Pandekten Rechts*, edited and translated by Nathaniel Lindley. Littleton, Colorado: F. B. Rothman, 1985 (1st published, 1855).

Thompson, E. P., 'The Moral Economy of the English Crowd in the Eighteenth Century.' *Past and Present* 50 (1971): 76-136.

——, *The Making of the English Working Class*, New York: Vintage, 1963.

Thoothi, N. A., *The Vaishnavas of Gujarat*, Calcutta: Longmans Green, 1935.

Tönnies, Ferdinand, *Community and Association, trans* C. P. Loomis, London: Routledge and Kegan Paul, 1955.

Tribhovandas Mangaldas Nathoobhai, *Lectures on Hindu Castes, Ceremonies, Customs and Inheritance: Includes Life Sketch of Mangaldas Nathoobhai*, Bombay: Education Steam Press, 1896.

Tripathi, Manahsukhram Suryaram, *Sujna gokulji jhala: eonun patrachitra sahit jivanacharitra tatha vedanta*, Bombay: Nirnayasagar Press, 1902.

Trivedi, Keshavlal Maganlal, *Pushtimarga kalpit chhe: etle vedabahya nirdhar chhe*, Ahmedabad: The Ahmedabad United Printing Press, 1910.

Trivedi, Navalram, *Samajasudharanun rekhadarshan*, Ahmedabad: Gujarat Vidya Sabha, 1934.

Vachha, Ratanji Framji, *Mumbaino bahar*, Bombay: Union Press, 1874.

Vaishnava dharmapataka, vol 1 part 1, 2, Bombay: Pushtimargiya Sahitya Prachara Karyalaya, Gordhanadasa Goculdas, 1916.

Varma, Sushma, *Mountstuart Elphinstone in Maharashtra 1801-1827: A Study of the Territories Conquered from the Peshwas*, Calcutta: K.P. Bagchi, 1981.

Ward, William, *A View of the History, Literature and Mythology of the Hindoos*, 3 vols, London: Kingsbury, Parbury and Allen, 1822.

Wilson, John, *Indian Caste*, 2 vols., Bombay: Times of India, 1877 (published posthumously, written in 1857).

Wilson, John, *The Religious Sects of the Hindus*, with additions from later sources by Reinhold Rost, London and Madras: The Christian Literature Society for India, 1904.

Yadunath Maharaj Suratvala, *Svadharma vardhak ane sanshay chhedak* vols. 1-17, 2nd ed. Ahmedabad: Haridas Zaverdas, 1911 (also spelt as Jadunath Maharaj).

Young, Iris Marion, 'Polity and Group Difference: A Critique of the Ideal of Universal Citizenship.' In *Theorizing Citizenship*, edited by Ronald Beiner, Albany: State University of New York Press, 1995.

—, *Justice and the Politics of Difference*, Princeton: Princeton University Press, 1990.

Index